EDNA O'BRIEN AND
THE ART OF FICTION

CONTEMPORARY IRISH WRITERS

Series Editor: Anne Fogarty, University College Dublin

Irish Studies is currently being vigorously rethought, not only in connection to major figures such as James Joyce, W. B. Yeats, Eva Gore-Booth, Flann O'Brien, Samuel Beckett, Elizabeth Bowen, and Mary Lavin but also within a larger framework, with particular attention to feminist issues, the environmental humanities, the perspectives of migrants in Irish society, nationalism and transnationalism, Northern Ireland and its writers, the Irish language, and the lively and often genre-crossing fiction, poetry, drama, and film of contemporary Ireland.

This series brings theoretically informed perspectives to a consideration of the work and lives of Irish writers. The volumes provide general discussions of interpretive issues and offer varied strategies for understanding them, with the intention of appealing to an informed audience—advanced undergraduates, graduate students, and general readers as well as scholars of Irish literature and culture.

Recent titles in the series:

For more information, visit www.bucknell.edu/universitypress.

EDNA O'BRIEN AND THE ART OF FICTION

MAUREEN O'CONNOR

Bucknell | UNIVERSITY
UNIVERSITY | PRESS
Lewisburg, Pennsylvania

Library of Congress Cataloging-in-Publication Data

Names: O'Connor, Maureen, author.
Title: Edna O'Brien and the art of fiction / Maureen O'Connor.
Description: Lewisberg, Pennsylvania : Bucknell University Press, [2022] |
    Series: Contemporary Irish writers | Includes bibliographical
    references and index.
Identifiers: LCCN 2021006642 | ISBN 9781684483358 (paperback) |
    ISBN 9781684483365 (cloth) | ISBN 9781684483372 (epub) |
    ISBN 9781684483389 (mobi) | ISBN 9781684483396 (pdf)
Subjects: LCSH: O'Brien, Edna—Criticism and interpretation.
Classification: LCC PR6065.B7 Z79 2022 | DDC 823/.914—dc23
LC record available at https://lccn.loc.gov/2021006642

A British Cataloging-in-Publication record for this book is available from the British
Library.

♾ The paper used in this publication meets the requirements of the American National
Standard for Information Sciences—Permanence of Paper for Printed Library
Materials, ANSI Z39.48-1992.

www.bucknelluniversitypress.org

Distributed worldwide by Rutgers University Press

Manufactured in the United States of America

In memory of Catherine L. Kasper

CONTENTS

PREFACE AND ACKNOWLEDGMENTS

This book is officially dedicated to the memory of a beloved poet and irreplaceable friend but was written with all of those who do the hard work of creation in my mind and in my heart. Every completed work represents challenges met and overcome, and this book is no different. It was regrettably, disappointingly dropped and picked up again numerous times, after job loss, the long fatal illness and death of my closest friend, and recurring periods of my own debilitating illnesses and hospitalizations. But now, here we are.

My interest in Edna O'Brien as a serious subject of critical inquiry began during my tenure as assistant editor of *Women's Studies: An Interdisciplinary Journal* (1998–2001), while a PhD student in Claremont Graduate University. In my editorial capacity, I had the honor of publishing essays by Kristi Byron, Eileen Morgan, and Helen Thompson, which went on to become canonical, authoritative sources in the yet-developing field of O'Brien studies. I must acknowledge the loving support and solidarity shared with a number of comrades from the journal who set me on my way, beginning with the publication's editor, Wendy Martin. Other brilliant women I worked with on the journal and who remain important presences in my life include Lisa Colletta, Janet Rathert, Danielle Hinrichs, Sharon Becker, and Jolene Zigarovich. I must also note the vital guidance and encouragement supplied by Marc Redfield in those Claremont years. Lisa Colletta and I coedited one of the first essay collections on O'Brien's work, which, due to the vagaries of academic publishing, appeared in 2006, the same year that the only other volume of essays on O'Brien appeared, which I coedited with Kathryn Laing and Sinéad Mooney, fellow English lecturers working in the area of Irish women's writing, whom I met at the National University of Ireland, Galway, after I relocated to Ireland in 2003. That collection was based on an international symposium the three of us convened at the university in 2005, the first to focus on O'Brien's work. These enormously precious collaborations, and the friendships that grew from them, have provided both emotional and intellectual sustenance to the present day.

A couple of years after these collections appeared, in 2008, I secured a MARBL travel grant from the Emory University Libraries, in Atlanta, Georgia, the location of the archive of O'Brien's papers, up to the year 2000. It was my first experience of that kind of dedicated, sustained archival research, and I will be forever indebted to the staff there, led at the time by Naomi Nelson. They were unfailingly helpful, enabling, and considerate, going so far as to invite me to their break room for the occasional cup of tea. Another benefit of my weeks in Atlanta was getting to know Geraldine Higgins, the professor who sponsored my time in

Emory University, as well as her lovely family, who kept me from feeling too lonely while far away from home and loved ones. Due to the vicissitudes enumerated above, it was quite a while before I was able to begin the actual writing of this book. A crucial step in that process was the foundational work completed during a 2017 research residency at the University of Nantes, an opportunity recommended to me by my brilliant, indispensable friend and Galway colleague Nessa Cronin, to whom I owe more, personally as well as professionally, than can be sufficiently conveyed here. In Nantes, I enjoyed the collegiality of welcoming scholars like Valérie Bénéjam and, especially, Marie Mianowski, who brought me into her lively and beautiful home. I would like to thank the students in Nantes who attended my talks and generated such stimulating discussions, as well as the students I spoke to at the University of Lille during this residency, at the invitation of another inestimably talented and thoughtful friend and scholar, Fiona McCann, whose wide-ranging Irish Studies interests happen to include Edna O'Brien's fiction.

The work of writing the book was begun and completed since I joined the Department of English at University College Cork, ten years ago, where I have the funniest, kindest, most dynamic, most gifted, and simply most dazzling in every way imaginable colleagues. I am especially grateful for the friendship and intellectual comradeship of Heather Laird, Pat Coughlan, Lee Jenkins, Barry Monahan, Adam Hanna, Orla Murphy, Clíona Ó Gallchoir, Claire Connolly, Laura Pomeroy, and Éibhear Walshe. UCC colleagues outside of the department have been just as important in providing continuing cheer and support, including Marie Kelly, Ben Gearey, Rachel McGovern, Piaras Mac Éinrí, John Borgonovo, and John Fitzgerald. In UCC, I have been teaching O'Brien's work to undergraduates and MA students, who have enriched and deepened my understanding of the work, including Lara O'Toole, Grace Collender, and Cristal Fernandez, who have written beautifully on O'Brien, and I want to thank those dedicated scholars as well. Without the encouragement, sympathy, and expertise of the luminous Anne Mulhall, I would never have landed in this nurturing academic roost.

Having thought and written about Edna O'Brien's work for twenty years, this book was bound to draw on observations, approaches, and arguments that have appeared elsewhere. I would like to thank every publisher and editor I contacted who has graciously granted permission for including revised versions of previously published material. Some elements that appear scattered across different chapters were originally part of the following: "Edna O'Brien: 'Psychic and Moral Historian,'" in *Clare History and Society*, ed. Patrick Nugent, Matt Lynch, and Willie Nolan (Dublin: Geography Publications, 2008); "'Becoming-Animal' in the Novels of Edna O'Brien," in *"Out of the Earth": Ecocritical Readings of Irish Texts*, ed. Christine Cusick (Cork: Cork University Press, 2010), "Not Telling," review of O'Brien's *Country Girl: A Memoir*, in *Dublin Review of Books* 34 (6 May 2013); and "Girl Trouble," review essay of O'Brien's *The Country Girls*, in *Dublin Review of Books* 55 (5 May 2014). Chapters 1 and 5 include some material that first appeared in "Animals and the Irish Mouth in Edna O'Brien's Fiction," in "Irish Ecocriticism" special issue, *Journal of Ecocriticism* 5, no. 2 (September 2013). Chapter 4 revises and expands on the previously published "'Extremely Nervous on This Earth': Fairy Tales and Madness in Edna O'Brien's *In the Forest*," in *Madness in the Woods: Representations of the Ecological Uncanny*, eds. Tina-Karen Pusse, Heike Schwarz, and Rebecca Downes (Bern: Peter Lang, 2020), and the same relationship obtains between chapter 2 and material that appeared in "Melancholy Ornaments in the House of Edna O'Brien's Fiction," in *The Vibrant House: Irish Writing and Domestic Space*, ed. Rhona Richman Kenneally and Lucy McDiarmid (Dublin: Four Courts, 2017). Chapter 6 draws on some sections included in "'The Most Haunting Bird': Unbeing and Illegibility in Contemporary Irish Women's Writing," *Women's Studies: An Interdisciplinary Journal* 44, no. 7 (September 2015). The editors of these publications have generously contributed to the refinement of my ideas and helped enormously in improving the way in which I write about literature, perhaps especially those who have become friends and continuing sources of reassurance and stimulation, Christine Cusick, Tina-Karen Pusse, and the redoubtable Lucy McDiarmid. I encountered these academics at conferences over the years and have benefited significantly from conversations and debates with a number of scholars at such conferences, particularly (though far from exclusively) two annual events, the Spanish Association of Irish Studies and the American Conference for Irish Studies, where I have learned from the lively, delightful, entertaining, deeply informed minds of many people, including Asier Altuna, Auxiliadora Perez Vides, Sara Martín Ruiz, Pilar Villar-Argáiz, Melania Terrazas, Luz Mar González-Aria, Irene De Angelis, Margarita Estévez Saá, Betsy Dougherty, Jennifer Slivka, Lauren Arrington, Kate Costello-Sullivan, Vivian Valvano Lynch, Ellen Scheible, Malcolm Sen, Anna Teekell, and Cormac O'Brien. The work of Dawn Miranda Sherratt-Bado, discovered in recent years, has been a signal influence on my thinking about O'Brien.

In my decades of conference attendance, I have been struck by the affection, even love, that marks the spirit of Irish Studies meetings. It was at such an event that I encountered Barbara Suess, someone who grew to be crucial to my emotional and psychic welfare. Were it not for the love of friends like Barbara, this book would never have been written, as they helped me work through a drawn-out, pulverizing experience of grief that threatened to drain me of motivation, as I struggled to find value in a world without Catherine Kasper in it. I do not know how many choirs get a mention in the acknowledgments of literary books, but the therapeutic benefit of singing every week with Choral Con Fusion in Cork can never be adequately quantified. My thanks to Tina O'Toole for introducing me to the group, as well as for her years of friendship, devilment, and intellectual exchanges. Though I have already thanked Heather Laird, she deserves another acknowledgment, as she has been there every step of the way with me, from the day I received the news of the initial hopeless diagnosis to the struggle I faced after Cathy's death, a struggle that caused serious health problems, which Heather helped me overcome. Of course, my handsome, loving husband, Tadhg Foley; his children, Jane and Denis; my parents, Jack and Colette; my brother Seán and his family; and my cousin Gene O'Hara were the core support and source of greatest comfort in those difficult times, but writing the preface to a book about negotiating women's challenges through the power of relationships and alliances with other women affords the opportunity to thank the many friends I am blessed to have, women who not only have provided models of ethical, humane engagement with the world but have, most significantly, given me hope and reignited my love of life. Foremost among those I have yet to mention are Mary Beth Hoerner and Carla Nuzzo, girlhood friends, to whom I remain umbilically connected. Caoilfhionn Ní Bheachain and her gorgeous young family make me feel loved and appreciated. Though we have met in the material world, in the virtual world, I have grown close to beautiful souls like Ellen McWilliams, Ida Milne, and Erin Kavanagh, willing to drop everything day or night to exchange gossip and complaint. I have a wonderful Galway squad, including Anne Karhio, Rebecca Barr (now in Cambridge), Muireann O'Cinneide, and Sarah-Anne Buckley, many of whom accompanied me in 2016, after having returned from the United States for my last visit with Cathy, to a memorable Elvis Costello concert, an event that reminded me of the joy to be derived from art, music, and the best of company.

I am grateful to Bucknell University Press, which continued to believe in the project since I first approached it with the proposal in 2013, when John Rickard was the series editor. It has been a delight to work with Suzanne Guiod and Pamelia Dailey, and I greatly appreciate the encouraging and insightful feedback provided by the anonymous readers. I hope the final product lives up to the promise they appeared to see in the chapters. Thank you also to Rutgers Press, to Kristen Bettcher for her kind and prompt attentions, to Vincent Nordhaus for the book's lovely cover design, and especially to Andrew Katz for his thorough and improving editorial work. Finally, I must thank Edna O'Brien for her generosity and cooperation all through this process, from my first time speaking to her in person, when she gave a standing-room-only reading in Ennis, County Clare, in 2005 to a visit to her iconic Kensington home in 2006 to frequent email exchanges ever since. She has kindly allowed me to reproduce passages from some of her unpublished work as well as brief quotations from a small selection of personal letters in the Emory University archive. She deserves all our gratitude for the personal sacrifices she has been making for decades in order steadily to produce her fiction, drama, biographies, journalism, and poetry that will for generations keep readers enchanted and scholars occupied.

EDNA O'BRIEN AND
THE ART OF FICTION

INTRODUCTION
Edna O'Brien, Leader of the Banned

I am moved by fear and childhood. I am sunken in my origin.

       Edna O'Brien was one of five finalists in 2018's "Clare's Greatest Ever Person" contest, sponsored by the county's radio station, Clare FM. Contestants were nominated by listeners. Even the extremely popular president of Ireland, Michael D. Higgins, who appeared in the top twenty, did not make the short list. The only woman included in the final count, O'Brien vied for first place with a traditional musician, two retired sports stars who played for the county, and a founding developer of Shannon Airport who devised the idea of duty-free shopping (and ultimately won the contest). That O'Brien is regarded with such respect and appreciation by the people of Clare represents a significant change since she published her first novel in 1960, *The Country Girls*, a sensation as much for what was at the time its original subject matter—the everyday lives of rural, Roman Catholic Irish girls and women—as for the scandal and outrage its appearance provoked in Ireland. This reaction built to near-hysterical intensity in County Clare, where O'Brien's own story, as do many of her early fictional narratives, begins.

       Born Josephine Edna O'Brien on 15 December 1930 to Michael and Lena (Helena, née Cleary) O'Brien of Tuamgraney, she was the youngest of four surviving children; she had two sisters and a brother. Several years younger than her nearest sibling, O'Brien often felt like an only child growing up. The family lived in Drewsboro House, on the road between the towns of Tuamgraney and Scariff, in County Clare. O'Brien's father had inherited the large house and a good deal of surrounding land, but his addiction to horseflesh and to drink meant that much of the land was sold off. By the time O'Brien was born, there were only threadbare reminders of former privilege and comfort, and so, while the family shared with most of its neighbors constant worry about money, in the O'Brien household, this anxiety was shadowed by resentment and a frustrated sense of entitlement. Beginning in childhood experiences, O'Brien has more than the literary in common with James Joyce, whom she calls her literary "mentor." The fiction of both self-exiled authors obsessively revisits the homeland that condemned them. The vividness of their re-creations of the place reveals the intensity of a complicated mixture of love and anger; both writers' depictions of Ireland, according to Michael Gillespie, "balance censure with raillery."[1] Like Joyce, O'Brien has been pilloried in Ireland for obscenity, accused of immorality, and banned by the Irish censors (among others), but the economic realities of the two authors' childhoods also bore some similarities: both had fathers who squandered their inherited fortune and standing, and O'Brien's father, like Joyce's, was listed as a bankrupt in *Stubbs Gazette*. While Joyce grew up in the country's capital, however, O'Brien's childhood was spent on the outskirts of a small rural, midlands town. She attended the National School in Scariff and then the Convent of Mercy in Loughrea, County Galway. Life in her "home town," O'Brien recalls, "was fervid, enclosed and claustrophobic."[2] She has described herself as coming "from a very wild place. People don't behave with the normal etiquette. It's like Chekhov's Russia."[3] O'Brien has often remarked, most recently when receiving the 2018 PEN/ Nabokov Prize, that W. H. Auden's observation about W. B. Yeats could be addressed to herself: "mad Ireland hurt you into poetry."[4]

In 1946, O'Brien moved to Dublin, where she first discovered Joyce's writings, attended night classes in pharmacy, and worked in a chemist's shop. While working there, O'Brien met Ernest Gébler through his father, who often came into the shop. Ernest Gébler was Irish born and of German-Czech background, a divorced father of a young son from whom he was estranged. An autodidact of impressive intelligence, will, and determination, he was at the time he met O'Brien also a successful writer whose first novel, *The Plymouth Adventure*, sold millions of copies in the United States and was made into a film starring Spencer Tracy and Gene Tierney in 1952. In 1970, his novel *Shall I Eat You Now* was also made into a film, *Hoffman*, starring Peter Sellers and Sinéad Cusack.[5] The couple married in 1954 and had two sons, Carlo and Marcus (known as "Sasha"). The family settled in England in late 1958.[6] Gébler and O'Brien separated in 1964 and legally divorced in 1967. O'Brien has never remarried. After her divorce, with two young children to support, following a difficult and protracted period of legal battles over custody, O'Brien had to earn a living. According to her 2012 memoir, *Country Girl*, her father's fortune was inherited from uncles, ordained priests who emigrated to Boston and made their money by patenting a medicine called "Father John's."[7] Beginning in the late 1960s, as resourceful and ingeniously self-promoting as her great-uncles, O'Brien crafted a public persona of a flamboyant red-haired colleen who appeared in shampoo ads, was photographed in yoga class, judged the 1972 Miss Beautiful Eyes competition, and featured in reports of "Swinging London"—in other words, a commodity for popular consumption.[8] This cannily ironic performance of national and gender stereotypes was frequently misunderstood—the fate of the Irish ironist since Jonathan Swift's *A Modest Proposal*—leading to imputations of "silliness," of frivolous shallowness, a lack of authorial integrity, impressions that have endured in some parts of the English-speaking world until recently.

Since 1958, O'Brien has resided principally in London, though for years she also maintained a home in County Donegal. She has always visited Ireland frequently. Official Ireland has been slow to appreciate O'Brien, though she has had dedicated Irish readers from the beginning. In a 1992 interview, she complained of Ireland, "They've never given me a prize; I don't have a great readership in Ireland, or major reviews, or anything like that, and it hurts a bit, yes."[9] It is only since the turn of the twenty-first century that she and her work have been widely received with approval in her home country, despite having been celebrated internationally for decades. A list of some of her major literary awards and their dates gives an indication of how belatedly Ireland came to officially recognize her worth: the *Yorkshire Post* Book of the Year Award (1970), the *Los Angeles Times* Book Prize for Fiction (1990), the Premio Grinzane Cavour (Italy, 1991), Guild of Great Britain Award for Best Fiction Book (1993), Writers Guild Award for Best Fiction (United States, 1993), the European Literature Prize (1995), Literary Award of the American Ireland Fund (2000), Irish Pen Lifetime Award (2001), the Ulysses Medal (University College Dublin, 2006), the Bob Hughes Lifetime Achievement Award in Irish Literature (Bord Gáis, 2006), Bord Gáis Energy Book Award, Irish Book of the Decade (2010), and the Frank O'Connor International Short Story Award, granted by the Munster Literature Festival (2011). O'Brien was inducted into Aosdána (an Irish association of artists considered exemplary contributors to their fields) and in 2015 was made a Saoi of that body (its highest distinction). *The Country Girls* trilogy was the 2019 choice of Dublin Libraries' "One City One Book" program, an initiative that receives national attention and comprises multiple cultural events around the city in a week-long festival. Always highly respected in France, she received the Irish Francophonie Ambassadors Literary Award in 2017. In 2018, she became a Dame of the British Empire for her services to literature and also received the PEN/ Nabokov International Award for a lifetime's achievement in literature. Her 2019 novel, *Girl*, received the Prix Femina Special, a prestigious French literary award, as well as the Kerry Group Irish Novel of the Year Award. In 2019, she also received the David Cohen Prize for Literature, generally regarded as "a precursor to the Nobel."[10] Just after her 90th birthday, late in 2020, she was invited to deliver the annual T. S. Eliot memorial lecture, and in 2021 was awarded France's highest literary distinction when she was named a commander in the Ordre des Artes et Lettres. As early in her career as 1973, O'Brien was invited to judge the Man Booker Prize, while in 2016 she was shortlisted for the Dublin Literary Award, for which she was longlisted the following year. She holds honorary degrees from the University of Limerick; the National University of Ireland, Galway; and Queen's University Belfast. Her record of achievement and recognition is especially significant, because she is one of the first successful Irish woman writers to come from a rural, Roman Catholic background and the first to grant such women a voice, to create an international place in literature for them.[11] According to Nuala O'Faolain, "Because Edna O'Brien existed, we are able to imagine a certain kind of Irish girl and Irish woman."[12]

Only a small number of scholars are aware of the breadth of O'Brien's international reputation—her work has been translated into at least twenty-five languages—and the astonishing scope of her output. Some of this has to do with the shifting nature of both her critical reception and her subject matter, as well as her longevity. The era of her greatest fame—or, perhaps, notoriety—ended roughly thirty years ago, so that it is necessary to be reminded of her onetime seeming cultural ubiquity in the United Kingdom. For example, O'Brien costarred with Patrick McGoohan and Lee Van Cleef in the forgotten but effective 1979 movie *The Hard Way* and appeared as herself in the first episode of the 1986 BBC television series based on Fay Weldon's novel *The Life and Loves of a She-Devil*.[13] In this period, she was also a popular chat-show guest—so much so that, on the publication of *Time and Tide* in 1992, the often hostile Nick Hornby could sneer, "television studio sofas everywhere are probably being prepared for the imminent arrival of the O'Brien bottom."[14] Years of celebrity, however, had little impact on her astonishing productivity. In addition to the numerous works of fiction for which she is best known (to date, eighteen novels and eight short-story collections), she has written several successful children's books, as well as plays, teleplays, and screenplays, and has published a volume of poetry. Her nonfiction books include biographies of the writers Byron and Joyce, *Mother Ireland* (a memoir / social history of Ireland, originally published with photographs by Fergus Bourke), *Country Girl: A Memoir*, books on Irish legend and myth, and the rarely discussed *Arabian Days*, published in 1978, a foresightful travelogue about Abu Dhabi, illustrated with photographs by Gerard Klijn, describing her impressions of a once "backward" country in the midst of becoming a modern, oil-rich nation. The juxtapositions created by sudden wealth provided O'Brien with ideal material, according to Anatole Broyard's review in the *New York Times*, which makes sly reference to the author's own professional tribulations: "Nothing could be better calculated to bring out Miss O'Brien's tolerant irony, which is the irony of someone who has herself tasted a full share of it."[15]

O'Brien has also produced dozens of shorter journalistic pieces on travel, cuisine, celebrity, war zones including Northern Ireland during the Troubles, and the everyday texture of women's lives in places like India, Cuba, and Fiji, as well as numerous book reviews. Her uncollected prose and poetry have appeared in journals, magazines, and newspapers around the world, nowhere with more consistent frequency than in the *New Yorker*, to which she has contributed over forty stories, beginning in the early 1960s. As this long-standing relationship with the *New Yorker* indicates, O'Brien has enjoyed consistent and enthusiastic support in North America, among literary figures as well as the reading public.[16] Some of her most eminent supporters include North American writers such as Alice Munro, Philip Roth, Mary Gordon, and John Updike. Henry Miller claimed that only the novels of Dostoevsky could compare to her literary achievement.[17] J. D. Salinger described her "matchless" stories as "worryingly" good.[18] Her long-time close friend and confidant, Philip Roth, has compared her to Colette and William Faulkner. So important a presence was O'Brien to Roth that she inspired the character Caesara O'Shea in his 1981 novel, *Zuckerman Unbound*.[19] Alice Munro claims to carry O'Brien's books around as if her "writing was a supply of oxygen" and insists that "no other writer is as brave and honourable and amazing."[20] According to Mary Gordon, "no one else writing today achieves what O'Brien does: the exploration of passionate subjects, and a deftness and precision of language accessible in our age most often to the chiefly cerebral, or to the detached."[21] In other words, O'Brien successfully and crucially bridges the perceived divide between "literary" and "popular" writing.

O'Brien began publishing in the 1940s (sometimes submitting work under the pseudonym "Dina Bryan"), when she first contributed occasional pieces to Dublin periodicals and newspapers including the *Irish Press*, and was particularly encouraged in her writing by the Irish revolutionary icon Peadar O'Donnell, then editor of the groundbreaking political-literary monthly magazine *The Bell*. After moving to London, her short stories began to appear in periodicals such as *The Spectator*, *Everywoman's*, the *Saturday Evening Post*, and *Ladies' Home Journal*. It was on the strength of her "sketches," published and unpublished, as well as the work she had been doing as a reader working for Iain Hamilton at the Hutchinson publishing firm, that she was offered fifty pounds in 1958 to write a novel with the support of Hutchinson in London and Knopf in the United States. The novel, *The Country Girls*, which she claimed to have written in the course of a few weeks, was completed the following year and published in early 1960.[22] In O'Brien's recent memoir, she recalls one particular prepublication response to *The Country Girls*. After a celebratory dinner with Hamilton and one of the manuscript's readers, the novelist Clifford Hanley, and buoyed by the enthusiastic praise the men had given the finished manuscript, O'Brien decided to leave a copy of the text for her husband on their hall table. Gébler surprised her a few mornings later "by appearing quite early in the doorway of the kitchen, the manuscript in his hand." What she records as his reaction was one that would become general all over Ireland: "You can write and I will never forgive you."[23] That was in 1959, and by the end of the following year, many people in Ireland would come to find the novel unforgivable.

The book's representations of sexual desire, sexual abuse, and even sexual humor set in a perhaps only too recognizable Irish rural location provoked public outrage and condemnation by, most publicly, John Charles McQuaid, Catholic Primate of Ireland and Archbishop of Dublin, and a government minister who would go on to become taoiseach (prime minister), Charles Haughey.[24]

McQuaid, whose purity campaign kept the Irish Censorship Board busy in the 1950s, inaugurated a decade of controversial persecution of Irish writers, which led to, among other things, the novelist John McGahern losing his position as a primary school teacher in 1965. In a comment McQuaid made to his press officer, Osmond Dowling, in 1966, he called O'Brien "a renegade and a dirty one."[25] At home in Tuamgraney, the reactions were shock, shame, and feelings of betrayal. O'Brien was denounced from the pulpit by the parish priest who was said to have conducted a book-burning in the chapel yard (though there is no evidence this ever took place). O'Brien's family, and especially her mother, felt humiliated and exposed. The scandal of O'Brien having previously eloped with a divorced "foreigner" compounded her family's sense of disgrace. Vicious letters were written anonymously from the village to the author, one local woman claiming to have been possessed by the devil as a result of reading the novel.[26] In several interviews, O'Brien recalls the discovery, after her mother's death, of a defaced copy of *The Country Girls*—dedicated to her mother in its first edition—in which words and passages were effaced, whole pages torn out. However, in the spring of 1960, when *The Country Girls* was first published, initial reviews and opinions in Ireland were favorable. Maurice Kennedy's review in *The Irish Times*, for example, described the novel as having "a fresh dewy sincerity about it, a nice accuracy of observation and feeling. . . . With any luck Miss O'Brien should have an immensely successful literary career."[27] Benedict Kiely, who saw the proofs in February 1960, remained her staunch champion for the rest of his life. Frank McEvoy, getting ready to launch *The Kilkenny Magazine* with James Delahunty, wrote to O'Brien in June 1960, congratulating her on a "marvelous achievement" and asking for a chapter for his fledgling publication of the next installment of what was already known to be the planned *Country Girls* trilogy. In the letter, he also asks whether she expects the novel to be banned, suggesting that this would be a great boost to sales.[28]

Banned it very soon was. *The Country Girls* was the first of six of O'Brien's novels that the Irish Censorship Board would judge indecent and obscene under section 7(a) of the Censorship of Publications Act, 1946. It would also be banned in Australia and New Zealand but was nevertheless enthusiastically received elsewhere in the Anglophone world. In the United States, where it was published by Knopf that same year, reviews called the book "brash and bright," "delightful," "charming," introducing "a writer of zestful humor and humanity." Even Dorothy Parker wrote a favorable notice for *Esquire* magazine.[29] In the United Kingdom, especially after the novel's second printing there by Penguin in 1962, it was received in similar terms. In O'Brien's correspondence with Hamilton about the future of her writing career at the time, she does not betray much concern about having been banned in Ireland, but she was not happy with Hutchinson's decision to issue the first edition in the experimental format of an expensive paperback rather than in hardcover, blaming this decision for a relative lack of early reviews. However, according to the *Sunday Times*, the novel was "a buoyantly youthful novel, with all the freshness in the world and undertones of something much more lasting."[30] The *Evening Standard* said the book offered an "excellent and highly unusual blend of bawdiness and innocence."[31] V. S. Naipaul in the *New Statesman* described it as "a first novel of great charm by a natural writer, . . . fresh and lyrical and bursting with energy,"[32] and Kingsley Amis claimed he was awarding it his first-novel prize of the year.[33]

In the sixty years since publication, *The Country Girls* made its author's lasting reputation. It is the one text of O'Brien's that makes at least some appearance in the official Irish literary canon and has never been out of print.[34] It usually appears as part of *The Country Girls Trilogy*, which was reissued with a newly written Epilogue in 1988. The novel has continued to define O'Brien, a fact she accepts and appreciates, as is evident in the titles of her 2012 memoir, *Country Girl*, and her 2019 novel, *Girl*. In 1986, she appeared on the cover of the magazine *Irish America*, under the title "Country Girl Revisited." In 1989, Seamus Heaney interviewed her for the RTÉ radio program *Off the Shelf*, a program listed in the *RTÉ Guide* as an interview with "The Country Girl." In 1991, the *Irish Independent* ran a feature entitled "Country Girl Goes Home," reporting O'Brien's receipt of an honorary doctorate from the National University of Ireland, Galway. O'Brien revisited the text herself when she produced a stage treatment of the novel for the Red Kettle Theatre Company production that toured Ireland in 2012 and was revived in an Abbey Theatre production in the spring of 2019. O'Brien can still incite discomfort in the twenty-first century. Some online reviews from the first theatrical run objected to the nudity onstage. In March 2013, in the "Diary" that Anne Enright regularly contributed to the *London Review of Books*, she discussed the history of Ireland's Censorship Board, suggesting that, in the case of McGahern and O'Brien in particular, it was the people at home in rural Leitrim and Clare, respectively, the ostensible subjects of the young novelists' early literary productions, who took most vigorous offense and umbrage at their work.[35] McGahern's local library board banned *The Barracks*, according to Enright, when the Irish Censorship Board never got around to doing so. She also makes the somewhat urban-centric claim that while "Edna O'Brien's erstwhile neighbours might have burned copies of *The Country Girls* in the churchyard . . . up in Dublin everyone who was a reader read it without a qualm."[36]

Nevertheless, for decades O'Brien continued to feel rejected and unforgiven by her home place and her own family. In 1929, in *A Room of One's Own*, Virginia Woolf, the subject of a successful 1981 play by O'Brien,[37] complained of the trivialization of "feminine" values in literature: "This is an important book, the critic assumes, because it deals with war. This is an insignificant book because it deals with the feelings of women in a drawing-room. A scene in a battle-field is more important than a scene in a shop."[38] If since Woolf wrote these words there has been an effort to accord the same status to the "domestic" and "personal," the private "feminine" concerns of sex, relationships, and family, as that granted "larger," traditionally "masculine" concerns of history and politics, even when considered by the male writer through family dynamics, the spheres remain strangely separate, if nominally equal.[39] According to Anne Fogarty, "Often writing by women seems to be considered unworthy of consideration in the Irish public sphere because it is viewed as lacking in universality and as being too particularist and concerned with the lesser issues of the domestic sphere."[40] Benedict Kiely has noted that, similarly in O'Brien's case, "it was not to be tolerated that a young woman educated, as we used to say, at one of the best Irish convent-schools, should come out, even in a fetching County Clare accent, with home truths or sharp statements about what we used to call sex."[41] O'Brien put it plainly when she stated, "I believe I was banned because I am a woman."[42] The Irish poet Eithne Strong, in a review of *A Pagan Place*, says of O'Brien's relationship with Ireland that "her reaction to former interdictions is not a McGahern anguish, rather it is a deliberate dwelling on previously forbidden ground, in a tacit insistence that it is as valid for writing about as, say, fitivation, the weather or anything else that goes to making up 24 hours."[43] Historically, O'Brien has caused offense by daring to be a woman who speaks uncomfortable truths

But just what did this novel do to stir up so much trouble and make O'Brien's fame? The narrative, loosely based on characters and events from O'Brien's own young life, follows the lives of two girls growing up in rural County Clare. The narrator, Caithleen (Cait) Brady, is an insecure, nervous child terrified of her feckless, drunken, abusive father. Her father's self-indulgence means that the family struggles to survive in a once-grand but badly run-down house and minimally producing farm with the help of a single farm hand. Cait, dreamy and lyrical about flowers and birds and the Virgin Mary, clings anxiously to her put-upon mother. Her friend Baba Brennan, on the other hand, is the daughter of a doctor, and so the prematurely jaded, wisecracking Baba enjoys rare privileges such as a shiny bicycle, new clothes, a modern house and motor car, and a cheeky attitude toward her own seemingly unconventional mother. Cait and Baba have a competitive, complex relationship that includes mutual sexual experimentation, providing Baba one of her many opportunities to threaten and torment shy, dependent Cait. The girls go to a convent school together—Cait on a scholarship—after Cait's mother disappears, presumed drowned. Cait has become infatuated with an older neighbor, known as "Mr Gentleman," an infatuation of which he takes advantage while the girls are away from home. Desperately unhappy, the girls get themselves thrown out of the convent by writing a dirty verse on a holy card and must then make their way in life without completing their secondary education. They head off to Dublin, share a room, and have various adventures there with men and boys, including a planned weekend away on the Continent for Cait and Mr. Gentleman, a tryst that never materializes. The novel is unsparing in its depiction of cruelty, privation, filth, misery, exploitation, and violence. It is also vivid and moving in its description of the natural world, childhood innocence, the all-consuming love between mother and child, the thrilling enticements of Dublin, the delight to be taken in the first flush of independence, and the joys and terrors of female embodiment. It is, above all, often raucously funny and irreverent about all physical experiences: sleeping, eating, eliminating, and sex in many forms. Despite its reputation, the novel is not salacious, nor does it ever blaspheme, even if the girls innocently attempt to; but the one revered object it does fail to take seriously is the sanctity of the Irish female. In O'Brien's novel, the Irish wife and mother is a resentful, unwilling slave to sexual demands and household drudgery, a fate shared by the downtrodden Mrs. Brady and the glamorous, "fast" Mrs. Brennan. Older men prey on young Irish girls, expose themselves to women and girls, fondle them, demand kisses of them, and threaten more serious attacks. Girls experience sexual desire for each other, for older girls in school, for nuns, for remote, idealized men, all objects of longing superior to any of the men Cait and Baba regularly encounter, who tend to provoke disgust or laughter or both. This laughter may be the novel's greatest transgression.

It is disturbing when surveying the contemporary reviews of *The Country Girls*, as well as the correspondence O'Brien received in both praise and censure of it, to note the repeated emphasis on the "youth," "freshness," and "girlishness," not only of the book's content and characters but of the author herself, a twenty-nine-year-old married woman and mother of two at the time of the novel's publication. This preoccupation with O'Brien's constitutively "immature" femininity could be aggressively unpleasant, as when her own husband asserted that her talent "resided in her knickers." He claimed to have written her first two books for her as she slept, rewriting and refining the silly gushing she had produced by day. He continued to insist up to 1988 that he had "held her hand, and taught her the ABC of narrative."[44] Gébler's campaign of defamation was later taken up by his nephew, the journalist Stan Gebler Davies, who repeated the charges as late as 1992 in a "review" for the *Evening Standard* of O'Brien's novel *Time and Tide*. After categorizing her work as "the sort of self-indulgent drivel written by housewives seeking to escape Wimbledon," he satirically commends his "former aunt's" good sense in writing about herself, that is, having continued to take her husband's advice that she run "her diaries through the typewriter. . . . It is a literary technique well known to all scribblers, and while it may not often produce high literature, it is frequently lucrative."[45] In reaction to O'Brien's response to this slander in a *Hot Press* interview, Gebler Davies, after accusing her of maligning him and referring to her as "Edna Average" and boring, advises she leave "malicious gossip" to "demented old ladies."[46]

Though O'Brien is often linked with McGahern as having suffered similar difficulties at around the same time and for the same reasons, there is an important distinction to be made between the writers' experience with condemnation and censorship.[47] Decades before McGahern's death in 2006, his reputation in Ireland had been thoroughly revised, and he has ever since been considered one of the most important Irish writers of the late twentieth century. O'Brien, on the other hand, is only recently receiving long-overdue acknowledgment in Ireland of her significant literary and cultural achievements, as detailed earlier. McGahern has been forgiven; it has taken much longer for Ireland to ask for O'Brien's forgiveness.[48] Though McGahern's novels are largely set in rural Ireland and frequently revisit characters from his own childhood, especially the brutal, domineering father and the saintly, doomed mother, his work does not draw the same accusations of overreliance on autobiography, or of "being stuck in a rut," that O'Brien's works have persistently received.[49] The sins McGahern committed do not appear to include having a range that is "narrow and obsessional," as one critic characterized it.[50] One of O'Brien's most vehement critics, Nick Hornby, laments her "ploughing the same emotional furrow" in her "airless joyless tales," which feature "little discernible modulation or progression" and stop "just short of evoking leprechauns."[51] This conflation of cheap Irish stereotypes with tedious repetition appeared as recently as a 2006 review of *The Light of Evening* in *The Observer*, which complained, "like the fiddlers who clog up Dublin's cheesier theme pubs you can't help but wish that occasionally O'Brien would change her tune."[52]

The early novels of the late McGahern were, like O'Brien's, popularly maligned and, in one instance (*The Dark*), officially banned. However, as noted, resentment and suspicion persisted much longer in O'Brien's case. As Benedict Kiely said in his 1969 endorsement of the embattled O'Brien, "while it's bad and very bad for a man to speak out and tell the truth, it is utterly unthinkable that a woman . . . should claim such a liberty."[53] Even in the United Kingdom, where sensitivities about national identity did not influence O'Brien's reception (though national stereotypes may have), initially positive critical attitudes began to change by the time the ironically titled *Girls in Their Married Bliss*, the final novel in what became *The Country Girls Trilogy*, appeared in 1964.[54] The trilogy follows the fate of the two young Irish women through disillusioning love affairs and unhappy marriages, and the books, appropriately, grow darker, more cynical and satirical, as the protagonists emerge from their adolescent dreaminess and mature, no longer girlishly "fresh" and "charming." The two novels that followed the trilogy, *August Is a Wicked Month* (1965) and *Casualties of Peace* (1966), are not set in Ireland, but both feature Irish women struggling with changing expectations for sex and marriage, a change often conveyed through the contrast between the rural girlhoods they have left behind and their more "sophisticated," but just as unfulfilling, urban lives. Even though the author had escaped her home country, her work continued to be haunted by it. *A Pagan Place* (1970) and *Night* (1972), as well as a number of short stories that appeared frequently in prestigious periodicals over the years (many of which were published in story collections), several of her well-received plays, including *The Gathering* (1974), *A Cheap Bunch of Nice Flowers* (1975), *Flesh and Blood* (1984), *Our Father* (1999), and *Family Butchers* (2005), and the stylized memoir/cultural history *Mother Ireland* (1976), are all set in Ireland.

Later "non-Irish" novels, such as *The High Road* (1988) and *Time and Tide* (1992), continued to feature Irish women poised between two worlds: one comforting and maternal yet blighted by sexual oppression enforced by church, state, and family; the other exciting and stimulating yet finally offering only sexual exploitation promoted as "enlightenment" and "liberation."[55] Superficial readings of these works, encouraged by the titillating fact of being banned in O'Brien's home country, secured her growing reputation as a writer of racy novels, a reputation that, along with her exceptional good looks and dramatic self-presentation and her occasional appearance on the margins of the "swinging London" scene of the 1960s and '70s, resulted in the trivialization and critical dismissal of her work as merely commercial, too transparently and wearily autobiographical, and preoccupied solely with "women's" personal concerns—that is, insufficiently socially engaged at a time when gender and social roles were in flux and identity politics was developing.[56] This dismissive attitude eventually crept into some American reviews of her work. As late as 1992, an American journalist opened an interview with the novelist, "Edna O'Brien has red hair and a scarlet reputation."[57]

The critical backlash O'Brien suffered was remarkably ad hominem, including remarks on her physical appearance and derogations of her "silliness" (the adjective "silly" appears in more than one critical assessment of her work).[58] She has noticed, "people review me rather than my books."[59] In speaking to Jan Moir in *The Guardian* in 1992, O'Brien admitted that, while she could withstand a great deal of criticism, it did bother her that some of her reviews "have a shockingly personal tone, a rabid personal tone."[60] Even the most positive interviews—and she has been interviewed dozens of times—cannot seem to avoid commenting on her eyes, skin, voice, hair, clothes. Even into her eighties, she continued to be subject to this kind of evaluation. Rachel Cooke, for example, declared in 2011 that "age cannot wither her," and Mary Kenny, in her 2012 review of *Country Girl*, described the author as remaining "glamorous and striking."[61] While O'Brien's official literary status in the United Kingdom began to suffer in the late 1960s through the 1970s, Irish commentators were divided in their opinion of this rising international figure at the close of the first decade of her fame. Benedict Kiely defended the "convent girl with her temper riz" against the censors and predicted great things for her,[62] while Bernard Bergonzi bemoaned her "feminine-primitivist rejection of intelligence."[63] John Mellors used the contemporary language of feminism against her, when he asserted that " out of sourness and sentimentality comes female chauvinist terrorism."[64] Sean McMahon deplored her "retardation" and her "neo-feminist propaganda,"[65] a painful irony at a time when feminists were largely denouncing her work, despite Anatole

Broyard's opinion that *The Country Girls Trilogy* is a "powerful argument for feminism"[66] and Julia O'Faolain's belief, stated in in 1974, that feminists "should be grateful to her. . . . Her stories are bulletins from a front on which they will not care to engage, field reports on the feminine condition at its most acute."[67] Pearl Bell noted the fact that "O'Brien has been criticized by feminists for her 'narrow' concentration on unredemptive pain. Yet her work is art, not tract. Where, except in a work of art, can we perceive the cruelest depths of a woman's world? Without such knowledge, how could we learn to care for a different way of being a woman?"[68]

Scandal certainly helped promote O'Brien's career initially. In 1967, her friend John Connery could ask in a letter, adopting a tone of mock concern, whether she was "still the leader of the banned," as Éamon de Valera had not mentioned her lately.[69] In 1972, she was identified in one of the letters collected for the compilation of the official British government publication *Pornography: The Longford Report*, alongside Henry Miller, William Burroughs, and D. H. Lawrence, as a "leading purveyor of insidiously pornographic and perverted views on sex,"[70] but her enduring international success has little to do with scandal or her reputation as a writer of "dirty" novels. As noted, she has been winning important international literary prizes from the beginning of her career and has had the support and admiration of eminent writers from the start, including some notable Irish figures: William Trevor, who observed that "rarely has an Irishwoman protested as eloquently" and described her as a "writer of wit and piquancy";[71] Derek Mahon, who identified her as a "culture heroine";[72] Seamus Heaney, who asserted that "Edna O'Brien is actually very important in the history of this country";[73] Declan Kiberd, who recognized the fact that "O'Brien was arguably the writer who made many of the subsequent advances in Irishwomen's writing possible, and . . . continued to craft a prose of surpassing beauty and exactitude";[74] Clare Boylan, who argued that O'Brien was "the first Irish novelist who managed to encapsulate the emotions of Irish Catholicism and the Irish convent influence with both humour and realism. . . . In her early novels she changes the image of Irish women";[75] and Anne Enright, who insists on the importance of "praising O'Brien because she has taken enough insults in her day."[76] Early in 2018, speaking at the PEN/Nabokov awards ceremony where O'Brien was honored, her fellow Irish author in voluntary exile Colum McCann referred to the novelist as a "legend" and a "treasure," a writer who "makes justice from reality. She refuses to live in stunned submission to the times. She imagines immensities."

At an event held in University College Dublin in September 2018, which celebrated O'Brien as Ireland's "greatest living writer," similar encomia were offered by a panel of writers including Frank McGuinness, Éilís Ní Dhuibhne, Sean O'Reilly, Danielle McLaughlin, and Louise Nealon.[77] Contemporary Irish writers appreciate her legacy, but O'Brien's Irishness has often provided a platform for much of the remarkably personal justifications for derogation of her work, even though her stated intention, from her first novel, has been to "eschew hypocrisy and stage-Irish rigamarole."[78] In an appreciation of her friend Samuel Beckett in 1971, she endorsed his condemnation of "the unctuous, gombeen, crubeen, twighlightis mistakenly thought to be Celtic,"[79] yet she has been described as cynically "curating a wild Irish persona" and as verging on "a parody of stage-Irish."[80] Despite her own repeated and strenuous objections to the "codology" of the "colleen image" that has attached to her,[81] she has been described as a "veritable flame-haired temptress"[82] and as "reading interminable prose-poems beautifully from under a chestnut-tree of red hair . . . adjusting her belt like a Connemara Dietrich."[83] She is "witty, candid, theatrical, she talks in legato Irish cadences and bright, feminine tones,"[84] and she "comes on like a brass band with cymbals clanging . . . speaking in a soft, sweet Irish brogue and looking like a cousin from the country."[85] Even the C-Span video recording of her acceptance speech at the 2018 PEN/Nabokov Prize ceremony is captioned, "a lilting bit o'magic spoken by author Edna O'Brien." One particularly incensed critic has deplored the novelist for being "an outrageous concoction of what foreigners expect an Irish person to be—mellifluous, volatile, wanton, irrational"—and chides "American critics [who] repeat the error of endorsing O'Brien's stage-Irishness."[86]

As noted, another recurrent complaint distinguishing critical assessments of O'Brien is the appearance of characters in her fiction considered to be too transparently autobiographical.[87] Despite McGahern also drawing on easily identified locals and family members in his fiction, he escaped what Amanda Greenwood has identified as the "unrelenting conflation of author and character" typical of commentary on O'Brien's fiction.[88] Such objections may indicate a discomfort with boundaries between author and text too emphatically made porous, as well as with the constructed nature of national and sexual identities—and the unacknowledged interdependence of those constructs—that such stylization of character discloses. O'Brien's theatricality self-consciously functions as social critique. In "The Books We Read" chapter of *Mother Ireland*, O'Brien recalls a childhood trip made to a Limerick cinema to see *For Whom the Bell Tolls*, a recollection that can be read as a commentary on her own work's reception: "The film's historic or political significance was cast aside, or never grasped, because what happened—so one was told—was that Ingrid Bergman loved Gary Cooper and had a baby inside her while he was most treacherously shot."[89] The real significance of O'Brien's fiction is often similarly overlooked by readers distracted by sex and celebrity. Just as Wordsworth, in the words of Oscar Wilde's barb, "found in stones the sermons he had already hidden there," reviewers expect the sameness in O'Brien that they claim to discover. In fact, O'Brien is ever citing and rewriting her own oeuvre even as she interpolates, ventriloquizes, and interacts with other writers and traditions. As Julia Obert argues, beginning with *The Country Girls*, O'Brien's work has signified "a desire to open the country to both Global feminisms and transnational textualities."[90] Obert is just one of a number of recent critics who have begun attending to O'Brien's practices of intertextuality.[91]

The novelist's "return" to Irish subjects at the turn of the twenty-first century, especially the controversial "state-of-the-nation" novels *House of Splendid Isolation* (1994), *Down by the River* (1996), *Wild Decembers* (1999), and *In the Forest* (2002), did not initially change critical attitudes, as she was deemed by a number of Irish critics, including, most consistently, Fintan O'Toole and Kevin Myers, to be out of touch with modern Ireland. As Peter Stanford argued in 2002, "logically, she should now be canonized for her foresight, but there is no logic in Ireland when it comes to Edna O'Brien."[92] Recent developments have vindicated O'Brien, however, including revelations about the role the Roman Catholic Church has played in the imprisonment and abuse of Irish women and children, as well as the rise and legitimation of the once-reviled political party Sinn Féin, whose former leader, Gerry Adams, O'Brien bravely defended in the early stages of the negotiations that led to the Good Friday Agreement. Her most recent collection of short stories, *Saints and Sinners* (2011), her memoir *Country Girl* (2012), and the novels *The Little Red Chairs* (2015) and *Girl* (2019) have been treated more generously, perhaps in part by dint of the author's longevity. Even Fintan O'Toole, one of her most severe Irish critics, in responding to the result of the 2018 referendum to repeal Ireland's constitutional amendment restricting abortion, made appreciative mention of her work's relentless exposure of the realities of Irish women's struggles under the concerted oppressions of church and state.

As O'Brien's elevation to one of the all-time greatest people in Count Clare by popular vote would indicate, all seems to be forgiven, though perhaps because largely forgotten, in her native county. This attitude reflects a national shift. Irish reviews of *Saints and Sinners* were laudatory to an almost suspicious degree. They exuded a slightly desperate air, a feeling that time is running out, that reparation and expiation are overdue. The former president of Ireland Mary Robinson reviewed *Country Girl: A Memoir* for *The Irish Times*, a choice that might constitute a surreptitious apology on behalf of the nation for the treatment the novelist has received from official Ireland. Certainly the conclusion of Robinson's review—"Perhaps now, on its publication, is the time for a proper reassessment of Edna O'Brien as one of the great creative writers of her generation"[93]— sounds like a call to her countrymen, a significant change from Kevin Myers's claim in 1985 that he "could willingly stick a hatchet in [O'Brien's] head only to be applauded by the nation."[94] Reviews of *The Little Red Chairs*, universally enthusiastic in the United States, the United Kingdom, and Ireland, share a largely unspoken assumption regarding O'Brien's significance, performing in some quarters a comforting amnesia about the history of her struggle to be taken seriously. Éilís Ní Dhuibhne, who reviewed the novel for *The Irish Times*, like her fellow novelist Anne Enright, will not allow the Irish reading public or its official literary experts to forget that, while now the recipient of the greatest honors the state can grant an artist, O'Brien's work was once "banned and reviled." Ní Dhuibhne concludes her review with the astonishing assertion that the novel is "arguably one of the most interesting and ambitious ever written by an Irish author."[95] O'Brien is not finished, however. She recently published her eighteenth novel, *Girl*, based on the experiences of the Nigerian school girls kidnaped by Boko Haram in 2014. Like the previous novel, *The Little Red Chairs*, the implicit internationalism of her fiction has become explicit, as her narratives are set in locations farther and farther away from Ireland.[96] In a 2019 BBC interview with Kirsty Lang about the new novel, O'Brien said that she would "like to write one more book."[97] In preparation for *Girl*, though O'Brien was in her late eighties, she traveled to Nigeria (with nearly £15,000 stashed in her clothing)[98] to conduct what she deemed the necessary research to explore once more, in yet another variety, her most enduring theme: the struggle for women to realize full personhood under patriarchal domination. Reviews of *Girl* echo this reading of the novel's place in O'Brien's oeuvre: Alex Clark, for example, notes the novel's "sense that women will be marked out for control and punishment wherever they are and in whatever circumstances or historical context,"[99] and Terence Rafferty's review forestalls any possible objections to the text's subject matter, its potential to "stir up a bit of a scandal": "That's something she has spent her whole long career learning to live with. She'll survive, in that room of her own where the words come to her, out on the rim with all her lonely girls."[100]

O'Brien's persistent theme of the struggles of girls and women organizes the chapters of this book, beginning with chapter 1, "Anti-Oedipal Desires," which traces O'Brien's relentless, career-long exposure of the psychological and social damage wrought by the patriarchal family, her systematic attempt to demolish a long-cherished illusion of ideological purity in Irish society. This illusion is challenged by the kind of alternative relationships imagined in O'Brien's' fiction, especially between and among women, though even these potentially liberating connections can become transactional and exploitative. According to Lynn Chancer, under the unjust social arrangements of patriarchy, sadomasochism inevitably emerges.[101] Chapter 2, "The Liberating Sadomasochism of Things," looks at the family home and the ways in which O'Brien uncovers a hidden history of Irish women's small refusals to submit to patriarchal expectations of total self-abnegation, a resistance registered through domestic interiors and everyday objects. Moving outside the home, chapter 3, "The Ungrammatical Sublime," considers the tensions between O'Brien's acknowledged debt to the Irish landscape as a signal inspiration and the implications of her reputation for "excessively" ornate descriptions of the natural world. This association with the "natural" has been used by some critics to devalue her work as something primitive and instinctual rather than truly literary and artistic, an implicitly gendered critique of her chosen subject matter and its effect on her style. Chapter 4, "Otherworldly

Possessions," evaluates the status of O'Brien as a "realist" writer, by considering the nonmimetic versions of perception and the "real" in her work, from dreams to mythologies, including Irish legends and tales. The effect of national myths and the work that feminist writers have been conducting since the 1960s to remythologize literature and history are central considerations in O'Brien's work, which exploits the liberatory potential in alternative, premodern systems of knowledge, while acknowledging the damage wrought by triumphalist inter-pretations of national destiny. Chapter 5, "Myth and Mutation," builds on the previous chapter's excavation of myth in the fiction, focusing on the frequent references to shape-shifting and the appearance of human-animal hybrids, a topos O'Brien frequently indexes to violation and exclusion, to uneasy alliances and imposed associations, including those that shape national identity. O'Brien's complex preoccupations with Irish identity are implicated in everything she writes. She has described her connection to her homeland as "umbilical," while also asserting the global relevance and resonance of Irish experience. Frustrated with the inadequate international response to the Northern Irish Troubles, she expressed a desire to be shot by the British army, understanding the impact of a "splashy" death.[102] Chapter 6, "Disorder, Death, and Dirt," analyzes the way in which the dead body figures as a fascinating object, even a source of wisdom, in O'Brien's work. It is at least as often the bodies of animals—considered to be detritus, to be treated with much more dispatch than is true for human corpses—that can speak most meaningfully to O'Brien's characters. The ostensibly dead body grounds the human in the greater world, insists on our connectedness to all elements of creation, and suggests that the line between life and death is a per-meable one.

In 2018, the same year that saw commemoration of the centenary of Irish and British women getting the right to vote, article 40.3.3 of the Irish constitution, which severely restricted women's access to abortion, known as the "eighth amendment," was repealed in a popular referendum, by a significant majority of over 66 percent of the electorate. At the time of that original amendment to the constitution in 1983, O'Brien remembers being horrified. She recognized the violence inherent in such legislation: "It is murder to the lives of women who are already born and trying to live their lives. The zealots never take into account the penalizing due to poverty and exhaustion that arises from having large families—the unhappiness for the mother, the damage that redounds on the children. They don't take that into account. I don't think much of Pope John Paul's opinions; he may be a charming man and a great traveller, but he's a dogmatist. Women's lot is hard anywhere, but an Irishwoman's lot is ten times harder."[103] In Eimear McBride's introduction to the latest reissue of *The Country Girls Trilogy*, she identifies the novelist's understanding of "the struggle for women's voices to be heard above the clamour of an ultraconservative, ultrareligious, and institutionally misogynist society."[104] O'Brien's anticipation of popular liberatory movements and attitudes is not confined to Ireland, however, as noted by Colm McCann, who observes that O'Brien has "been #MeTooing for the last fifty years."[105] What Anne Enright has said of O'Brien's protagonists is true of the novelist herself: they are "completely honest, completely courageous, and heroic on the slenderest and most absolute of terms." Despite a career that started in scandal and a body of work often characterized as sex obsessed, to quote Enright again, "what was actually remarkable about her writing, what had been remarkable all along: it was not sex, at all, but honesty." [106] More recently, Enright has observed that "for Edna O'Brien, courage has never been in short supply."[107] Her honesty and courage are why O'Brien has endured and continues to inspire.

1 · ANTI-OEDIPAL DESIRES

The women of Fiji enshrined my view of the great desirable matriarchal society.

When interviewed in 1965 for the BBC television program *Panorama* on censorship in Ireland, in response to the question of whether it bothered her that in Ireland her work is considered "obscene or indecent," Edna O'Brien responded, "I'm not over sensitive about it because all the censors and bishops and judges are all men, and the Irishman's attitude to sex is very strange."[1] Helen Gurley Brown, author of an infamous 1962 novel, *Sex and the Single Girl*, and longtime editor of *Cosmopolitan* (a literary magazine that Gurley Brown reshaped into a lifestyle guide for the "liberated" single woman), asked O'Brien in 1967 if she would be interested in writing a piece for the magazine on the topic of "being a daddy's girl." The author responded, "I don't know what it means to be a daddy's girl."[2] O'Brien's subjects do not include loving father-daughter relationships. As Patricia Coughlan has noted, in O'Brien's fiction, "the father-function tends, disastrously, to be strong and weak at the same time: weak in empathy and protective love, strong in regulation, assertions of control, and the making of inappropriate demands."[3] Of her own father, O'Brien has said, "he murdered in me each and all of my tiniest inclinations, so that I walked with a stoop, thought with a dread."[4] O'Brien's protagonists inevitably duplicate this oppressive dynamic in their adult relationships with cold, controlling men, while often drawing emotional sustenance from other women. The complex but enduring friendship between Cait and Baba of *The Country Girls* (1960), and the novels comprising the trilogy, established a pattern of alliances between women found in other texts, such as Willa and Patsy in *Casualties of Peace* (1966), Mary and Mona in *Down by the River* (1996), Cassandra and Imelda in *In the Forest* (2002), and Maryam and Buki in *Girl* (2019). The most primal, most intense woman-to-woman connections, however, are between mothers and daughters, though that relationship is also a source of frustration and pain, destructive in its own way. In the same unpublished piece in which O'Brien describes her father as soul-destroyer, her mother emerges as another stultifying force: "whenever I wandered abroad ... [she] called me back to that world of stirabout and bowel movements, to the cold, dark rooms reeking of vomited drink, to the cold dark rooms waiting for their next hideous commission of sin."[5] O'Brien's depiction of the traditional Irish family consistently features a needy, undermining mother, whose emotional overinvestment threatens to cripple her daughter, alongside a distant, violent father, sometimes capable of rape and murder.[6] Contemporary families in her fiction tend to consist of young parents on the verge of a breakup, a wife and children emotionally abandoned (and minimally sketched) by a philandering father, or an anxious single mother with sons. O'Brien's most potent and persistent act of cultural transgression has been her relentless exposure of the psychological and social damage wrought by the patriarchal family, her systematic attempt to demolish a long-cherished illusion of ideological purity in Western, and especially Irish, society.[7]

The sanctity of the family comprises one of the foundations of the post-independence Irish nation-state and Irish identity, reliant on both a self-image of a distinctive and fervent Roman Catholic piety and the maintenance of "traditional" filial virtues of hearth and home. As Gerardine Meaney has observed, "In post-colonial southern Ireland a particular construction of sexual and familial roles became the very substance of what it means to be Irish."[8] In the twenty-first century, the Irish public has been forced to confront the consequences of the regime of control of sexuality, especially women's, that has been historically central to the institutions of family, state, and church. News reports and reopened investigations have kept the enormity of the treatment of Irish women and children in the last century before the public in this century, phenomena about which O'Brien has been writing from the first. Hundreds of allegations of child sexual abuse by Catholic priests were identified in a series of reports in the first decade of the twenty-first century, commissioned by the Irish government, such as the Ferns Report in 2005, the Murphy and Ryan Reports, both in 2009, and the Cloyne Report in 2011. Clerical sex abuse is a key plot point in both *A Pagan Place* (1970) and *In the Forest*. The historian Catherine Corless's suspicions about the unrecorded burial of children on the grounds of the "mother and baby" home in Tuam, County Galway, run by the Bon Secours nuns, were confirmed in March 2017 when the remains of nearly eight hundred babies and toddlers were found in a long-disused septic tank,[9] and more evidence regularly emerges about the practice of selling babies born in such homes to childless couples, especially Americans (recent revelations include the illegal registration of adoptive couples as biological parents).[10] The women imprisoned and used as slave labor in the Magdalene laundries were belatedly honored and recognized in an apology for their treatment from the president, Michael D. Higgins, in June 2018. O'Brien has been referring to the Irish system of incarceration of unmarried pregnant or otherwise sexually suspect women and girls for years. For example, in *Girls in Their Married Bliss* (1964), Baba expresses defiance in face of her drunken, estranged husband with a sneering remark about him expecting to find her in "the Magdalene laundry";[11] in *August Is a Wicked Month*, published in 1965, the first novel to appear after the *The Country Girls* trilogy, the character of Ellen describes herself as having "been brought up to believe in punishment; sin in a field and then the long awful spell in the Magdalen laundry scrubbing it out, down on her knees getting cleansed";[12] while the narrator of the short story "House of My Dreams" (1974) recalls her sister being sent to a Magdalene laundry after an unsuccessful attempt to self-abort an "illegitimate" pregnancy.[13] Preparations are made in *A Pagan Place* to send the narrator's unmarried sister to a mother and baby home, where "it was already arranged that Emma's baby would be handed over to the State a few seconds after it was born."[14] *Down by the River* was based on the "X case" of 1994, in which a fourteen-year-old rape victim, impregnated by a family friend, was stopped from traveling to England for an abortion.[15] In O'Brien's novel, the rapist is the victim's own father. Reaction to the X case resulted in a change to the law, to allow travel abroad for terminations, an "outsourcing" of abortion services that ultimately fueled greater outrage about Ireland's cruel and hypocritical treatment of women. As noted, the Eighth Amendment of the Irish Constitution Act 1983, which severely limited access to abortion, would go on to be repealed entirely by public referendum in June 2018. Earlier in 2018, Irish police reopened the 1984 Kerry Babies case, a notorious miscarriage of justice, in which Joanne Hayes, a young single woman, was accused of giving birth to and murdering two babies whose bodies were found miles apart and one of whose blood type was incompatible with the purported mother's. Hayes wrote about her own experience in *My Story* (1985). In the same period, after meeting with Hayes several times while spending months in County Kerry,[16] O'Brien wrote a play and a screen treatment based on the case, though neither was produced.

Against this background of systemic abuse, no happy marriages or healthy traditionally Oedipal families appear in O'Brien's fiction. Women in these texts act as though obliged to pursue heterosexual romance but often betray the self-hatred aroused by this same pursuit, as when Cait, toward the end of *The Country Girls*, preparing for a date, simply states, "I hate being a woman,"[17] or when the mother in "Rose in the Heart" cries out, "Why be a woman?"[18] or when, in an unpublished passage from a draft of *Time and Tide* (1992), the narrator says of Nell, "She could not bear to be a woman. . . . She could not bear to think of down there without freaking out."[19] According to Helen Thompson, "O'Brien's canon testifies to the failure of heterosexual relationships and nuclear families and instead suggests that women's salvation lies in their relationships with each other."[20] It is not only friendships between women that offer relief and even escape from the pressures and restrictions of patriarchal imperatives but also erotic relationships, which are littered throughout O'Brien's work. In *The Country Girls*, Cait and Baba play sexual games with each other as children; Patsy in *Casualties of Peace* fondly remembers a sexual relationship with her cousin Pauline, in which "the pleasure was sweet and tickly, even sweet to remember";[21] Mary Hooligan, the narrator of *Night* (1972), lazily recalls love letters including one in which she wrote, "you touched my cunt and I touched yours";[22] Clarissa in the story "Manhattan Medley" has "female lovers as well as male";[23] the unnamed protagonist of "The House of My Dreams" "seduces" another woman and describes it as "a strange sensation, as if touching gauze. . . . They were both wet; Her fingers inside the woman would leave a tell-tale for all time";[24] Nora, the narrator of *Johnny I Hardly Knew You* (1977), recalls a female lover, whom she describes as a "little damson . . . tart to the taste," whose "quim was as warm as jam that had just been lifted off a stove";[25] the narrator of "The Mouth of the Cave" entertains an elaborate romantic, sexual fantasy about a young woman she sees on a walk; Eleanora in *The Light of Evening* (2006) invites Bertha, her therapist, to dinner and, after experiencing a "clandestine thrill" at the sight of Bertha removing her hat, scarf, coat, and gloves so that, though fully clothed, she appears as if "stark naked," dances in her arms, "find[ing] such a freedom in it and even, perhaps, such pleasure";[26] and *The High Road* (1988) centrally features an intense emotional and sexual affair between two women. "Sister Imelda," "Rose in the Heart," *A Pagan Place*, *Down by the River*, and *The Country Girls* all include the experience of a young girl at convent school falling passionately in love with a nun, a love rendered physical and erotic with the exchange of evocative gifts; physical signals passed between girl and nun; secret, illicit meetings; the expressed but frustrated desire for physical contact; and the girl's fantasies both about how the nun's body looks beneath her habit and of living in exclusion with the object of her desire. In O'Brien's 2012 memoir, *Country Girl*, she reveals the origin for this recurring story from her own time as a convent pupil when she experienced her first love, an ardent devotion to one of her teachers, a young nun. O'Brien describes this love as drawing her "into the wild heart of things."[27] In her latest novel, *Girl*, nuns provide Maryam, the young victim of kidnapping and sexual violence at the hands of the terrorist group Boko Haram, the sanctuary and potential salvation that even her family deny her. For O'Brien's young women raised in oppressive, patriarchal families, nuns offer their first intimation of an "undomesticated female body," to use Elaine Marks's term for the kind of "provocative counterimages" necessary to "both destroy the male discourse on love and redesign the universe."[28]

As already noted, in *The Country Girls*, other girls and nuns, and sometimes remote, idealized men, are objects of longing superior to any of the men Cait and Baba encounter in their daily lives. In the 1980 essay "Compulsory Heterosexuality and Lesbian Existence," Adrienne Rich offers some insights into the source of many of the frustrations, desires, and alliances experienced by and between women in O'Brien's fiction. Rich calls for recognition of the unacknowledged "breadths of female history and psychology which have lain out of reach as a consequence of limited, mostly clinical definitions of 'lesbianism.'"[29] This recalls

O'Brien's regret, expressed in a 1964 interview with Nell Dunn, regarding the "ugliness" popularly associated with the word "lesbian," which she describes as part of every woman's experience, especially every woman's "love of girlhood" and "girlish things," noting that "on the whole women are more touched by the external things of women like petticoats or dance shoes or something than by the external things of men."[30] The longing that Anna, the repressed protagonist of *The High Road*, feels for Catalina culminates in a physical affair but can only initially be acknowledged as an almost disembodied desire for Catalina's essential womanliness: "I wanted to hold her, be held by her, but in her sleep, so that our night selves might reach out and give each other that thread of sustenance that we craved, that invisible sustenance, not what we sought from men, something other-womanly, primordial."[31]

In talking to Dunn about the primal, insatiable mother-hunger that is common to all sexual desire and that renders heterosexuality an inevitable disappointment for women, she concludes, "I think a woman can never rely on a man the way she can on another woman, because to a great extent, man is a woman's enemy."[32] In this revealing interview, conducted only a few years after O'Brien's first publishing success, she articulates a version of what Rich would call the "lesbian continuum," that "range—through each woman's life and throughout history—of woman-identified experience; not simply the fact that a woman has had or consciously desired genital sexual experience with another woman. [A range that can be] expand[ed] to embrace many more forms of primary intensity between and among women including the sharing of a rich inner life, the bonding against male tyranny, the giving and receiving of practical and political support."[33] Rich describes the "lesbian existence" as "both the breaking of a taboo and a rejection of a compulsory way of life. It is also a direct or indirect attack on male right of access to women,"[34] a description that could also summarize much of O'Brien's oeuvre. O'Brien shares Rich's understanding of "the covert socializations and covert forces which have channeled women into marriage and heterosexual romance."[35] O'Brien's Irish contemporary Nuala O'Faolain, scandalously bisexual when few people in Ireland knew what the word meant, describes the culture of brutal enforcement of conformity in which she and O'Brien grew up: "Lives were ruined at that time, thousands and thousands of them, quite casually, by the rules of patriarchy made for young women."[36] As Caroline Moorehead noted in 1980, O'Brien's "recurring theme" is that "we live in a world run by men for other men."[37]

Despite the explicit connections between O'Brien's fiction and feminist concerns and issues, with few exceptions, Irish feminism has been slow to reevaluate O'Brien's cultural significance. O'Brien, for her part, has remained suspicious of official versions of feminism, having been the victim of some of its second-wave limitations. As she describes her experience in the early 1970s, "Feminists and academics . . . were tearing into me for my supine, woebegone inclinations."[38] In a 1973 interview, she claims to "sniff a certain dogmatism about the women's lib-eration movement."[39] The reasons for such reactions are complex and implicate not only gender politics but also questions of national identity. For example, among the attacks leveled against O'Brien when *House of Splendid Isolation* was published in 1994 was *The Guardian's* Edward Pearce labeling her "the Barbara Cartland of long-distance Republicanism."[40] The elision here between O'Brien and the romance writer Barbara Cartland—an instance of one enduring trope in criticism of O'Brien—in juxtaposition with the Troubles and sectarian violence (however ironic its intent) reveals more about the real subject matter of her fic-tion than the reviewer realizes. From the earliest novels, many commentators have noted that desire is at the core of O'Brien's narratives. The true irony in such observations lies in their frequently blinkered understanding of what constitutes that desire, reducing it to a heteronormative, Barbara Cartland–style pursuit of "romance." While the characters themselves may think this is what they hunger for, the text inevitably opens up vaster sources of insatiable longing. The histori-cal disfigurement of Irish womanhood—whether it is the torn and bleeding vic-tim of rapine; the bitter, suffocating mother who cripples her children with the guilt that both church and state rely on her to perpetuate; or the "virago" scan-dalously claiming her sexual and political rights—rather than the clichéd story of the "wronged" individual (indeed, self-obsessed) woman O'Brien is accused of endlessly retelling, constitutes the particularity of the "loss" that is, in the nov-elist's own words, her "central theme." In the early 1980s, O'Brien described her own work as "concerned with *loss* as much as with love. Loss is every child's theme because by necessity the child loses its mother and its bearing."[41] Loss in the fiction can be both transformative and paralyzing.

The much-discussed mother figure in O'Brien's fiction is an intensely cathected "love object" who is nevertheless fiercely resisted due to her complic-ity in the enforcement of patriarchal constraints. In the first pages of *The Country Girls*, young Cait is "protected" by two oppressively self-sacrificing women: her own flesh-and-blood mother—who, in order to ensure her daughter does not choke on a sweet she has fallen asleep sucking, forgoes her own night's sleep so that the next morning her blue eyes are "small and sore"[42]—and the "Blessed Virgin," who glares "icily from a gilt frame" and whose worship impels the self-abasement and sacrifice of getting "out of bed six or seven times every night."[43] As Heather Ingman has noted, "in Ireland . . . the patriarchal construct of the Virgin was used to control and define women,"[44] a "feminine ideal embodied in inaccessible perfection," according to Julia Kristeva, only achievable "by way of exacerbated masochism."[45] The especially intense Mariolatry that distinguishes Irish Roman Catholicism lent power and authority to the practice of locating responsibility for national identity and moral maintenance with the mother, ever struggling and necessarily failing to live up to the ideal of virginal maternity. It is not only the individual mother who figures in the writer's preoccupation with loss, however, but also "Mother Ireland." In a particularly disturbing scene in *The Light of Evening* (2006), a young Irish woman crossing the Atlantic to a new life in America flings her newborn baby into the sea, just as so many of Ireland's children have been cast from their motherland never to return.[46] In an interview with Julie Wheelwright, O'Brien described the novel as "umbilical,"[47] and in *Mother Ireland*, she characterizes the link between the diasporic Irish and their homeland as a "tie that is more umbilical than among any other race on earth" yet also says that there is "something secretly catastrophic about a country from which so many people go, escape."[48] The mother is not only the source of love and despair but also, or perhaps therefore, the source of artistic creation, according to O'Brien: "One's themes always spring from the matrix."[49] The relationship to both mother and motherland under such conditions is one that is traumatized, broken, destructive, and yet passionate and enduring. Like La Malinche of Mexico, another Roman Catholic country known for its devotion to the Virgin Mary, "Mother Ireland" is the nation as victimized woman responsible for her own ravishment and therefore contemned, an allegory that allows for the sublation of unsanctioned desires for surrender and absorption, even as it serves as scapegoat for failures and betrayals. *Mother Ireland* opens with the assertion that "countries are either mothers or fathers. . . . Ireland has always been a woman," a woman repeatedly violated "body and soul,"[50] and this theme of conquest and invasion as gendered phenomenon is endemic to the process of Irish history in O'Brien's work, a political fate with implications for every realm of experience. O'Brien recognizes the family as a political institution, like Rich, and like Teresa de Lauretis, O'Brien is aware of the role of maintaining rigid hierarchies of sexuality, gender, class, and race in "the defence of the mother country and of (white) womanhood [that] has served to bolster colonial conquest and racist violence."[51]

Representations of the intense mother-child relationships that distinguish so much of O'Brien's fiction, and the related erotic charge frequently invested in relationships between women, even when not explicitly represented as sexual, constitute the locus for O'Brien's career-long critique of the Oedipal nuclear family as a significant, originary source of psychological, cultural, and political dysfunction. A number of recent psychoanalytic analyses of O'Brien's fiction make productive recourse to Julia Kristeva's theory of the abject in excavating the tangled roots of desire and identity of the intense and ambiguous interfemale attractions—even obsessions—manifest in so many of O'Brien's protagonists.[52] Such readings revise earlier frustrated feminist responses of despair at the "passivity" of O'Brien's female characters, by positing incomplete abjection as a source of a perverse liberatory potential in the "split" or "severed" female subject under patriarchy central to O'Brien's work. Also of use in this regard is Jack Halberstam's theory of "shadow feminism" that "speaks in the language of self-destruction" and is grounded in "negation, refusal, passivity, absence, and silence, offers spaces and modes of unknowing, failing, and forgetting as part of an alternative feminist project, a shadow feminism that has nestled in more positivist accounts and unravelled their logic from within."[53] The positivist accounts Halberstam refers to here, especially, are those that organize ideas about inheritance, genealogy, and family, "a concept deployed to gloss deeply reactionary understandings of human interaction."[54]

O'Brien's protagonists, despite popular characterizations to the contrary, resist the fate of wife and mother, their role as "repositories for generational logics of being and becoming,"[55] a resistance often instantiated in reactions to female embodiment ranging from discomfort to revulsion, and even terror, but specifically to those modes of female embodiment implicated in heterosexual erotics and reproductive imperatives. In the Nell Dunn interview, O'Brien, at this time the mother of two young sons, says, "I have some sexual terrors that still maim me. I'm frightened of breastfeeding a baby, I'm frightened of having my nipples touched."[56] Kristeva, in "Stabat Mater," describes constructions of maternity shaped by worship of the Virgin Mary as confining mothers to "the uttermost sphere of sublimation, alienated from her own body."[57] Many women in O'Brien's fiction appear to be so alienated from their own bodies as to find breasts and breastfeeding a source of unease. For example, the narrator of the story "The Love Object" admits to being "squeamish" about her nipples, while Cait/Kate in The Lonely Girl, the unnamed mother in A Pagan Place, Tessa in "The Favourite," and Dilly in The Light of Evening all find breastfeeding uncomfortable, if not revolting. Childbirth is depicted as brutal, abject, even tragic. Among the horrors of the LSD trip described in Country Girl is O'Brien's conviction that her waters have broken (though she is not pregnant) and are ceaselessly cascading from her. A more memorably gruesome scene occurs in the 1978 short story "A Rose in the Heart of New York." A woman gives birth; the midwife informs the drinking husband and cronies in the kitchen, and the men rush upstairs at the news: "The father waved a strip of pink flesh on a fork that he was carrying and remarked on its being unappetising. . . . The mother felt green and disgusted and asked them to leave her alone."[58] Once they are gone, the midwife begins "stitching down the line of torn flesh that was gaping and coated with blood."[59] The memoir reveals an origin of this scene when O'Brien tells the story she has heard of her own birth: "My father and his brother Jack were downstairs drinking, and on being told the good news they staggered up, bringing strips of goose they had just cooked."[60]

Speaking to Dunn, O'Brien claimed to be "very frightened" of sex, which makes her think "of daggers and needles": "I think [from] early on, from when I can't remember, the connection between sex and operations and medical things were all linked together."[61] In a later interview with Philip Roth, she still remembers that "sexual excitement was to a great extent linked with pain and separation."[62] O'Brien has used the word "butchery" to describe the emotional damage she sustained in childhood, which led her to distrust her own body and its desires.[63] Despite the historical tendency to reduce O'Brien's fiction to uncomplicated autobiography—inaugurated by her husband's well-publicized denial of the originality of her first novels—this attitude toward the body that O'Brien diagnoses is more than personal. As Ingman argues in a discussion of *The Country Girls*, Cait's relationship with a divorced "foreigner" threatens the "integrity of the nation": "Her female body and the Irish nation are conflated so that it becomes her community's business. . . . They are preserving one Catholic girl from foreign ways but also safeguarding the purity of their nation."[64] Christianity's traditional distrust of the body is intensified in Catholic Ireland, which Cheryl Herr has described as "desomatized": "Ireland has literally eroded, in the sphere of representations that constitute social identity, a comfortable sense of the body."[65] The representation of female desire as exceeding traditional family-centric norms in O'Brien's work is political, as understood by Gilles Deleuze and Félix Guattari when they argue that "the most erotic of desires brings about a fully political and social investment, engages with an entire social field."[66]

The significance of O'Brien's representations of heterosexuality as less than a romantic ideal was recognized by some insightful readers as early as the 1970s, such as Pearl Bell writing for the *New Leader*, who suggested that O'Brien's work was "more profoundly and subtly revelatory about women's sexuality than all of Erica Jong's boisterous calisthenics,"[67] and Anthony West, who, in *Vogue*, described O'Brien as an "almost frighteningly brilliant" writer who "acknowledged the dark side of sex" and fearlessly delivered the "bad news for women about what being a woman means."[68] Recent feminist reassessments of O'Brien note the discrepancy between the novelist's reputation for frivolously titillating themes and the serious social critique she actually undertakes. The series of Penguin paperback editions of her novels from the late 1960s and into the '70s, featuring Barry Lategan's photographs of female breasts and haunches, may appear to instantiate this ironic distance between cover and content, but women's fragmented, alienated experience of embodiment is central to O'Brien's work. Mary Gordon observed in 1990, in a live interview with O'Brien at the Irish Cultural Centre in New York, that she combines "a fastidious ear with a voluptuous eye" and "brought the body into literature in a new way."[69]

It is a particular element of embodiment and not the body itself, then, that creates neuroses and trauma for women in these texts. Much of the humor in *The Country Girls*, for example, is bodily, even scatological. A moment that inspires laughter between Cait and her mother is their shared memory of the latter being surprised by a man on a bicycle when she is peeing in a ditch; he collides with her, and his front tire ends up between her legs. In the memoir, O'Brien recalls her own mother smelling the chair seats after male visitors to the house, "to see if they had farted."[70] The body is, in fact, a frequent site of pleasure as well as pain, and appetite can be relished, as when in *The Country Girls* Baba and Cait gorge themselves on treats in food parcels while pupils in the convent or delight in treats like ice cream and restaurant dinners once they escape to Dublin.[71] Such satisfactions are frequently eroticized, displacing bodily enjoyment—most frequently to the mouth—from heterosexual genital contact, which, in O'Brien's fictional world, can be difficult to separate from violence, invasion, and loss. O'Brien frequently renders desire for the other as arrested at the oral stage. Love objects and rivals (male and female) are both ingested and ingesting. In *Night*, for example, the narrator, Mary Hooligan, describes a successful liaison with a "Finn" as the lover "turn[ing] . . . the flesh itself into a luscious stew."[72] O'Brien's put-upon rural mothers are consistently depicted as self-sacrificing, usually typified in depriving themselves of food. But the mouth is site not only of the mother's self-denying love but also of her potential for violence. In the story "My Two Mothers" (2011), the narrator has a recurring dream of her own tongue being cut out by her mother, an image displaced onto the mother slicing into an "ox tongue" in the earlier story "Savages" (1982), which leads the narrator to think in a self-pitying identification, "poor oxen had not much of a life either living or dead."[73] In "Rose in the Heart," the mother frequently appears as delectable food to the young daughter. When the girl has her first sexual experience years later, it is recounted entirely in oral terms: she and her lover "devour each other's faces. . . . But these orgies only increased her hunger, made it into something that could not be appeased."[74]

The desiring mouth in O'Brien is infantile and unformed, hungry for soft, babyish food, even as it is savage in its masochistic and cannibalistic desires. The female narrator in the story "Over" (1974) desires to consume young flesh but equates toothlessness with eating another, perhaps an example of Halberstam's radical "masochistic passivity" as critique: "I want all my teeth drawn out of me and other teeth, molars if you will, stuck back into my gums. I want to grind these new teeth, these molars to a pulp. Perhaps I want to eat you alive."[75] The sadomasochistic sequence of extraction, insertion, pulverization, and violent consumption suggests a regression or atavism that obeys its own chronology; the very act of chewing undoes itself, a paradoxical "unchewing." This sadomasochistic defiance in the face of expected modes of development also emerges in the fiction as violent undoings of the "natural" order of reproduction—what Halberstam refers to as "an interruption to generational modes of transmission that ensure the continuity of ideas, family lines and normativity itself."[76] The continuity of family lines is often threatened in O'Brien's fiction. Early readers occasionally expressed alarm at the deaths of children in her work, especially sons. A young German boy, Otto, drowns in *Time and Tide*, while the young son of estranged parents dies in an accident in *August Is a Wicked Month* when in the care of his father, when his mother is on a decadent, sex-filled holiday.[77] Another son drowns in *Time and Tide*, and in *Johnny I Hardly Knew You*, Nora is on trial for the murder of her much-younger lover, a friend of her son's, a kind of surrogate for her own son, about whom she has entertained incestuous fantasies, characterized as a chance "to reunite."[78] There are also children who do not make it as far as being born or only survive a few days, as when in *The Light of Evening*, the young woman, Mary Angela, who has given birth on a ship to the United States from Ireland, drops her baby into the sea, striking "fear and foreboding into" the crew and other passengers.[79] In *Down by the River*, Mary, the young, pregnant incest/rape victim, is released into renewed, exhilarating possibilities when she miscarries. Josie in *House of Splendid Isolation* undergoes a secret, illegal, torturously painful abortion in order to frustrate her abusive husband's desire for an heir. In an echo of Cait (now Anglicized into "Kate" by her husband, "Cait" being too "Kiltartan"), who, in the last installment of the *Country Girls* trilogy, *Girls in Their Married Bliss*, has herself sterilized, in *Casualties of Peace*, Patsy fantasizes about the ultimate freedom: to never conceive at all. Patsy dreams of being a bird, a radical "othering" being the only way in which to stage a rebellion that she otherwise dares not attempt: "Away with the clouds. Coming down for food and a little spring wooing. As the semen darted in her she would fly, letting it spill out in a wild jet of betrayal. No aftermath. Freedom, freedom, freedom!"[80] In these instances, O'Brien imagines fatal disruptions of the hierarchy of transmission, the determinative "generational logic" identified by Halberstam as crucial to maintaining the oppressive status quo.

When sexual pleasure is not displaced but fully enjoyed by O'Brien's protagonists, it is not reproductive and rarely phallic. Adrienne Rich refers to the need to "understand the erotic in non-phallic-female terms, . . . not confined to any single part of the body or to the body itself."[81] Erotic encounters with men are most powerful when imagined or anticipated or safely nonphallic, as when, in *The Little Red Chairs*, Fidelma, who is feeling restless in her childless marriage to a much-older man, goes to a hotel in the hope of getting pregnant by a man she knows only slightly; in skittish anticipation, she becomes overwhelmed at the thought of "seeing his armpits for the first time."[82] Her lover's sexual attractiveness and attentiveness is signaled by his statement to the waiter serving them dinner that "the libido is in the taste buds."[83] The most explicit sexual details in O'Brien's fiction are found in scenes of oral sex, most often fellatio performed by one of her protagonists. "The Love Object" is a notable exception, not least because achieving a kind of sexual parity and reciprocity brings the affair to an end for the man, who feels he has lost his power by orally pleasuring his lover. In *Johnny I Hardly Knew You*, however, very early in the novel—a first-person narrative in which Nora reviews her life while awaiting trial for murder—Nora remembers one of her emotionally unsatisfactory married lovers performing cunnilingus, represented as an act of sly vengeance on all men who have wronged her: "Shame was banished . . . and I was pleasured in both channels, and in my mind able to bask in the wantonness of it without apologizing and thinking of him. Haven't I always been attending to a him, and dancing attendance upon a him, and being a slave to a him and being trampled on by a him?"[84] The novel is an astonishing narrative of rage and sexual violence recalled by Nora, whose own act of murder by suffocating her much-younger lover, when finally revealed, is, ironically, one of the least aggressive acts in the text, even though it is committed in defiance of "all fathers, who soiled [Nora's] mother's bed, tore her apart, crushed her and made her vassal,"[85] indeed, possibly revenge against all men, "stampeders of our dreams."[86] The history of psychological and physical abuses that Nora has suffered at the hands of men has so affected her that even an erotically detailed lesbian experience is ultimately exploitative and without meaning, modeled on the kind of heartlessness and power imbalance she associates with sex. After making love with Nora, the unnamed woman asks if they "will get to know one another," but Nora recalls, "Like any male philanderer I found myself wriggling out of it, voicing an excuse, inventing an appointment. . . . She meant nothing to me."[87]

Very early in the text, in the second paragraph, a mysterious woman, Dame Dora, appears but never clearly emerges as important to the story. She "mow[s] men down with her glacial beauty" but melts for no one, being "too cunning to be wholehearted."[88] Elke D'Hoker, who describes Dame Dora as a "femme fatale,"[89] takes Nora at her word when later in the narrative, contemplating how to carry herself in the courtroom, Nora says she does not want to appear "as a crazed woman. Neither as a Dame Dora."[90] A passage from O'Brien's typescript of the novel puts words in Dame Dora's mouth that do not appear verbatim in the published version but that inform the simmering rage of the text, when Dora refers to "bulls of men who would put a hacksaw through you as quick as their organs, nay both if the mad orgiastic rage took possession of them. Rabies they had, in the loins and in the brains."[91] In O'Brien's handwriting in the margin of the typescript at this point is the word "Lesbian." Dame Dora's textual function remains somewhat mysterious, though she is at the very least the kind of survivor that Nora is not, in a world of relentless, violently threatening misogyny. Despite the marginal note, neither in the typescript nor in the published text is there anything blatantly homoerotic about the relationship between Nora and Dame Dora, whose names nevertheless chime evocatively.[92] If, as D'Hoker suggests, Dame Dora is an alter ego for Nora, or, perhaps, a fantasized ideal, she is in some sense mirroring Nora, a tempting but occluded—because forbidden or misunderstood?—example of the possibilities of Rich's liberatory "lesbian existence."

With the exception of this signally angry novel, however, lesbian sex in O'Brien's fiction is tender, comforting, and restorative for the women involved, even as fully realized lesbian relationships resist representation. The arms of other women offer refuge from patriarchal brutalities and deprivation, however temporary the relief for women characters, who, in the words of Bernice Schrank and Danine Farquharson, lack the "social awareness or political consciousness" necessary to imagine radical alternatives and positively transform their lives.[93] The retreat from heterosexuality, wherever it falls on the "lesbian continuum," provokes repercussions in service of restoring heterosexist imperatives and reasserting male control and dominance, which can be extreme, such as the murder of Willa by a jealous husband in *Casualties of Peace* or of Catalina by an estranged, abusive husband in *The High Road*. In both instances, the "wrong" woman is killed, not the intended victim, reflecting a misogyny that renders women ultimately interchangeable. Hearing that Catalina has been killed, her lover Anna first suspects Catalina's father. Catalina has told Anna that her father hates her for not being a son: "he always wanted to break me."[94] She has reported his revolting views, including a shrugging dismissal of rape as not serious and a conviction that women are "the stupidest creatures on God's earth."[95]

The misogyny that culminates in Catalina's murder is reflected in one of the novel's epigraphs: "God that berreth the crone of thornes / Distru the prud of womens hornes," identified as a "Curse." The two lines are from a medieval poem, probably of fourteenth-century Irish origin, preserved and reproduced by John Swayne, Archbishop of Armagh in the fifteenth century. John Seymour translates the two lines as, "May God who wears the crown of thorns destroy the pride of women's horns,"[96] a literal reference to the sinful "excess" of women's fashionable headgear. The longer medieval text is a diatribe against women, arrogant instruments of the devil who endanger man's salvation through their beastly incitements to lust. The poem's rage, however, seems to be more acutely directed at women's proud independence, expressed through extravagant fashions, such as the horned headpiece in question, as well as long-trained gowns, neither of which would appear to be designed to be especially sexually tempting. Paradoxically, the poet's frustration appears to be with women dressing for themselves, without regard for the male gaze, even possibly in defiance of heterosexual desire. Such defiance possibly informs the implicit meaning of "women's horns," suggestive of an "unnaturally" sexually endowed or appetitive female, the kind of transgressive woman labeled "puta," "whore," and "lesbos" in *The High Road*,[97] set hundreds of years after the church fathers quoted in the novel's epigraph condemned shameless women of their time.

The romance between Anna and Catalina is the most sustained representation of a lesbian relationship in O'Brien's fiction, "the most positive note in O'Brien's work so far in the context of her challenge to Ireland's masculinist nationalism," according to Heather Ingman.[98] However, the relationship is deeply flawed, finally disabled by economic and cultural differences exacerbated by Anna's solipsism, her ironically "colonizer" mind-set. Anna, the narrator, is an Irish writer holidaying on a Spanish resort island who falls in love with Catalina, a young maid working in the hotel where Anna is staying. The imbalances in age, privilege, and power between the women will have consequences for their separate fates. Examining the eight short stories in the earlier 1968 collection *The Love Object*,[99] Schrank and Farquharson regret the ways in which, even when stirred to seek satisfaction outside the existing "romantic gestalt," the women of the stories cannot find positive alternatives to it, "even though the idea of 'coming out,' of moving beyond and into the public sphere provides the only territory as yet unexplored by these women."[100] Throughout the collection, the male love object's "spectacular insufficiency demonstrate[s] the need for a social vision commensurate with the dreams and longings with which the characters are beset."[101] Anna and Catalina entertain such visions, but the novel's unblinking realism recognizes the near impossibility, in the shadow of violently enforced heterosexual norms, of any full or lasting realization of alternatives to traditional family formation. Kathryn Stockton describes this kind of limitation as women's alienation "from a future body owed to them. These are bodies women have not been allowed to see, fashion, or to listen for."[102]

The threat these women's relationship poses is instantiated in Catalina's cross-dressing and the pride she takes in her androgyny. In the course of a walk through the marketplace that marks the beginning of the women's intense emotional connection, Catalina repeatedly asserts her lack of "femininity," from laughingly displaying "her overworked nails" to a vendor selling nail polish,[103] to insisting "she had no liking for finery" and whistling for a taxi with an air "full of bravura,"[104] to boasting about her ability to be her father's "son" by meeting every physical challenge he sets and by protesting, "what would I do with nice dresses or mantillas.[105] Despite all of this, Anna pictures the younger woman in taffeta and stockings, unable to understand her own desire outside of heterosexual gender categories. She impulsively offers Catalina the earrings she is wearing. Catalina accepts just one, puts it on, and places the other in Anna's ear, so that they mirror each other, a moment of intimacy that leads to their first thrilling physical embrace: Catalina borrows a motor bike to bring Anna back to the hotel, announcing herself Anna's "chevalier."[106] As they near the hotel, Catalina suggests they extend the adventure and visit other towns, admitting to "longing to be in some strange country, alone, free, independent, unfettered."[107] But, while thoughtlessly enjoying all of the desirable conditions that Catalina enumerates, Anna responds defensively, however unconsciously, pettishly demonstrating that she is, in fact, fettered when says she has an appointment she must keep. Catalina's evident disappointment and abrupt departure leave Anna fearing she is "unsporting" and lacks "daring,"[108] an oblique reference to her fear of defying conventional norms.

Marjorie Garber credits the transvestite with "considerable power to disturb" and "transgressive force,"[109] as the figure "emblematizes the disruptive element that intervenes, signaling not just another category crisis, but—much more disquietingly—a crisis of 'category' itself."[110] In relation to Anna, Catalina occupies subordinate class and age positions, which can be addressed, according to Garber's analysis of the transvestite, by "traversing the boundary from female-to-male [which] also involves trespassing on the terrain of another class."[111] Catalina's seductive performance of capable masculinity is necessary to overcome Anna's own border-crossing anxieties. Accustomed to trading on her "feminine" desirability, Anna is nevertheless vulnerable as a woman traveling on her own and subject to exploitation. She is uncomfortably aware on the one hand of her privilege, especially when meeting Catalina's family on their farm, yet on the other hand insecure about her Irishness when in the company of fellow visitors and voluntary exiles, most of whom are English. Even as she acknowledges her privilege, Anna qualifies it by describing Ireland dramatically as "permeated with an emptiness redolent of the greater emptiness, giving a sense of having been stranded, left behind by history and the world at large, a severed limb of a land full of hurt and rage."[112] O'Brien is alert to the irony of Anna's own performance of abject, historically victimized Irishness while exploiting the emotional resources of the island she has sailed to on an utterly self-serving, "healing" mission. Catalina provides the kind of "primitive" balm to the jaded, metropolitan visitor Anna that the savage but soulful Irishman traditionally offered to the repressed, overly civilized Englishman of the nineteenth century.[113]

As Amanda Greenwood points out, in *The High Road*, O'Brien "identifies the convergence of 'essential' 'femininity' and 'Irishness' as crucial to the commodification of her protagonist," a commodification "according to femininity and nationality" that she shares with Catalina.[114] After the marketplace stroll, Anna visits one of the English "settlers" in the village, with whom she has been socializing, and grows uncomfortable in the sterile, cultivated surroundings: "For some reason I imagined invalids sitting there, looking out at the beautiful roses, plaintively. I did not want to be there, I wanted to be with Catalina; I yearned to be with her, on the scooter, on the farm, milking the goats with her, anything, because here in this deserted and luxurious place there were whiffs of despair, reminding me too pointedly of my own life."[115] Not only is Anna potentially a kind of emotional colonizer, then, but she is also a version of O'Brien's Irish "mother," complicit in maintaining the patriarchal hierarchies, in this case, comfortable social structures from which Anna benefits, turning to a younger "daughter" for the emotional sustenance of which she is deprived. Anna is a visitor to the island where Catalina must live and work, both in the hotel and at home, to maintain a minimum level of sustenance. The role of the pressures of capital in the novel's tragic and violent conclusion is accounted for in the uneven and disproportionate experience for each of the women of the escape from everyday life that they enjoy in each other's company.

Anna, feeling that she has fallen in love with Catalina, organizes an official, heteronormative "date." Before their meal, after which they dance together, Catalina goes for a swim while Anna, still timid, watches. Catalina emerges from the water, "shouting with glee," and asks, "Do I look like a boy? . . . Take a look and tell me. . . . Someone, some young man down there, thought I was a boy."[116] Even undressed, Catalina asserts her androgyny. When the women meet again and spend the evening exchanging songs and stories from their respective cultures, the figure of androgyny dominates Anna's account of the sexual union that such emotional intimacy inspires, an experience that powerfully and erotically allows both women to exceed the limits of sexual identity:

> I stretched out and cleaved to her, through her opening to life; arms, limbs, torsos joined as if in androgynous sculpture, the bloods going up and down merrily, two bloods, like mercury in a heated thermometer, even the cheeks letting go of all their screams and all their grumble and all their thousand unspent kisses, tenderness, rabidness, hunger back, back in time to that wandering milky watery bliss, infinitely safe like wine under a skin or sap inside a tree, floating, afloat; boundaries burst, bursting, the mind as much as the body borne along, to this other landscape that was familiar yet unfamiliar, like entering a picture, or a fresco, slipping through a wall of flesh, eclipsed inside the womb of the world, and throughout it all, her words, faint, sweet as vapor.[117]

The love between Anna and Catalina bursts every boundary, releasing both women into a new relationship with more than each other. Bracha Ettinger's theories of "matrixial" transsubjectivity are useful here, as they allow for a revised approach to the "maternal," especially the connection of the self to "mother." Prior to the phallic and to individuation, and underlying both, the matrixial is a shared space of consciousness and experience.[118] Even the originary mother-love shadowing every lesbian encounter, evoked in the phrase "milky watery bliss," gives way to a larger landscape, an apprehension of the world itself as matrixial, an uncanny experience at once fleshly and cosmic, aesthetic and earthy, intimate and impersonal.

This utopian moment is necessarily brief, as too many boundaries are crossed, and it is the working-class Catalina, not privileged, timid Anna, who will bear the full weight of patriarchal discipline. The coming danger is hinted at when the women dance, attracting catcalls from young men watching them with disapproval. After that first evening together, even before they have had sex, Anna receives another warning, an unsigned note: "She'll doe it and doe it and doe it till dawn."[119] Messages conveyed through other anonymous notes and insults scrawled on walls indicate the amorphous yet organized power of communal condemnation seeming to seep from every surface. Catalina, who never entertained "illusions about family love, whether it was among people or beasts,"[120] is murdered by her estranged husband, who claims to have intended to kill Anna. At the funeral, Anna meets Catalina's grandmother, the woman who raised her. The older woman knows who Anna is and hands her a package of Catalina's thick dark hair, which had hung down her back and has been a repeated object of Anna's fascination and admiration from their first meeting. Cutting away her hair restores to Catalina the androgyny that her husband attempted to erase in his assertion of masculine ownership and control of her. The woman's gesture also acknowledges Anna as her granddaughter's lover, with a right to one of Catalina's few valuable possessions. The grandmother kisses the hair, saying, "muy precioso . . . muy precioso," or "very precious," which Anna "translates" as her saying, "to love one must learn to part with everything,"[121] a jarringly self-romanticizing interpretation of the older woman's grief.

If the women in O'Brien's fiction are unequipped to see a way out of what Christine Holmlund has called the "impasse of heterosexuality,"[122] the novelist's own scope and vision are wider. What Holmlund has said of the work of the French feminist Luce Irigaray can apply to O'Brien's fiction: "the lesbian, the mother, the daughter, the heterosexual female lover all function as nodal points for the subversion of patriarchal discourses and the creation of feminist alternatives."[123] As O'Brien understands, however, patriarchal neoliberalism is insidious and not so easily overthrown. Her protagonists are materially comfortable, if emotionally starved, and have internalized an erotics of power imbalance and cruelty. The revolution is still a long way off.

2 · THE LIBERATING SADOMASOCHISM OF THINGS

Gifts of trinkets and things, these signals of an outside, cosmopolitan world.

At the conclusion of Edna O'Brien's novel *The High Road* (1988), at the funeral of her lover Catalina, Anna receives a memento of the dead woman. Not knowing at first what she has been handed, other than "something in a scarf,"[1] Anna is unnerved that it feels "warm": "I thought it was a dead bird or entrails, a curse, but . . . I saw Catalina's hair, so vibrant, so alive."[2] In *Girl* (2019), the hair of another victim of fatal male violence manifests uncanny animation. A horrific description of a woman's death by stoning ends with the observation, "The strangest thing of all was her hair, so long and luxurious, it seemed to bristle with life."[3] This chapter considers the liveliness assigned to the "inanimate" in O'Brien's work, a quality noted over the course of her career by many fellow writers. Philip Roth in a 1984 interview described his friend's work as creating "a net of perfectly observed sensuous details," suggesting to her, "you seem to remember the shape, texture, color, and dimension of every object your eye may have landed on while you were growing up."[4] In a 1968 review of the short-story collection *The Love Object*, Paul Scott recognized the fact that "the love object . . . may be a man [or] a piece of furniture."[5] Isobel Murray has described O'Brien as having "a piercing sense of the physical,"[6] while Clare Boylan, in a 1990 review for *The Irish Times*, admired her "almost sentient particularity of detail," the "astonishing power in her descriptions of inanimate settings and objects, as symbols to trigger superstitious imaginings."[7] Anne Enright describes O'Brien's books as "great acts of reclamation' in which "we stumble across . . . the perfect object, perfectly recalled."[8] According to Éilís Ní Dhuibhne, in her 2015 review of *The Little Red Chairs*, "[O'Brien's] most distinctive talents are her astonishingly acute powers of observation and her ability to describe in the most simple and appropriate words people, things and places, which gives her writing its uniquely beautiful texture—rich, sensuous, alive and colourful as a medieval tapestry."[9] In a review of *A Fanatic Heart* for the *Los Angeles Times* in 1984, Mary Gordon observed of O'Brien's themes that they "flower in a soil teeming with lively and portentous objects. Clothes, stuffs, foods, medicines in her hands turn into vessels brimming with meaning and value. And her language itself takes on the texture of a precious thing, precious and yet familiar, held close to the body, kept, always, in the center of the home."[10] Like the woman-to-woman connections discussed in chapter 1, the most vividly rendered objects of O'Brien's fiction supply brief occasions of comfort and retreat, especially for those women whose lives are most severely curtailed, limited to the horizon of the domestic. O'Brien reveals her sympathy with seeking solace in things to Nell Dunn: "I shall resolve . . . to survive everything, and look out the window . . . and sink, not even sink into, but be glad of inanimate things, trees and sewerages, and advertisements and cigarettes. Glad of the prevailing thing, rather than putting such hope into what is after all and must be by its very nature, a very transitory thing, like fresh love."[11] In O'Brien's fiction, human relationships can prove less enduring and hopeful than connections to the faithful inanimate.

Bill Brown, in his foundational essay "Thing Theory," takes up the distinction made by Heidegger (in his turn, responding to Kant) between objects and things, arguing that an object requires a subject, while a thing is independent of human consciousness: "The story of objects themselves as things, then, is the story of a changed relation to the human subject and thus the story of how the thing really names less an object than a particular subject-object relation."[12] The distinction between not only the thing and the object but even between the object and the subject can be difficult to decide in O'Brien's early work, which features women who, as Sinéad Mooney has pointed out, manifest "recurring anxiety" over the "boundaries . . . between the I and the not-I."[13] When Anne Enright argues that O'Brien "knows the precise emotional weight of objects, their seeming hopefulness and their actual indifference to those who seek to be consoled,"[14] suggesting tension between hopeful subject and indifferent object, she hints at a kind of sadomasochist (S/M) intimacy that animates representations of the ostensibly *in*animate residing in the houses of O'Brien's fiction. The S/M dynamic in O'Brien's representations of all kinds of relationships was referred to in chapter 1. The novelist has asserted that "the best relationships are based on SM," and other commentators have noted the sadomasochistic dynamic that characterizes many primary relationships in her work, an observation sometimes used by critics to characterize her fiction as frivolous, drearily preoccupied with doomed heterosexual romance. Jack Halberstam, however, argues that the adoption of radical "masochistic passivity" can function as critique.[15] Similarly, Shirley Peterson observes of *The Country Girls Trilogy* that its "subversive S/M narrative" can act as a "strategy for interrogating male-dominated society."[16] In O'Brien's fiction, sadomasochistic defiance in the face of expected modes of development emerge as violent undoings of the "natural" order of reproduction. This chapter extends the sadomasochistic dynamic to include relationships between the animate and the inanimate, demonstrating the variety and complexity of possibilities for connection in O'Brien's fiction. Such human-nonhuman entanglements distribute agency in challenging configurations and exert additional pressure on the subject-object divide, an already unstable boundary in O'Brien's representations of intrahuman connection. The poignant attempts by O'Brien's abused and lonely wives and widows to vivify domestic interiors uncover a hidden history of small refusals to submit to patriarchal expectations of women's total self-abnegation in post-Independence Ireland.

Of O'Brien's sensitivity to the liveliness of things, Enright asks, "Is this the root of the (usually male, let's face it) unease about O'Brien; the worry she might become untethered from the real? It is the tension between the actual and the metaphorical that gives her sentences their enormous energy and restraint."[17] O'Brien's "untethered" treatment of the nonhuman material world collapses the aesthetic distance between subject and object, as well as between the real and the metaphorical, a distance necessary to the violence of figuration. There is more than one way of "being" in O'Brien, which introduces a number of instabilities into her fiction, instabilities that expose what her biographer Amanda Greenwood identifies as the novelist's persistent critical target, Irish "cultural matricide."[18] According to Greenwood, a constitutive linking of "Irishness, suffering and maternity" is evident in a "cultural ideal of maternity ... threatened by the bodily functions which it struggles to deny,"[19] exemplified in the impossible model offered by the Virgin Mary, simultaneously maternal and untainted, as discussed in the introduction and chapter 1.

Mary is at once a connection to the animist pagan past of Irish religious practice that invests every element of creation with liveliness and a model of supreme Christian womanhood as disembodied fetish or idol.[20] The irony of this unrealizable ideal, dominant in Ireland's mariolotrous Catholic culture and reflected in the iconography of long-suffering "Mother Ireland," is that the country must "always be motherless."[21] This sadomasochistic attempt to deny the undeniable mother fuels the homicidal rage of the killer, Michen O'Kane, in O'Brien's 2002 novel In the Forest. A man simultaneously obsessed with and infuriated by the maternal, O'Kane murders a woman he has idealized into his fantasy mother and daydreams about being an IRA terrorist, drawing an implicit connection between personally and nationally self-inflicted violence. Ireland's centuries-long struggle for independence was marked by cycles of betrayal and self-destruction, evident even after independence was achieved. O'Brien often evokes this history in the self-conscious and insecure co-optation and occupation of the Irish "Big House," as in House of Splendid Isolation (1994) and The Light of Evening (2006), figured as reflections of the crisis of Irish male identity.[22] The Oedipal implications of the bloody wrenching apart of the union between the kingdoms of England and Ireland, traditionally figured as a marriage between John Bull and Caitlín Ní Houlihan, make for shameful regrets and longings, insecurities, and suspicions of illegitimacy (always the result of a "sinning" mother), another historically situated reason for O'Brien's resistance of the Oedipus plot as a model for organizing family and state, as discussed in chapter 1. The forensic attention O'Brien brings to her descriptions of houses and their furnishings inevitably reveals the wounds inflicted by a damaged postcolonial masculinity, reasserting itself through the subjugation of women in post-Independence Ireland.[23]

Beginning with the publication of *House of Splendid Isolation* in 1994, O'Brien's fiction has been once more primarily set in Ireland after a period of over twenty years (since the publication of *A Pagan Place* in 1972) during which none of her novels but some short stories and dramas have been set in her native country, as enumerated in the introduction. O'Brien's earliest works are not usually recognized as belonging to the category of Big House fiction,[24] but nearly all of the rural Irish homes of her imaginings resemble to differing degrees her family home, Drewsboro. The early writing, in particular, draws significantly on the author's life. O'Brien opens and closes her recent memoir with descriptions and recollections of her childhood home, "a large two-story house, with bay windows . . . approached by two avenues, an old and a new. The goldish sandstone of which it was built was from the burnt ruin of a 'Big House' that had belonged to the English and that had been burnt in the Troubles, during the 1920s."[25] The destruction of the Big House was carried out by a group of rebels that reportedly included O'Brien's own father, Michael, who nevertheless aspired to the elegance and status of the Protestant Ascendancy, whose example influenced the building of his own home (a story ascribed to family patriarchs in *A Pagan Place*, *House of Splendid Isolation*, and *The Light of Evening*). The mirroring dynamic reinforcing patriarchal authority in the family and the nation has been summarized by Gerardine Meaney, when she observes that for contemporary Irish women writers, "the legacy of the Big House tradition . . . is a metonymic relation between domestic and national narrative."[26]

Even the earliest texts, then, can be seen as responding in some way, however indirectly, to the Big House tradition. It is useful in this context, therefore, to note what Maud Ellmann has observed of the work of a more readily recognized Irish Big House novelist, Elizabeth Bowen: "Things, in Bowen, offer none of the expected comforts of solidity; they stand, like Freudian fetishes, as monuments to lack and loss. Nothing, by contrast, bears down on her imagined world with a weight more oppressive than materiality."[27] In Bowen's fiction, objects remember and even enact loss in their uncanny liveliness. In 1984, O'Brien said of her own work, "Loss is every child's theme because by necessity the child loses its mother and its bearings. . . . So my central theme is loss."[28] The bereft women inhabiting O'Brien's early fiction, embedded deeply in the physical and emotional worlds of the author's childhood, want to believe in the power of the object to effect some kind of transformation. As the narrator of "My Two Mothers" (2011) says of her mother, she has a "strange childish gratitude for things."[29] These magician-mothers find their ideal audience and coconspirator in the young girl central to much of this work. Together, mother and daughter entertain assuasive visions of a nurturing domesticity unlike their immiserated reality. As in Bowen's fiction, in O'Brien, the object "magnetized into being," as Ellmann describes it, externalizes some unrealized desire or painful memory.[30] The ordinary but ornamental object, obtained with difficulty and carefully set aside, falls into David Lloyd's category of "kitsch," which he describes as representing "a desire for ornament and surface that belongs with savagery and is deeply antagonistic to aesthetic distance."[31] The kitschy paper fans and chocolate boxes cherished by the women in the texts are at once a source of comfort and a symbol of something unobtainable; they "preserve the melancholy recognition of the insuperable distance between desire and its objects" that Lloyd describes and yet also offer instances of "the congealed memory of traumas too intimate and profound to be lived over without stylization and attitude."[32] These special objects mutely express both pain and pleasure. For all of their personalized talismanic power, however, nearly all of the fetishized objects preserved and often hidden in the domestic spaces in O'Brien's early fiction are strikingly impersonal, anonymous, mass-produced, even things that might be considered rubbish in a more comfortable home, like empty sweet wrappers and chocolate-box lids.[33] These things are further unmoored from atomized experiences and individuals by the fact that they recur with regularity across texts.

The vibrantly signifying objects under consideration wield an apotropaic power, promising escape from the evils of drudgery, poverty, and domestic abuse, but the respite is temporary and contingent, when not illusory. O'Brien's interest in Ireland's pre-Christian traditions is well documented, and her rendering of domestic detail evokes a kind of pagan animism. Nearly all the objects mimic organic forms: flowers, fruit, animals, the material bodies of saints, extensions through time of the otherwise perishable (with the possible exception of certain saints' remains), recalling Alison Landsberg's category of "prosthetic memories,"[34] those memories that belong to no one and everyone at once. Elizabeth Freeman argues, however, in her deployment of Landsberg's theory, that "S/M may literalize the prosthetic aspect of *all* memory";[35] in other words, such memories rely on props, objects used in a performance of identity and community, rendering both private and shared experiences plastic, subject to interpretation. Prosthetic memories extend beyond the personal into cultural memory, potentially transcending individual trauma, according to Freeman, by both "bind[ing] and unbind[ing] historical subjectivity."[36] The possible curative power of S/M, its dark promise of sharing the desire for release, including release from the trammels of self, is suggested when O'Brien says, "All masochists are just sadists waiting to be cured," an assertion quoted by Shirley Peterson in her discussion of sadomasochistic desire in *The Country Girls Trilogy*.[37] According to Lynn Chancer, whom Peterson finds insightful in understanding O'Brien's S/M dynamics, the hierarchical structure of the sadomasochistic relationship is erected on an unjust social arrangement, and Chancer argues that sadomasochism inevitably emerges under conditions of patriarchy,[38] an especially oppressive version of which prevails in the mid- to late-twentieth-century Ireland of O'Brien's fiction.

The psychologically immature or incomplete O'Brien protagonist, who invites and even performs self-annihilation, occupies, according to Peterson, a metonymic position vis-à-vis the "sadomasochistic impulses that drive the mid-century Irish sociopolitical agenda" a relationship that can be extended to "a kind of global abjection," another indication of the way in which the figure of loss in O'Brien potentially ramifies beyond the individual context.[39] Accepting the significance of "thing-power," Jane Bennett argues, registers resistance to the kind of "individualism [that] lends itself to atomistic" formulations of the self and in its place endorses a radical "congregational understanding of agency."[40] Such an "understanding of agency as confederation of human and nonhuman elements [can] alter established notions of moral responsibility and political accountability."[41] The associated political implications of S/M are noted by Chancer, who reveals the instability of the implicit S/M hierarchy, as it is an inherently codependent relationship in which positions of dominance and submission can become interchangeable: the sadist needs the masochist, and so the masochist can exert a kind of paradoxical control. The subversive potential of weakness and passivity contributes to what Jack Halberstam has identified as "shadow feminism," a practice distinguished by, among other qualities, a "refusal of mastery."[42] Halberstam associates this kind of feminism with "negative forms of anticolonial knowing."[43] Feminism under colonial/postcolonial conditions may, according to Halberstam, "find purpose in its own failure,"[44] resorting to "a radical form of masochistic passivity that not only offers up a critique of the organizing logic of agency and subjectivity itself, but that also opts out of certain systems built around a dialectic between colonizer and colonized,"[45] systems of especial significance in a postcolonial Irish context. As Terence MacSwiney, one of the leaders of the Easter Rising in Cork, famous for his martyr's death on hunger strike, is credited with saying, "It is not those who can inflict the most but those who can suffer the most who will conquer."[46] If masochistic passivity can be seen as conducting a "critique of the organizing logic of agency and subjectivity itself," a focus on "things" or "objects" is also necessarily at the very least questioning the distinction and distance that traditionally obtains between subject and object, a distinction on which all technologies of power are predicated.

The typical protagonist of O'Brien's early fiction, to whom many critics have historically objected, is read as lacking a confident, independent "self," a failure to comply with foundational expectations for the Western subject. For these characters, the porous, borderless "self" of infancy is only partially repressed in adulthood. Rebecca Pelan, among others, has identified the primary "love object" for O'Brien's protagonists as the mother, whose replacement her daughter hopelessly seeks in inevitably disappointing heterosexual partners.[47] As discussed in chapter 1, the adored and put-upon mother of O'Brien's early novels and short stories is a hardworking, self-denying country woman, usually married to a feckless alcoholic; she is, nonetheless, "house-proud." Bernice Schrank and Danine Farquharson have tracked a "subtle yet dense network of echoes and anticipations" that creates a web of recurring and overlapping objects and images in O'Brien's early work.[48] This network links several representations of the typical O'Brien mother. The particular objects produced in evidence of the pride she attempts to take in her home, despite its usually decrepit state of neglect, vary little across the early fiction: ornamental mirrors hung too high to be useful; a chocolate box or paper fan in the unused fireplace; seashells; a "what-not" (small ornamental set of shelves); wax or paper flowers; a dust-collecting stuffed or china animal figure; as well as holy statues. That these items are often kept enshrined in a "good" room that is never, or very rarely used—or not in a room at all but at the landing of a stairs—heightens the poignancy of their tawdry, faded prettiness, the frailty of the private bulwark they present against the harsh reality for women of Irish rural domesticity. According to Enright, O'Brien and her characters are "in thrall to artifice, the way it holds desire."[49] These precious objects, however battered, retain a kind of glamour and potency, a numinous quality that Bennett refers to as "the invisible field that surrounds and infuses the world of objects,"[50] a vibrancy emanating from the "denied possibilities" inherent in their promise of "nonidentity," that is, evading the determining power of dominant gender and sexual identities: "thing power may be a starting point for thinking beyond the life-matter binary, the dominating organizational principle for adult experience."[51] The volatile, ontologically ambiguous object in the secret world of O'Brien's rural women undermines numerous received truths about social and domestic order.

O'Brien's first novel, *The Country Girls* (1960), establishes figurative and emotional patterns in home ornamentation. Many of the early chapters take place in Cait Brennan's childhood home, where "things were either broken or not used at all,"[52] including the wedding present of Doulton plates kept in a dresser: "we never use them in case they'd get broken."[53] Their use as a screen against reality is literalized in its function as a hiding place for "hundreds of bills. Bills never worried Dada, he just put them behind the plates and forgot."[54] The "breakfast room," never used, or at least not for its ostensible purpose, serves as Cait's mother's sanctuary. Her life is a never-ending round of labor: "She was dragged down by heavy work, working to keep the place going, and at nighttime making lampshades and fire screens to make the house prettier."[55] The (sado)masochistically self-sacrificing mother who serves everyone else first, who eats dry toast while others breakfast on eggs and bacon, keeps a personal stash of biscuits behind a curtain in the "breakfast room," where she also sneaks the occasional cigarette. Cait obsesses painfully over her mother's self-denial. When her mother seems to have disappeared, later to be presumed dead, Cait reluctantly follows her friend Baba, who has brazenly let herself into the breakfast room in search of a treat: "The room was dark and sad and dusty. The whatnot, with its collection of knickknacks and chocolate-box lids and statues and artificial flowers, looked silly now that Mama wasn't there. The crab shells that she used as ashtrays were all over the room."[56] In the first half of the novel, before the girls begin the convent education that will spark their rebelliousness, self-satisfied, middle-class Baba adheres faithfully to the hierarchies of capital and patriarchy. Her "masculine" gaze diminishes the beauty of the room's decorations in the eyes of Cait, who had up to now greatly admired her mother's "taste." The barely concealed trauma "congealed" in the kitschy ornamentation of the room is exposed in the shamefully dirty seashell-ashtrays, redolent of death and decay, an exposure from which Cait shrinks, downplaying the décor's significance with the gendered adjective "silly."

Objects lose their glamour, reclaim their thingness, whenever the deep mother-daughter bond is broken, to be replaced with the loneliness of enforced normative heterosexuality, usually the daughter's pursuit of romantic relationships, consistently represented as exploitative and sterile, often ending in an unsuccessful, usually brief marriage. In a story first published in the New Yorker in 1963, "The Rug," the final disappointment caused by a household object presages a future loss of just this kind, a foretaste of abandonment and isolation for the mother. The house in the story is one typical for O'Brien in this period, with its contrast between the near-derelict "masculine" face of the house's exterior and the "feminine" domestic interior of the home, a space of compensatory, hopeful plenitude:

Though all outside was neglect, overgrown with ragwort and thistle; strangers were surprised when they entered the house; my father might fritter his life away watching slates slip from the outhouse roofs—but, within, that safe, square, lowland house of stone was my mother's pride and joy. It was always spotless. It was stuffed with things—furniture, china dogs. Toby mugs, tall jugs, trays, tapestries and whatnots. Each of the four bedrooms had holy pictures on the walls and a gold overmantle surrounding each fireplace. In the fireplaces there were paper fans or lids of chocolate boxes. Mantle pierces carried their own close-packed array of wax flowers, holy statues, broken alarm clocks, shells, photographs, soft rounded cushions for sticking pins in.[57]

Into this mixture of wax flowers and broken clocks, in an unmarked parcel, comes a sumptuous thing, a hearth rug that is not imitation, not ersatz kitsch, but "real sheepskin, thick and soft and luxurious."[58] Mother and daughter delight in puzzling over the identity of the mysterious person who has somehow "decided upon just the thing she needed."[59] In this instance, it is not the rug itself that signifies independently, which may indicate that it is not a proper resident of the house, that is, a thing rather than an object; instead, it testifies to the existence of a tasteful and thoughtful friend or relation elsewhere, evidence of connection, that the narrator's mother is actually admired, appreciated, and understood as she deserves. This diverting speculation ends with the discovery that the postman has made an error. The mother's "whole being drooped—shoulders, stomach, voice, everything."[60] There is no escape from the domestic misery detailed earlier in the story, summarized in the narrator's observation of her mother that she "never expected things to turn out well."[61] Her hopeless, familiar, mechanical gesture of constraint and submission closes the story: "she undid her apron strings, and then retied them slowly and methodically, making a tighter knot."[62]

This object confirming love, comfort, and glamour rightfully belongs in another woman's home. Other women's homes are objects of fascination and envy for many of O'Brien's characters. Visits to and even uninvited surveys of other women's houses, featuring a detailed inspection of design elements and sumptuous objects, occur in a number of short stories, including "New in Manhattan," "Nomads," "An Outing," "The Conner Girls," "The Small Town Lovers," and "Green Georgette." In "Green Georgette," objects collaborate in inspiring an ultimately violent erotics of sadomasochistic longings. This story, which first appeared in 1978 in the *New Yorker*, was republished in the 2011 collection *Saints and Sinners*. The young narrator and her mother are thrilled by an invitation to the Coughlans, a somewhat mysterious, childless, middle-class couple, subject to gossipy speculation in the parish. The Coughlans are known to have a piano, and the husband works in a bank. He is considered eccentric for not using his car to commute, preferring to walk, carrying his "lizard-skin attaché case,"[63] while his wife, "the cynosure of all," is "like a queen. There is not one woman who is not intrigued by her finery."[64] Her attraction lies predominantly in her "variety of smart fitted outfits and oodles of accessories and broaches,"[65] detailed descriptions of which fill most of a page. This is in contrast to her drab sister, Effie, who lives with the Coughlans and is rumored to be a former nun, boasting of "only two outfits, both tweed."[66] The narrator confesses that "being invited is a miracle," and so the mother and daughter relish imagining various versions of the

Coughlans' interiors and what the conversation and food will be like when they arrive.[67] On the day, they are ushered into Mrs. Coughlan, who "sat upright on a two-seater sofa with gilt-edged side arms. She wore green georgette and a long matching scarf."[68] Her setting is appropriately theatrical: "There was a fire in the room, with an embroidered screen placed in front of it. The various lit lamps had shades of wine red, with masses of a darker wine fringing. It was like a room in a story, what with that fire, the fire screen, the fenders and fire irons gleaming, and the picture above the black marble mantelpiece of a knight on horseback."[69] The narrator is especially arrested by Mrs. Coughlan's beautiful shoes: "they were cloth shoes of a silver filigree, with purple thread running through the silver, and there was a glittery buckle on the instep." Her appreciation is more than aesthetic, recalling religious ecstasy: "I could have knelt at them."[70] The masochistic self-abasement and submission of the narrator's imagined posture before the "divine" shoes is echoed by her mother's repeated, embarrassing offers of service, suggesting she sew or bake something for the Coughlans, offers that do not stimulate much conversation.

The mother and daughter have been granted their audience with Mrs. Coughlan as a gesture of thanks for just such a servile exchange. The Coughlans earlier threw a fancy dinner party (to which no one from the parish was invited), in the middle of which they sent their maid to the narrator's house for cream. The terms of polite condescension ruling the resulting visit are not immediately evident to the narrator or her mother but begin to emerge when disappointingly inferior shop cake and buns are served, though on an "exquisite" china set. The strain of the visit erupts into bizarre and explicit rudeness when Mrs. Coughlan leaps up claiming to need to see a doctor about a rash, though it is evening, well after hours. Mrs. Coughlan and her sister abruptly leave, and the narrator and her mother are unsure how to respond. Deciding to linger, they take the opportunity to assess the contents of the room more carefully. The mother estimates the cost of all the furnishings, claiming that "she would not give tuppence for the piano."[71] The revenge of this disparaging evaluation is meager and short-lived, however, as the mother and daughter finally return to their own home, noting with dread that the lights are out, a sign that the narrator's father has retired early and will have to be placated to avoid problems in the morning. The reality of her and her mother's domestic servitude piques a rebellious hunger in the girl for a modest, but denied, luxury, tinned peaches: "Mixed in with my longing was a mounting rage. Our lives seemed so drab, so uneventful."[72] The thrilling yet humiliating visit, the frustrating exposure to desirable, withheld objects, rouses in the narrator a sadomasochistic fantasy of destruction. This vision of devastation that affects animals, things, family, and neighbors closes the story: "I prayed for drastic things to occur—for the bullocks to rise up and mutiny, then gore one another, for my father to die in his sleep, for our school to catch fire, and for Mr Coughlan to take a pistol and shoot his wife, before shooting himself."[73] The childhood family home, whether real or ideal, intimate or strange, from which the O'Brien protagonist flees or is ejected, inspires mutinous fantasies that both employ and destroy beloved objects, as guilty yet regretted as any human occupant of the remembered domestic space.

Even as O'Brien's novels become increasingly urban and tend to be set outside of Ireland, the vibrant childhood home nevertheless still appears in some of her best-received short stories, like "Green Georgette." Another example, "Rose in the Heart," which also first appeared in the *New Yorker* in 1978, is littered with things and provides a detailed narrative of the profound, doomed connection between mother and daughter. O'Brien's memoir reveals that the horrific birth scene opening this story is based on accounts she heard of her own birth. The room in which the birth takes place in the short story is the "blue room," a room with "distempered walls" in which the fireplace is fronted by "the lid of a chocolate box," echoing details of where O'Brien herself was born, also called the blue room: "walls weeping quietly away from endless damp and no fire, even though there was a fire grate, ridiculously small compared with the size of the room, in which the lid of a chocolate box had been laid as an ornament."[74] After the difficult birth and what seems to be a period of postpartum depression, the mother and daughter in "Rose in the Heart" become intensely close: "The food was what united them, eating off the same plate, using the same spoon, watching one another's chews, feeling the food as it went down the other's gullet. . . . Her mother's knuckles were her knuckles; her mother's veins were her veins, . . . her mother's body a recess that she would wander inside for ever and ever."[75] The mother and daughter are united against a brutal father and husband who, among other cruelties, threatens his wife with a hatchet. Against the ugliness, the mother constructs oases for sharing beauty and stolen self-indulgences with her daughter:

> On the big upstairs landing, . . . the felt dog still lorded it, but now had an eye missing. . . . Also on the landing there was a bowl with a bit of wire inside to hold a profusion of artificial tea roses. These tea roses were a two-toned colour, were red and yellow plastic and the point of each was seared like the point of a thorn. . . . In the landing at home too was the speared head of Christ. Underneath Christ was a pussy cat of black papier mâché which originally had sweets stuffed into its middle, sweets the exact image of strawberries and even a little leaf at the base, a leaf made of green glazed angelica.[76]

This promiscuous assemblage respects no boundaries, including that between the sacred and profane, as objects exchange qualities with each other and mimic other absent things. Plastic flower petals evoke the crown of thorns associated with the image of an "endlessly commiserat[ing]" Christ, unselfconsciously juxtaposed with an empty cat-shaped sweet container that yet retains the memory of remarkably strawberry-shaped sweets made of "heavenly" material, angelica.

The recurrence of holy pictures and statues among such miscellanies of ornamentation in O'Brien's domestic interiors suggests the mystical "latency" and
"excess" of all things, as Brown argues: "what remains physically or metaphysically irreducible to objects, . . . their force as a sensuous presence or as a meta-
physical presence, the magic by which objects become values, fetishes, idols, and
totems."[77] The endlessly circulating economy of elusive references and referents
in these scenes provides numerous instances in O'Brien of the ongoing mutual
exchange described by Brown, in which the object shapes and possesses the subject, and vice versa.

In this story, this process extends to the house as a whole, which is described
on the first page as having "a strange lifelikeness as if it was not a house at all but
a person observing and breathing."[78] This uncanny domestic subjectivity, remi-
niscent of the watching, reproachful houses found in Bowen's fiction, will return
in the final paragraph, a subjectivity entirely suffused with the memory and history of the mother-daughter bond. The grown daughter comes home after her
mother's death and longs to be in touch with her once more: "She looked to see
some sign, or hear some murmur. Instead a silence filled the room and there was
a vaster silence beyond as if the house itself had died or had been carefully put
down to sleep."[79] The house and the mother have retreated into an elusive thingness. Having grown estranged from her mother over the years, the daughter no
longer feels the human-nonhuman connection so vital to her mother's survival.
According to Tim Ingold, "Remembering is not so much a matter of calling up
an internal image stored in the mind, as of engaging perpetually with an environment that is itself pregnant with the past."[80] The daughter has lost the specific
knack of engaging with the environment and memories that she once shared
with her mother and cannot make sense of the fragments she discovers in search
of the lost love object. Rifling through drawers, the daughter can only find "bits"
of the older woman's life: "Wishes. Dreams contained in such things as a gauze
rose of the darkest drenchingest red. . . . Never having had the money for real
style her mother had invested in imitation things—an imitation crocodile bag
and an imitation fur bolero."[81]

The investment here goes beyond the monetary, so cruelly limited by the
mother's unremunerated drudgery and servitude. Where, after all, was she ever
likely to go carrying a crocodile bag or, indeed, wearing a fur bolero? There is an
entirely other, alternative set of experiences being "remembered" by and through
these objects, not by the daughter but by the woman who carefully stored them
away. Men are implicitly excluded from the bond between women created by a
certain aesthetic, usually referred to as "style" in O'Brien and communicated by
vividly signifying, immediately recognizable "props" of glamorous, undomesticated femininity. The life being commemorated in the gauze rose, the crocodile
bag, and the fur bolero never existed. Memory is, according to Freeman, "not

natural or organic at all, but depends on various prompts or even props. In turn, S/M shows us memory can prop up projects unrelated to the history it supposedly preserves."[82] The mother's carefully archived, unused and unusable "mementos" are the stage dressings for a lacerating yet liberating drag performance, disconnected from, indeed, alien to her own lived experience and expectation. This imagined performance of femininity at once relishes and regrets the mysterious pleasures of a denied version of womanly embodiment. From O'Brien's first novel, *The Country Girls*, she has presented femininity as performance, inspiring both appreciation and resentment: "It is the only time that I am thankful for being a woman, that time of evening when I draw the curtains, take off my old clothes, and prepare to go out. . . . I shadow my eyelids with black stuff and am astonished by the look of mystery it gives my eyes. I hate being a woman. Vain and shallow and superficial."[83] Mooney describes O'Brien's explicit deployment of traditional drag—that is, a man dressed as a woman—in the novels *Down by the River* (1996) and *August Is a Wicked Month* (1965) as not only highlighting the arbitrariness of the cultural order but also offering the transgressive possibility of simultaneously articulating and eliding individuality,[84] a liberatory potential it shares with sadomasochism's painful pleasures.

In recent fiction, O'Brien has considered the unhomeliness of the modern home, bereft of well-used, richly associative objects, and extended it to a global context. In "Inner Cowboy," a story written for the collection *Saints and Sinners*, an ecological disaster is brought about by Celtic Tiger greed, fueled by macho posturing and competition. Men are "grabbing, buying up every perch of farm, bog and quarry," and have "destroyed a sacred wood with its yew trees, bulldozed it in order to make pasture to fatten livestock."[85] The massive oil spill perpetrated and then covered up by one of these men is witnessed by the childlike, sensitive male protagonist, Curly (his very name suggesting "deviance"),[86] who has a complex relationship to objects, as does his grandmother. Curly's grandmother's shed, where he goes in order to hide something for his shifty cousin Donie, "beat all for clutter":

> There was stuff in it going back hundreds of years, an old sidecar with a trap wedged over it, milk churns, milk tankards, breast slanes and foot slanes from when turf was cut by hand, and fenders and picture frames and old chairs and a horsehair sofa with the leather slashed and the coarse hair spilling out. There was a hole in the floor under the sidecar, where his great-grandfather hid his pike in Fenian times and his grandfather hid the bottles of poteen and where [Curly] would hide his bag.[87]

As Brown has observed, things can gothically intervene in traditional chronology, which is collapsed and inverted here through the placement of things with no regard to hierarchical and temporal significance: farming implements, household furniture, weapons of insurrection, and illicit distilling.

The interior of Curly's grandmother's house is similarly disrespectful of "proper" order, as a guard who visits her home at the end of the story discovers: "[The guard] was amazed at the amount of clobber she had accumulated, every single chair and armchair a throne of old newspapers and bags and flattened cardboard boxes. There were bits of crochet, dolls' prams, and a multitude of small china animals along the mantelpiece, above the unlit stove."[88] Curly shares his grandmother's promiscuous love of things, her "childlike" resistance to categorizations and priorities of aesthetic pleasure. However, Curly's relationship to the nonhuman is ultimately tentative and destructive rather than reassuring. To protect his grandmother, Curly retrieves his cousin's bag from the shed and takes it to the bog, the place he learned in school where treasure and bodies were traditionally buried. Curly's treatment of this bag as a person/corpse makes sly reference to bog bodies and the way in which corpses become objects when displayed in a museum setting. He places the bag into his own wardrobe and buttons it into a jacket and puts a hat on it "so that it looked like a dead person, a dead person with the legs sawn off."[89]

The bag/body hovers in that liminal zone of "thingness," the "threshold between the nameable and the unnameable, the figurable and the unfigurable, the identifiable and the unidentifiable."[90] Dressing the bag in men's clothing, a kind of drag performance that crosses the human-nonhuman divide, illustrates a significant difference between Curly and the female characters discussed thus far. Unlike them, Curly struggles to conform to "manly" expectation of behavior and attitudes, a struggle with implications for his connection to things. Curly feels compelled to perform adult masculinity, reflected in his dressing up of the bag; but his efforts are unconvincing, and he is no more able to "pass" as an appropriately masculine adult than the bag wearing a hat is. Dressing up the bag recalls a child playing with dolls, and one particularly uncanny category of objects in O'Brien's fiction is toys, which often take on a life of their own, and in such a way as to voice characters' melancholy dread or feelings of helplessness.[91] An Elmo doll in "Inner Cowboy" articulates the inescapability of an oppressive and compulsorily violent masculine heteronormativity, which leads to Curly's death. Curly has been bullied into acting like a "man" and risking his own (and his grandmother's) safety for his cousin's sake in hiding the bag, which contains money and/or drugs, an act that has driven Curly to despair as he hears his own voice emerging from a neighbor child's doll: "There was a girl two doors down that got a toy at Christmas that could talk. It was clothed in red fur, the mouth open and the tongue hanging out. It had two plastic knobs for eyes and an orange fur nose, and every so often it said 'Elmo wants you to know that Elmo loves you.' He was Elmo, only it was him saying it to himself—*I am so far in I can't get out*. It wouldn't stop."[92] As at other times in the story, Curly struggles here with the imperative to replace an ethic of love with one of brutality. Obeying this command takes him to the brink of psychosis, which perhaps leads him to throw himself in the bog along with the bag, though whether his death is a suicide, an accident, or something more sinister is never discovered.

Curly's body is found by a walker who responds to a call, not a human or animal call but the mechanical cry of a mobile phone, which, when she picks it up, feels "alive in her hand."[93] Curly's last communication is through an object, an "inappropriately" gendered light-pink phone, retrieved by a woman, attuned in some unspoken way to the cries of the nonhuman. Curly has been missing but rejoins the community as a corpse, a thing, whose reentry is enabled by a living, "speaking" object, an instance of what Bennett calls our "cyborgization," the "agentic assemblage" that comprises human agency, always an assemblage of the human, nonhuman, animate, and inanimate:[94] "there was never a time when human agency was anything other than an interfolding network of humanity and nonhumanity."[95] In O'Brien's fiction, telephones, like toys, demonstrate an uncanny liveliness, a quality that can be unsettling, even menacing, sometimes acting as extensions and intrusions of malign force.[96] In the story "House of My Dreams" (1974), the narrator, fearing the removal of her children by their vengeful father, watches telephones "where they lay, somehow like numbed animals, black things or white things, or a red thing, that has gone temporarily dead."[97] In *Time and Tide* (1992), Nell fears the same kind of call from an estranged husband, an animating dread that renders the phone "a dark cobra waiting to pounce" or "like a panther." So fierce is the instrument's vitality that Nell finds she must exert pressure to control it: "her elbow weighed on it as if she were holding down a writhing animal."[98] Josie, in *House of Splendid Isolation*, is paradoxically struck by the telephone's "lifelessness," despite it being "a viper, grey-black."[99] In "Manhattan Medley" (2011), a telephone kiosk looks to the narrator to have been "someone's abode," littered with objects including a "dirty baseball cap, punched cans, orange rinds, and a cassette tape in such a tangle that it looked as if it might presently scream."[100] It is, of course, the abode of the telephone itself and has become the resting place of various rejected objects, including an abused and suffering cassette tape on the verge of expressing its pain.[101]

Recognition of the vibrant, signifying other is an ability accorded largely to women in O'Brien's fiction. Curly's tragedy emerges from his attempt to refuse the support of and connection to his grandmother and all of the older "homely" values she represents. He has been bullied and shamed into rejecting the comforts of home, filled to bursting with friendly objects, sometimes capable of replacing the human, as when his Granny reacts to her husband's death by "crochet[ing] a beautiful white bed shawl," which "kept her alive."[102] Curly is excluded from the transcendent magic inhering in the object, not only by his gender but also due to his positioning in twenty-first-century modernity, an era of increased disposability that has attenuated our attachment to loved objects, an attachment now associated with childishness and nostalgia. A passionate relationship to things in O'Brien's domestic interiors, however, especially the impoverished interiors of midcentury rural Ireland, allowed the women trapped within to imagine revolution on a personal level as well as communally, to dare defiance and to glimpse dangerous freedoms along the edges of the life-matter divide.

3 · THE UNGRAMMATICAL SUBLIME

Nature is so unsinful, unpunishing, so silent and time to itself.

Edna O'Brien's "Inner Cowboy" (2010) is a story with an ecological disaster at its center. Its environmental concerns are made explicit from the opening paragraph, which introduces the landscape as well as Curly, the protagonist, who admires that landscape in an entirely unselfconscious way, though he fears being jeered at for his "feminine" receptivity to natural beauty, his aesthetic, imaginative response to the scene. O'Brien's descriptive powers, her specificity of detail, are most often recognized in her descriptions of landscapes and the "natural" world. In a 1958 essay for the journal *The Writer*, written two years before the publication of *The Country Girls*, O'Brien describes the act of writing as necessarily collaborative, a process that harnesses, in Jane Bennett's phrase "nature as creativity":[1] "In the subliminal depths of my writing, me, I am aware of a yearning to make contact. And I remind myself that we are all of the earth. We have felt rain, heat, cold, wind, etc. We have all known grass under our feet, stars overhead. We have all touched trees, flowers, water, rock, etc. There on the earth somewhere my characters and I meet. I feel something about the part of earth they come out of."[2] The kind of empathy with and connection to the natural world described here is often understood as "feminine." Curly's boss regularly calls him a "retard," the kind of person who admires the mist rising, "like a grand lady lifting the veil of her hat."[3] Curly is out of step with thrusting alpha-male dominance, which never notices mist rising and certainly does not entertain fanciful metaphors to describe natural phenomena but, on the contrary, requires the destruction of the natural world, as a demonstration of power, as well as in order to satisfy greed and bolster status.

For O'Brien, literary creation relies on the landscape, on contact with elements of the natural world, both inanimate and animate, wind as well as trees. From this early description of the "subliminal depths" of her writing, she has continued to describe the writing process as partly inexpressible, not entirely under her control. This is not simply naïve romanticism about inspiration[4] but, as O'Brien articulated in the excerpt from *The Writer* from sixty years ago, a recognition of what Val Plumwood has more recently described as "the creativity of earth others," an acknowledgment of "multiple agencies in the more-than-human world."[5] This refusal of "mastery" and a defense of something beyond the coldly rational as vital to imaginative recreation, a defiance of rules of propriety and rational organization, affect both content and form in O'Brien's work. The lush qualities of O'Brien's prose, especially when describing the natural world, have sometimes been dismissed as excessive, even ludicrous, an implicitly gendered critique. As Catherine Nash has observed, the "feminization of the field of vision," which links "the landscape, the colonized, [and] the looked-upon," effects the "exclusion of women from knowledge production."[6] For decades, O'Brien was excluded from the ranks of "literary" writers, at least in part, as already discussed, because of her focus on "women's" concerns.[7] This chapter considers the radical messiness of the novelist's prose, sometimes characterized as irrational and unconscious, therefore too "feminine," too "natural" to be taken seriously. Few commentators have understood O'Brien's attempts to break through the linguistic barriers between human and nonhuman experience in those moments when her prose partakes of the evocative, extralinguistic powers of verse, a result of her deep understanding of writing as a communal project, of the writer as working in creative collaboration with the natural world, whose language is rarely articulable in a traditional sense.

The derogation of sensitive Curly recalls the way in which the murderer Michen O'Kane of *In the Forest* (2002) is berated as a child by bullies in the schoolyard. At the death of O'Kane's mother, he is haunted by the memory of the jeering reception that met his claims then to be "a true son of the forest," when his classmates called him, instead, "a mammy's boy, a patsy, a pandy, a sissy, and a ninny." The association of woman and nature in shared degradation, in this instance, equates weak effeminacy with idiocy, as Curly's imaginative impulses are indexed to his lack of manliness. This childhood treatment of O'Kane will be repeated by other defenders of masculinity, including the police officers who finally arrest him. Suffering a breakdown in prison, O'Kane receives visitors:

> The staff shot the pheasant that kept him company because they were jealous of it. He got his revenge. He had birds coming in the window whistling tunes and he whistled back. Then one day six or seven red hens from home came and he talked to them and asked them if they were laying well. He had great times with them. He learned the chookchookchookchookchookchook that they did after they laid. One morning they didn't come and he cried. Pigs came, but they got stuck, they got wedged between the bars, their pink hairy rumps not able to get out. They taught him grunts, and the screws listened outside the cell and looked through the spyhole, made bets whether he was or was not a pig. Instead of Fattie they called him Piggy.[8]

As happens often in her late fiction, through animals, O'Brien locates an almost shocking, somehow chilling poignancy in what should be an utterly unsympathetic male character.

In these texts, ostensibly irredeemable characters betray a surprising and ironic humanity when they communicate via nonhuman language, whether open to learning and understanding "chookchookchookchookchook," like O'Kane, or versed in the "non-words, horse words"[9] as is James, the rapist-father of *Down by the River*, who uses horse words to help a mare deliver her foal. The hens and pigs, emissaries from O'Kane's unfulfilled dreams of domesticity, love, and mother, offer only fleeting comfort; in fact, they invite further abuse, as the prison guards, representatives of patriarchal social control, act like O'Kane's earliest tormentors, boys learning to be "hard" men at the expense of mothers and animals, those designated worthless because most threatening to self-similar male subjectivity. The danger posed by desire for and sympathy with the "other" is accounted for in Kristeva's theory of abjection: "The autonomy or substance of the subject is called into question, endangered. I am solicited by the other in such a way that I collapse. This solicitation can be the result of fascination, but also suffering of the other disgusts me, I abhor it, it is—we are—waste, excrement, a corpse: it threatens me."[10] As discussed in chapter 2, Curly, unlike O'Kane, retains some of his sensitivity, indexed in the story to his openness to solicitation by the other—whether that other is a human, a corpse, a cow in calf, or a child's doll—though he does so at a terrible cost to himself.

As in the examples of Curly and O'Kane, O'Brien does not romanticize connection to the nonhuman world, for women or men, as simply regenerative or innocent, however essential or undeniable it may be. In an early unpublished piece about returning to her native County Clare, O'Brien describes a harsh landscape reflective of unrelenting domestic realities: "Always a wind. Calves shelter around reeks of hay, and trees have long since learned to bend and accommodate themselves to the drinking bouts of men."[11] Nash provides the "historical contexts" for reading the Irish landscape in this way, the "efforts to control an 'essentially female race' and post-independence attempts to employ notions of femininity, rural life and landscape in the construction of Irishness and the subordination of Irish women."[12] Nature and women "bent" by the violent masculine imperative to ownership that assumes an equivalence between the appropriation of women and of land are often the subject of O'Brien's fiction. A subdued, "throttled" landscape, eerily silent, frequently signals sexual abuse or exploitation for her female protagonists, including in *August Is a Wicked Month* (1965), *Johnny I Hardly Knew You* (1977), *Wild Decembers* (1999), the short story "Plunder" (2010),[13] and *The Little Red Chairs* (2015). In *Red Chairs*, a rape/abortion, set in an abandoned house amid unused fields at the edge of an empty bog, is conducted with a crowbar and described as "slewing and tilting, then raking, as if raking earth."[14] Trees are sacred and inspirational to young Maryam in the more recent *Girl* (2019); they are the subject of a prized school essay, but they seem to betray her when she is kidnapped and driven deep into the wilderness: "We enter dense jungle, trees of all kind meshed together, taking us into their vile embrace."[15] Eventually, however, after one of many rapes she endures, Maryam recovers her healing relationship to the landscape as it takes pity: "The top of the big tree stands patient against the sky and the leaves murmur as before rain. Then a breeze from the forest, a cool breeze that heralds rain is blowing all over my body and down along my legs like silk. The rain came in great noisy squalls, sheets of it coming down to wash everything clean, rain is fierce and sudden and merciful."[16] A restored kinship with the natural indicates Maryam's own resilience, the possibility of surviving her ordeal.

The sympathetically muted landscape is especially poignant in *Down by the River* (1997), when the young girl Mary is being raped by her father: "Not a sound of a bird. An empty place cut off from every place else, and her body too, the knowing part of her body getting separated from what was happening down there."[17] The helpless silence of the abused girl/woman finds an analogue in an evacuated, "denaturalized" nature. The "empty place" is not only the "down there" of "unmentionable" female sexuality but also the "down there" of the earth itself, particularly the treacherously "feminine" Irish bog. The father preparing to sexually assault his daughter in this lonely, remote place, "struck out with [his metal tape] then waved and dandled it to verify both his powers and his riches which had lain so long, prone and concealed, waiting for the thrust of the slane."[18] Patriarchal structures of church and history, including mythology, implicitly sanction the father's sense of entitlement as he swings the tape "in an apostolic arc . . . pronouncing his claim over the deserted but fabled landscape."[19] O'Brien's other late-twentieth- and early-twenty-first-century state-of-Ireland novels also figure the land as a feminized victim of violent masculine subjugation, threatening in its intimacy with both birth and death. The prologue of *Wild Decembers*, in which two men violently compete over their rights to land and to a young woman's loyalty and love, recounts a local history of "fields that mean more than fields, more than life and more than death too, . . . fields that translate into nuptials, into blood; fields lost, regained and lost again."[20] The centuries-long battle for "ownership" of Ireland, in which the IRA gunman on the run in *House of Splendid Isolation* (1994) is yet embroiled, haunts a parallel, domestic struggle for dominance and independence remembered by the elderly Josie, whose house the gunman has chosen as his refuge. Josie's late husband, who entertained fantasies about participating in that same armed national struggle, raped her nightly. The novel opens with a monologue by "The Child," who appears to be speaking from beneath the soil and might be the spirit of Josie's defiantly aborted fetus. The Child describes the earth as "so old and haunted, so hungry and replete. It talks. . . . A girl loves a sweetheart, and a sweetheart loves her back, but he loves the land more."[21] The mutually reinforcing dynamic of the sexualizing of the land and the objectification of women inevitably provides the foundation for violent destruction in O'Brien's late fiction.

The last of the state-of-the-nation novels, *In the Forest*, prompted *The Irish Times* journalist Fintan O'Toole to castigate O'Brien for her "lack of discretion," in a review-length complaint about the novelist's failure to know her place, in the sense not only of observing the proprieties but also of having been out of Ireland too long to write sensitively or perceptively about it. Throughout, he accuses O'Brien of lacking a clear critical grasp of her role as a chronicler of modern Ireland.[22] Some critics feel differently about O'Brien's "disobedient" tendencies, such as Mary Leland, who, also writing in *The Irish Times* about the novelist, though a decade earlier, "thank[s] god" that the novelist "breaks the rules." Leland and other women readers acknowledge that O'Brien "gave us back the right to recognize ourselves, to find ourselves worthy of appreciation,"[23] by regularly betraying ideals of chaste and proper womanliness, a state of moral disorder that critics once claimed to find reflected in the writer's very diction and syntax. In post-Independence Ireland, one channel through which ideological hegemony is maintained is the hegemony of normative representational structures. In texts such as the travelogue/memoir *Mother Ireland* (1976), the novel *A Pagan Place* (1970), and the Epilogue (1986) to *The Country Girls Trilogy*, O'Brien deploys one of her distinctive formal experimentations, the use of second-person narration, a diffuse and disorientating representational mode that lays bare the fictive metaphor of narrative "person." O'Brien undermines the textual conceit's strategy of what Dennis Shofield describes as its "naturalization and anthropomorphism which acts to maintain particular normative ideological/discursive structures,"[24] just one example of the novelist's interrogation of "natural" structures of dominance even as they occur at the level of language itself.

Kristi Byron has argued that the use of second person in the Epilogue establishes an "oral, colloquial, intimate tone," which implicitly "creates gendered positions for both narrator and narratee,"[25] a gendering that also distinguishes the narrative effect of person in *A Pagan Place*, a novel about sexual secrets furtively held by women struggling to assert limited control over their lives. Byron recognizes O'Brien's canny manipulation of narrative techniques and genre, also the subject of Elizabeth Chase's reading of the novels in the trilogy, which, Chase claims, reject genre and are the first steps in the novelist's career-long "revisionist project."[26] As in Byron's discussion, Chase genders her structural analysis: "Boundaries of genre offer her women no escape. . . . As problematic as O'Brien's techniques may have been to feminists, her purpose is to critique literary structures from within. . . . By utilizing and revising an established genre, O'Brien points to the genre's inadequacies and devastatingly chronicles the effects such conventions have on the female protagonist and on the women who read her story." According to Chase, the challenge that O'Brien "presents to the boundaries of the literary text"'[27] recalls traditional colonial stereotypes of the recalcitrant and rebellious Irish, ready to attack from their hiding places, sunken in the bog or treacherously hidden in the trees.

This association of the intractable Irish and their ability to disappear into the pleats and shadows of the landscape can be seen in critical assessments of O'Brien's prose style. Some critics see O'Brien herself as performing the "pictur-esque," a category of landscape aesthetics that prizes oxymoronically careful disorder. For example, Nicholas Wroe describes O'Brien's hair as "tousled immaculately,"[28] while Robert Nye dismisses her prose as "good words for the most part in the right order, or plausibly Irish in their rhetorical disarray."[29] She is also seen to enact the more exhilarating aesthetic extreme of the "sublime," as when Lorna Sage refers to O'Brien's work as "splendidly untidy."[30] The associa-tion of disarray, irrationality, and untidiness with Irishness is a familiar one. The colonial stereotype of the filth-loving Irish, living in dunghills and swinesteads and snatching their food out of ditches, is one that goes at least as far back as Sir John Davies and Edmund Spenser in the sixteenth and seventeenth centuries. Spenser described the Irish as wild beasts, "living subhumanly in bogs."[31] This figuration of the Irish as wild savages, irremediably estranged from culture, underwent some moderation in the nineteenth-century discourse of Celticism, which presented a "feminine," childlike Celt, full of soulfulness, poetry, and emotion. However, whether children or savages, the "bogtrotting" Irish, literally mired in the landscape, were incapable of self-control, in need of instruction and direction.[32] The Irish Literary Revival attempted a further redemption of the ste-reotype, characterizing country life as oral, organic, and closer to nature. But this version of the Irish peasant, when presented on the stage of W. B. Yeats's Abbey Theatre, could provoke riots, as happened at the first performance of J. M. Synge's *The Playboy of the Western World* in 1907, convincing Yeats of the need to "cultivate" the aesthetics of the audience, to discipline the unruly crowd, who were in the habit of "disgracing" themselves,[33] a project similar to Eugene Gail-lard's for Caithleen, the woman whose name he prunes and "civilizes" to "Kate" in O'Brien's *The Girl with Green Eyes* (1964). By the novel's conclusion, after Eugene has begun to reproach Kate for her lack of discipline and order, her need to develop self-control and practice better hygiene, he will express contempt for her "country soul,"[34] an echo of Sage's evocation of "passionate ruts and boggy tracks" to express despair at O'Brien's thematic limitations.[35]

O'Brien's offenses against propriety have been both personal and literary. She traces her resistance to regulation and obedience to childhood in her memoir, when she recalls the harrowing experience of the lancing of an infected dog bite on her neck when she was about four years old. Several men held the little girl down, clamping her mouth closed with rough-skinned, tobacco-reeking hands.[36] She has continued to fight others' desire for domination from when she first screamed and struggled under patriarchal pressure. She has painfully chronicled the complexities and contradictions of twentieth-century Irish masculinity, insecurely supported and justified by exerting control over women's bodies, their purity, their responsibilities for reproducing the nation within the sanctified family, as discussed in earlier chapters. As Nash has demonstrated, "The metaphor of land/body has been used to justify both approaches to women and the environment and to legitimize colonisation."[37] Postcolonial "approaches to women and the environment" did not change in Ireland post-Independence, however. According to David Lloyd, "Irish nationalism and British imperialism largely concur . . . in associating self-government and 'manliness,' at the level of the individual person as at that of the nation,"[38] and in O'Brien, this can be seen even at the level of discourse. She has regularly been accused of linguistic irregularity, as when Gabriele Annan observed that her "grammar can be wonky."[39] According to John Broderick, "She is a silly and sloppy writer. The darling of the semi-literates";[40] Lorna Sage often complained of her "untidy idiom";[41] and Denis Donoghue denounced her as a "damnably appalling sloppy writer who writes in the words of the Irish tourist board,"[42] the last yet another example of O'Brien's Irishness somehow enabling derogation of her craft. Even admiring critics make recourse to O'Brien's national origins in explaining her idiosyncratic style, if to different ends, as when Jan Moir refers to O'Brien as having "her countryman's Byzantine eloquence"[43] or when Terrence Rafferty, in a review of *The High Road* for the *New Yorker*, says of the novelist, "she's a superb craftsman of traditional realist English fiction, yet there's always something wild and unmannerly—Celtic in the best, most primitive sense—trying to break the surface."[44] Similarly, Thomas Cahill links the unorthodoxy of O'Brien's writing with her national origin, again associated with the premodern, the not-fully-civilized: "Her best work has the sound of something prehistoric. . . . It is indeed not prose, at least not in any modern manner. . . . She writes [as] one of a long procession of prophetic Irish women."[45] Victoria Glendinning's *New Yorker* review of the short story collection, *Rose in the Heart*, after describing O'Brien's language as both effective and peculiar, bluntly states that "by conventional standards she does not write 'well.' She writes, often, very badly. Her punctuation is all to hell, and she abuses both grammar and vocabulary." However, Glendinning ends the review by suggesting that O'Brien's apparent lack of fully conscious self-control might, ironically, be subject to expert and deliberate manipulation, asking whether "she has learned consciously and professionally to harness this unself-consciousness to her purposes."[46]

Glendinning's paradoxical suspicions regarding O'Brien's self-aware "unself-consciousness" points to a reading of the novelist's purported stylistic deficiencies as defiance of formal authority and its determinate structures. Gerardine Meaney has argued that "as women claim and change their roles and seek a different identity for themselves as women, they will also change the meaning of national identity. . . . No longer the territory over which power is exercised, women, in exercising power, may redefine the territory."[47] The power to define territory is one that O'Brien has long striven to wrestle from established author-ity, as Anne Enright observes in a review of *Girl* for *The Irish Times*, where she argues that "O'Brien has always written with a kind of recklessness; her sen-tences undo and redo language as they go. . . . This dive into the possibilities of language is not just a dive into the self, it is a creative disruption, one which allows new shapes and possibilities to form."[48] According to Karen Barad's analy-sis of the questionable primacy granted to the linguistic in authoritatively deter-mining meaning, feminists and social scientists are belatedly developing the kind of skepticism that was always evident in O'Brien's writing: "The belief that grammatical categories reflect the underlying structure of the world is a continu-ing seductive habit of mind worth questioning. Indeed, the representationalist belief in the power of words to mirror preexisting phenomena is the metaphysi-cal substrate that supports social constructivist, as well as traditional realist, beliefs. Significantly, social constructivism has been the object of intense scru-tiny within both feminist and science studies circles where considerable and informed dissatisfaction has been voiced."[49] Barad joins O'Brien in understand-ing the implications for beings that have traditionally been understood as excluded from the symbolic, seen as incapable of literate communication, including the nonhuman. As Alicia Ostriker has argued, "to justify their exploi-tation and destruction, women and nature must be seen both as morally evil and metaphysically non-existent,"[50] that is, incapable of self-reflection. The archaic "wildness" of O'Brien's prose, trapped in some inarticulate Celtic twilight, is best suited, in many critics' opinion, to passionate outbursts of irrational emotion and ornate descriptions of the natural world, unconnected to intellection or the creation of meaningful art. A review of *August Is a Wicked Month* says of "her prose" that it "coos with all the lovesickness of a woman's magazine story," sug-gesting a bird brain making meaningless, inarticulate sounds.[51] Unlike the case of her predecessor James Joyce, whose flouting of grammar signals his genius and originality, O'Brien's apparent ignorance of those same rules signifies per-sonal and professional failure.

The kind of textual dissonance that distinguishes O'Brien's literary practice does evoke moral failures, but not the author's own. In provoking self-consciousness in the reader by bringing a text's textuality to our attention, her prose can potentially destabilize the normative dynamic and distance "proper" to the relationship between author, character, and reader, as in the opening pages of *Down by the River*. The narration luxuriates in descriptions of an unremarkable country road that nonetheless inspires lyrical description, featuring "entwined undulations of mud," "young shoots surgent in the sun," and light "dappled and filtered through different muslins of leaf." Into the middle of this first paragraph erupts a disconcerting apostrophe to the sun: "O sun. O brazen egg-yolk alba-tross."[52] According to Hilary Mantel, O'Brien's language in the novel is "ornate and sometimes florid," especially at this moment, which, Mantel sardonically warns, may cause "queasiness."[53] However, when this formula is repeated a few pages later, during the novel's first rape, it does not raise a smirk. Its recurrence is accompanied by a shift in narration to second person: "It does not hurt if you say it does not hurt. It does not hurt if you are not you. . . . O quenched and empty world."[54] Who is speaking and to whom is discomfitingly unclear. Is this Mary, the girl being raped, or the older Mary remembering, or the narrator? The passage does not appear in quotation marks. When the rape is over, the disinterested third-person narration resumes. In this harrowing passage, an "inappropriate" outburst of archaic language returns and, as in its first appearance, is punctuated flatly, a simple declarative, not an exclamation, defying structural expectations of such an address to the natural world, here the setting for an "unnatural" violation. This moment's varying layers of signifying dissonance cause a kind of textual stumble and interruption that should jolt the reader into confrontation with the brutality of what is being described. It also asks what language *is* appropriate to describe a father's rape of his adolescent daughter.[55] The language strains at the limits of the representable as it collapses points of view and confuses narratorial perspective, at the same time encouraging a recursive rather than linear reading practice. The iteration of "O" requires reconsideration of its initial usage, and the entire first paragraph takes on new significance. For all of its lyricism, the opening description is not celebrating "nature" as a retreat or flattering backdrop to human activity but is describing mud and rubbish and weeds, the smell of a dead donkey, and the rust on a rotting car, itself a "shrine" to a drunken suicide in this spot. The contrast between content and style established from the outset, exaggerated in the disjunctive formal address to the sun, is deliberately extreme in preparation for the unbearable scene to come, which eludes representation. As is often the case in O'Brien's fiction, reality exceeds traditionally "tidy" modes of articulation for women's experience.

O'Brien chooses a rural landscape that promises the picturesque only to refuse it, in order to stage a confrontation between form and content, a confrontation that challenges easy ascriptions of "natural" and "unnatural," "human" and "bestial." O'Brien's rule-breaking, both personal and linguistic, defies the "purity rules" identified by the anthropologist Mary Douglas as essential to supporting the "division between nature and culture." The purity rules "constrain" expression, "import judgements of their own about the relation of nature to culture."[56] Both Douglas and O'Brien interrogate the mechanisms of power that inhere in such rules and the vested interest that social control has in disavowing an understanding of "ourselves as things in nature."[57] The structures of exclusion subtending oppression require, ab initio, a "constructed world of nature," wherein "the contrast between man and not man provides an analogy for the contrast between members of the human community and the outsider. In the most inclusive set of categories, nature represents the outsider."[58] According to O'Brien's recent memoir, her sense of being an outsider informed her belief that from birth "the

words [were] always there," suggesting that the "cultural" is a bodily phenomenon. Her outsiderness also nurtured her relationship with the natural world, a
relationship always inextricable from the literate since childhood, when, she
says, "in my daft ambition to be a writer, I was studying nature."[59] O'Brien's use
of landscape recalls Nash's promotion of representation of the natural "as a shifting strategic source of identity without implying the adoption of a masculinist or
fixed natural or inherent identity," by understanding the constructedness of
identity, Irishness, gender, and even "nature" itself, constructs imagined by and
projected from more than one source.[60] As Bennett demonstrates, "culture is *not*
of our own making, infused as it is by biological, geological and climatic forces."[61]
From childhood, O'Brien has experienced the "cultural" as emerging from the
Irish countryside.

From the start of her career, O'Brien has recognized the damaging effects of
the culture/nature divide for women, traditionally identified with the dispar-
aged, subordinated side of that opposition, even as she has embraced and celebrated an association with the natural. Subject to a patriarchal calculus of value,
women, children, and animals are caught in the same trammels. In an Irish context, the potentially fatal consequences of systematic dehumanization have been
part of discussions of recent revelations regarding the imprisonment of mothers
and babies, as discussed in earlier chapters. For example, the *Sunday Independent*
journalist Gene Kerrigan has described the attitude of the church toward "dis-
graced" women and their children as reducing them to "shameful mistakes" to be
"melted down and recycled,"[62] while TD (member of Irish Parliament) Bríd
Smith likened the government's financial support of carceral religious institutions to the Bon Secours nuns receiving "headage payments as if they were cattle
or sheep for each child."[63] Women and girls in O'Brien's fiction are consistently
evaluated in terms of livestock, an assessment intended to be demeaning,
whether ostensibly positive or negative. In *Girl*, the kidnapped girls are both
"corralled" like cattle before being raped and "appraised" later "as if [they] were
cattle" when being chosen as trophy brides for warriors.[64]

Kristeva's "abject" accounts for the othering of the female body, the way in
which it is rendered constitutively monstrous, defined as other to the (male)
human subject. Jane Ussher's analysis of the female body, including the mother's
body, as repulsive and threatening relies on the theories of abjection. According
to Ussher, the leaking, swelling female body is seen as "uncontained" and, therefore, associated "with the animal world which reminds us of our mortality and
fragility."[65] In *The Country Girls*, Caithleen reacts to admiringly being called
"plump" by stating, "I hated the sound of the word. It reminded me of young
chickens when they were being weighed for the market."[66] Her description of an
elderly woman only a few pages later unconsciously deploys the same figure for a
woman's sexualized body, in this case, a woman no longer sexually relevant and,
therefore, even more inspiring of disgust: "the yellow skin stretched over her

old bones and her hands and wrists were thin and brown like boiled chicken bones."[67]

O'Brien's Irish characters are rural, even if they have moved to London or beyond. A typically instrumentalist attitude toward domestic animals is extended to wives and daughters on the farm. In *Mother Ireland*, O'Brien refers to "madwomen" whose "brothers or keepers put harnesses on them,"[68] like Eily, the unmarried pregnant girl in "A Scandalous Woman" (1974), whose father wants "to put a halter on her."[69] When Mary, the young rape victim in *Down by the River*, reveals to her neighbor Betty that she is pregnant, her terror registers with Betty as "not that of a little girl at all but an animal, animal eyes staring out from the noose of a trap."[70] The dominating James of *House of Splendid Isolation* demonstrates his power over his wife, Josie, in the marital bed, where "he arched up and down in mimicry of riding his favourite filly." Over the course of their marriage, he increases the sexual humiliation by "holding her lips shut with one hand, clamping the way he might clamp an animal. . . . He calls her muddy, short for mother and mud,"[71] making explicit his reduction of Josie to mere matter, the insensate incubating body, on the same level as the fructifying earth beneath his feet, with which she shares an "abject fecundity."[72] When Josie does become pregnant, she is determined to disappoint James's dynastic ambitions and undergoes a dangerous illegal abortion.

Looking back on the experience, Josie recalls her fear of the housemaid's suspicions, because she "bled like a pig,"[73] a resonant simile. The pig, an insulting symbol of the Irish in the eighteenth and nineteenth centuries, until Darwin's theories made the ape a more popular shorthand for the unevolved Celtic "race," has wider significance as a reviled, polluted animal, metaphor for the poor and working classes, as in Edmund Burke's phrase "the swinish multitudes," and subject to dietary prohibition for centuries in Abrahamic religions.[74] In O'Brien's fiction, screaming, trapped, or butchered pigs often figure women's entrapment, objectification, endangerment. In *A Pagan Place*, using second person, the narrator remembers a violent scene between her parents: "your father had a pitchfork raised to your mother and said I'll split the head of you open."[75] A few short paragraphs later, the narrator describes the herding of animals to be butchered by her father, including pigs: "He slit their throats and then held them upside down over a container to catch the blood. . . . You seldom watched but you heard. The squeals of each particular pig reached you no matter where you hid, no matter where you happened to crouch, and it was heart-rending as if the pig was making a last but futile effort for someone to save him."[76] In this novel, the narrator's unmarried older sister, Emma, is referred to by gossiping neighbors as having "a porker" on the way.[77] Not only the whole village knows about the family's shame but also, even more humiliating, farmers from beyond the village who would not have known except for the fact that "there was a pig fair on."[78] Cait and Baba intentionally disgrace themselves in *The Country Girls* in order to be sent way from their convent school, a plan Cait regrets, as it means the girls have to support themselves, which they cannot do in their small hometown. As they prepare to leave for Dublin, where new excitements and sexual dangers await them, Cait is saying a heartbroken good-bye to all of the sights and sounds, including those of "a pig fair around the market-house": "the pigs grunted and stuck their noses through the holes in the creels, trying to get out."[79]

A similar scene is recounted by O'Brien in *Mother Ireland*: "Pigs kept in creels squealed non-stop, slipping and slithering all over the place."[80] Animals that struggle and lose their footing under the rough hands of brutal men appear at least briefly in nearly all of O'Brien's fiction, cows as well as pigs, both of whom share with O'Brien a tendency to be "slipshod," according to Sean McMahon, who uses the word to describe the novelist's own writing.[81] Something about the crazed response of animals to their restrictions speaks with special clamancy to O'Brien's women, as when, in *Casualties of Peace*, Willa, psychologically abused by a man who has taken her from her family and is keeping her isolated and dependent, timidly rebels by releasing a cow, who tosses her head wildly and shits "contentedly over the new snow," making a "crazy shape" that defiles the fresh fall.[82] In *August Is a Wicked Month*, Ellen, another isolated woman far from home, witnesses a road accident and finds herself "vanish[ing] back into child-hood and the dark springs of her terrors. [She] saw bogholes into which animals stupidly plunged, and a mountain lake where two mad women drowned them-selves."[83] In O'Brien's 2012 memoir, she recalls the monthly cattle mart in Dublin, where the cattle "were hectored out of the back of lorries, roaring and bawling, an almost human plaint to their cries, chafing against their new confines, some refusing to be herded, running loose, as the drovers, with their ash plants and their bludgeons, walloped them on their heads and on their shins. . . . All of it brought back the reek and constraints of home."[84] Solidarity with the animal can comfort and reassure even as it reaffirms the near inevitability of entrapment and abjection.

As in the opening of *Down by the River*, the decomposition of a donkey in *A Pagan Place* marks a significant space of death and decay, sources of power in O'Brien, as will be discussed in chapter 6. Many titles of O'Brien's novels suggest human relation to a natural setting, including words such as "river," "tide," or "forest." Like *In the Forest*, *A Pagan Place* is named for a recalcitrant, uninviting natural site no more than incidentally linked to the human, a "fort of dark trees" that "was a pagan place and circular."[85] The place is primeval, unchanged since time immemorial, according to the child narrator, whose own historical aware-ness only goes back one generation: "Druids had their rites there long before your mother and father or anyone you'd ever heard tell of." Not only does the remarkable smell of animal rot render the scene antiromantic, but the small wood also discourages human lingering: "The ground inside was shifty, a swamp."[86] As Nuala O'Faolain observes of the novel's landscape, "nothing is warm or easy or picturesque."[87] The small wood is also memorable for the fabled sighting of an unrestrained, improperly dressed woman, "a lady ungirdled,"[88] one of a number of mysterious women associated with nature of whom the child narrator hears tales, like "the woman who did cures," rumored to be a witch: "She picked plants and stones and when foraging she cackled to herself."[89] A widow, she is no longer constrained by reproductive imperatives and can act with less regard to social norms and expectations of propriety. The novel, named for a natural site that is too small, dark, and uncomfortable to be of exploitative or scenic interest, is a text preoccupied with the ways in which women's lives are kept small, contained, and hidden. The fort of trees offers retreat and comfort, but only temporarily. The narrator's relationship to her childhood haven changes as she becomes aware of her own position as trapped in her role as a resource for ideological and sexual reproduction. Her fate is narrowly determined, grounded in cultural constructions of her "natural" function.

In the early part of the text, the narrator inhabits her own younger, uninformed perspective, describing, in particular, the travails of her older sister, Emma, glamorous and initially resented, who becomes pregnant. Emma defies attempts to force her to marry and refuses to feel any shame or regret for her actions, including giving up the child for adoption and getting on with her life. The narrator also recalls her own sexual abuse by a priest and being physically beaten by her father, who blames the girl for the assault. The narrator prepares to enter a Belgian convent to become a nun at the end of the novel, the only alternative her world offers to the servitude and drudgery of marriage and motherhood. The use of second person throughout makes for a disorienting reading experience and has the paradoxical effect of distancing the narrator from various traumas beginning in young childhood while conveying the suffocating inescapability of the effects of those traumas. The memories being recounted are neither entirely subjective nor objective; they register as partly impersonal and externalized yet unshakable, as if stalking the narrator from multiple directions. Do these memories belong to more than the narrator, and what does a potentially distributive shaping of recollected events, suggested by the use of second person, which can be both singular and plural, mean for justice and responsibility?[90] The "naturalness" of narrative voice is belied by awkward textual self-consciousness, as relationships between writing and remembering, between individual and community, become tenuous and ambiguous. Renate Lachmann, on the memorializing function of literature, refers to art's transformation "of mourning into a technique. The finding of images heals what has been destroyed, ... restores shapes to the mutilated victims and makes them recognizable by establishing their place in life."[91] A Pagan Place's narrative, on the contrary, wields its literary techniques, including tropes of remembering, in order to deny the possibility of wholeness, to challenge models of subjectivity and even consciousness as solitary and singular, bounded and separate from the environment.

The text's use of second person structurally embeds this plurality, an example of one of Gretchen Legler's "emancipatory strategies" for women writers who aspire to "reimagine nature and human relationships with the natural world." Legler endorses the "erasing or blurring of boundaries between inner (emotional, psychological, personal) and outer (geographic) landscapes, or the erasing or blurring of self-other (human/nonhuman, I/Thou) distinctions."[92] The novel's narrator regularly disrespects such boundaries, grants the nonhuman world properties usually associated solely with the human. Early in the novel, she consults dandelions to know the time in a child's game of clock.[93] This language of seeking advice from the natural world recurs late in the novel after the narrator has been savagely beaten by her father and is raging against captivity, becoming more "like Emma, with a secret sewn into you."[94] Increasingly disillusioned with both present life with her family and the future she has been trained to anticipate, she "no longer skipped to see if [she] would marry a man called John" and instead "consulted frogs as to what you should do, asked frogs their opinion. Frogs had learnt the knack of being stealthy. Frogs had very good camouflage."[95] The narrator's relationship with the nonhuman has begun to change at this point in the text, as she realizes the extent of patriarchal power's reach and its appetite for domination, but just as every woman in the novel nurtures a secret, so does the natural world retain secret strategies to evade the depredations of men, secrets it might be willing to share with a fellow sufferer.

The narrator asks of dandelions and frogs questions she can ask no one else. All knowledge must be gained obliquely, stealthily. According to O'Faolain, the novel's "plot proceeds by association, as in remembering: and the language is faultlessly faux-naif—a recreation of the idioms of a child's thinking, or quoting of the phrases which strike at her from the adult world. The desired effect is one of tranced recall."[96] The disembodied trance-like narration offers another example of disparity between form and content that threatens to rupture the smooth surface of ideological reproduction, as the narration dreamily recounts brutalities committed in order to maintain the authority of family and church, to quell rebellious acts and deny inconsistencies and hypocrisies. The associative rhythm does not conform to traditional plot structure but does collect appalling incidents and exchanges, accumulates details of blighted lives, including those glimpsed in the margins, like an unnamed mad woman; a shamed girl in the parish engaged to a man with a family in England; the family's neighbor Hilda, who hysterically performs an idealized femininity; Lizzie, who comes home from Australia with "yellow jaundice" and whose attempts to conform to beauty standards fall short; and the school teacher Miss Davitt, who, on the way to being committed to a mental institution, escapes from the car and drowns herself, to the narrator's bemusement. A visiting guard (policeman) who relays the gossip of the suicide, tells the narrator's parents, "she was always a screw loose."[97] The guard's dismissive aside is, with some difficulty, associatively made sense of by the narrator. She is an inveterate eavesdropper, who, for all of her careful attention and detailed recording, must piece together information, as propriety dictates she be kept ignorant and not ask direct questions. There is the suggestion, however, of effective modes of understanding and communication other than the verbal. Though her mother repeatedly will tell her to shush "and put her fingers to her lips though there was no one listening,"[98] the narrator claims to know much without being told, like the story of her own birth, including the "bad job" the midwife did in stitching up her mother, as well as the crude birth-control methods her mother employs when obeying her husband's sexual demands: "Before she went across to the landing she put tissue paper in the inside of her pussy. It made a crinkly noise. Even without a candle you knew what she was doing."[99]

As in this midnight-dark scene, throughout the text, images of obscurity and illumination contrast the stifling indoor world with the freedom of the outdoors. The narrator says of a neighbor's blinds, "They made stripes along the floor, stripes of light and stripes of shadow. You didn't like them because you couldn't see out properly, the world outside got divided up into segments, the sky got reduced."[100] She revels in that expansive world outside while still a child, before the struggle begins between her parents and Emma for control over Emma's body and independence and before the narrator is sexually assaulted: "The cropped grass was like a carpet. The high stalks danced and waved. You danced with them. You touched them. That was your way of saying hello. Yellow flowers predominated. Yellow flowers were your favourite, the warm bells and the warm disks." The fort of trees, separate from the world of interdiction, is full of magic in these young unmarked years: "When you passed your throne you sat because that was good luck. Every time you passed it you had to sit. Sometimes to avoid it you made a detour. It was a tree stump, a seat of happiness with briars round it. You had a place trampled down for your feet. Elsewhere the briars flourished, were its garland. Birds called to each other in the grass. Some were melodious, some were not. There was whirring, that was grasshoppers."[101] This "seat of happiness" is protected by a barrier of thorny briars, like the growth that springs up around the castle in the tale of Sleeping Beauty, keeping intending suitors at bay. The pagan place fails to protect, however, when a visiting cousin, a stranger to the narrator, menacingly demands that she come to his room:

"You ran out the front door and down the fields and through the fort and through the lily swamp to the open callows. . . . You kept running away, away from the house where he was packing to leave. The night went under the trees. Under the trees began to be vast dimensionless places—trees frightening. . . . You shouted help. . . . There was no response save the rushing of water and the bats and in the distance dogs and other carnivorous things."[102] Once again, the natural world falls silent, rendered as helpless as the sexually threatened girl, a silent echo of the narrator's fear for her sister, Emma, at the hands of her family and the community when earlier in the novel they meet to decide her fate: "The world was empty. The world was deserted. You didn't hear a dog or you didn't hear a bell, you heard nothing only your heart hammering."[103]

Unlike the narrator, Emma's preservation instincts drive her to disassociate from the farm and its landscape. She insistently identifies with New York, where she was born, but does not actually remember. When the novel begins, Emma is home from her secretarial job in the city. She walks into town several times a day to show off her clothes and is chided by a neighbor for paying too much attention to her nails during mass. She affects an accent and comments on the "balmy" country air as though she is a tourist. She calls her family home "This Dump!" and expresses a desire to get back to her friends in the city. The only appreciation of the "natural" she expresses is in reference to her preferred bath oil: "She described how it made a veneer on the surface of the water and how it had the perfume of the woods. The woods Emma conjured up were not like the ones beyond the window where the old trees reigned and the badgers roamed and the dogs convened at night. Emma's woods were bright and blossomy as in an operetta."[104] The manufactured stagecraft woods of Emma's city-fired imagination reflect her own brittle performance of sophisticated womanliness throughout the novel, a performance that includes frequent costume changes for what she hopes is the overawed audience of hometown yokels whom she might distract from the fact of her increasingly apparent pregnancy. Though she manages to defy her parents' desire that she reform her godless ways and stop behaving like a "harlot" with various admirers, she nevertheless continues to pursue the admiration and approval of men.

The narrator's final maturation and move away from the family home follows a different trajectory that does not require she entirely renounce her pagan place. Just before she announces her religious vocation, having received a letter from Emma telling her that "there was no scope" for her in the city,[105] the narrator makes a final visit to the fort of trees that allows her to unite with the variety of sensations there: "There was an overall smell but you could separate them out the way a prism separates light. There was a smell of bark, of green branches, of nettles, of dung, of fresh earth, of fungi and the elder flower that grew profusely. . . . There was a smell under your arms. She enjoys a deep connection as boundaries dissolve, including between consciousness and unconsciousness: "The flutter of the leaves brought on your trance. Hundreds of thousands of sycamore leaves all obeying the same wind, their wide green palms opening, tightening, letting in and keeping out the light changing the prospect from indoor to outdoor to indoor, forever altering. It was the most lonesome hour just before dusk with all the colours going, all the streamers, pinks and reds, and violets and indigoes and blues, the lovely laneways of vanquishing light."[106] In this synesthetic trance, all barriers between human and tree, inside and outside, smell and sight dissolve.

There are colors in the landscape that seem to be visible only to women in O'Brien's novels, a spectrum only they can register. For example, according to the narrator in *The House of Splendid Isolation*, the colors we think we see are deceiving: "blue would seem to be the nature of the place though the grass is green, different greens."[107] In *Johnny I Hardly Knew You*, Nora buys her young lover a shirt because "it had the colour and texture that one thinks of the earth as having, the real earth, that is, that lies hidden under the earth we tread on."[108] Women in most of O'Brien's novels carry an enriched, interior vision of fields and trees and animals that evoke contrasting memories and feelings. In *Mother Ireland*, the novelist frames her return to County Clare as a longed-for reunion, more potent than the painful scenes endured with her disapproving parents: "The world outside and the rolling countryside seemed to emanate a beauty and the very hills seems to breathe. All the deprivation had been worth it for this release, this return to the natural world. . . . The further away I went from the past, the more clearly I returned inwardly picturing meadows, grasses, some animals caught under briars, cuckoo spit, etc."[109] In a piece for an Irish newspaper in 1990, O'Brien claims that "more than anything in nature trees carry a sense of continuity" and makes a direct connection between her own rootedness in the trees of her youth and the pencil with which she is writing.[110] As Seamus Heaney remarked on the occasion of O'Brien's receipt of the Bob Hughes Lifetime Achievement Award in 2009, "she has a strong sense of the idiom of Ireland."[111] That idiom is the untamed and recalcitrant idiom of the natural world of County Clare, its trees and winds and animals, all of which, however, can appear to act in league with the forces that would control nature and all those associated with its suspicious, fathomless forces. Heaney could confidently assert his intention to write with as much masculine force of ownership as his father could wield a spade, when he concludes his poem "Digging" with the stanza, "Between my finger and my thumb / The squat pen rests. / I'll dig with it."[112] The narrator of *A Pagan Place*, in contrast, enjoys a much less secure and dominating relationship to her writing tool and the ambivalent power of creation: "The pencil was so sharp it ate a hole in the page."[113] O'Brien's sense of shared powers of creation with the nonhuman retains a humble, respectful awareness of and receptivity to the powers beyond the human and the mystery of our place in the world.

4 · OTHERWORLDLY POSSESSIONS

I am told that I conversed with trees, stones, and mounds.

Edna O'Brien told David Haycock that her ambition in writing *A Pagan Place* (1970) was to produce "an extremely non-literary book." "Non-literary" in this context means that the narrative is not structured according to normative expectations for the literary novel, as discussed in chapter 3, but is indebted instead to the kind of "organic" storytelling the novelist experienced in childhood: "I was brought up very much on mythology and on folktales and on verse."[1] Decades later, in a piece written for the *Irish Independent* in 1990, O'Brien again refers to mythology when revealing a connection between her younger self and the narrator of *A Pagan Place*: "I grew up surrounded by trees (among other things) and trees are important to me. My mythology instilled in me the notion that they were sacred. In Ireland, around our house, we had huge, primeval groaning trees. There was a fort of oak trees that I believed were Druidic."[2] The narrator of *A Pagan Place* behaves like a Druid, reading the natural world for signs and portents, a turning to alternative sources of understanding, and away from the dominant, orthodox modes of inquiry and communication that order and contain her sister's life and her own. O'Brien's protagonists often read portents in the material world as well as in their dreams. Echoing O'Brien's ambitions to exceed the expectation of the "literary" book, Elke D'Hoker challenges conventional readings of O'Brien as a realist or naturalist writer, claiming that the purported realism of her narrative is "a thin veneer covering an underlying symbolic structure, which dramatizes recurrent psychic patterns and processes," processes that D'Hoker sees as "indebted to Freudian theories of the unconscious as well as to the archetypal psychic patterns that are contained in the myths and fairytales."[3]

Other twenty-first-century critics have also reassessed what Jane Elizabeth Dougherty describes as the "ambiguous relationship between text and reality" in O'Brien's fiction.[4] Mary Gordon's 1990 assertion that O'Brien "extended our ideas of womanhood . . . from the inevitability of the body to the openness of dreams" is an early acknowledgment of the novelist's nonrealist aesthetic.[5] Dream logic is as reliable and insightful as any other source of understanding or knowledge in the fiction. Dreams are not the exclusive domain of women, but access to otherworldly visions and powers associated with dreams is valued and even trusted by women, like Biddy Early, often referenced by O'Brien, a nineteenth-century healer—from Clare, O'Brien's home county—officially accused of witchcraft and even brought to court where no one dared testify against her. Legendary women like Early inspire marginal figures in O'Brien's work, like the witchy widow in *A Pagan Place* "who did cures."[6] These shamanic figures demonstrate, in the words of Mary Douglas, the "special powers of healing that come to those who can abandon rational control for a time."[7] In "Shovel Kings" (2011), the laborer Rafferty, stranded in London at the end of his working life, longing to be back in Ireland, remembers the women of his youth, his mother and first love, both associated in his memory with a particular shade of blue, which is also the color of the famous "bottle" that granted Biddy Early a witchy second sight, power connected to the natural world, as discussed in chapter 3.[8] O'Brien transvalues the reading of such characters as mad, aware of not only the shamanic figure's history across several cultures but also the tradition of "mythic insanity" in Irish writing.[9] Patsy in *Casualties of Peace*, Nell in *Time and Tide*, Mary in *Night*, Nora in *Johnny I Hardly Knew You*, Josie in *House of Splendid Isolation*, Breege in *Wild Decembers*, and Maryam in *Girl*, as well as numerous women across the short stories, are troubled by dreams, warned and counseled by nighttime visions. The fact that Curly, in "Inner Cowboy" (2011), has a similarly emotional, reactive relationship with his dreams is one among many qualities pointing to his failure to achieve normative masculinity.

Michen O'Kane of *In the Forest* (2002), who occupies the realm of dreams and visions to a disabling, dangerous extent, is more systematically and tragically brutalized into conforming to heterosexist norms of manliness than Curly is, as noted in chapter 3. In the opening pages, the novel's imagery, themes, and dark outcome—O'Kane, a victim of years of physical and sexual abuse, murders three people—are foreshadowed in a dream by Ellen, another insightful widow: "[She] did not join in the search when the men and women set out with their dogs and their sticks, clinging to the last vestiges of hope. Yet she dreams of it, dreams she is in Cloosh Wood, running back and forth, calling to those search parties whom she cannot reach, the tall trees no longer static but moving like giants, giants on their grotesque and shaggy roots, their green needly paws reaching out to scratch her, engulf her, and she wakens in a sweat, unable to scream the scream that has been growing in her."[10] As noted, trees are mythic presences for O'Brien and in many spiritual traditions. In *Girl* (2019), Maryam, though nominally Christian, believes in the local deity, the "Tree Spirit." In a prize-winning essay for school, she writes, "Ancestors who have died live there and govern lives. They ward off evil. If those sacred trees are harmed or lopped or burnt, ancestors get very angry and sometimes take revenge."[11] Clair Wills has argued that the generation of Irish women who feature centrally in most of O'Brien's fiction are situated at a "juncture between the values of enlightenment and tradition" and that it is not, therefore, possible in such a context "to dissolve the realm of fantasy and myth." The feminist critic needs "to be wary of the argument that the truth of individual women's experience can undercut the myths and mystifications which have surrounded her image in Irish culture."[12]

O'Brien has written directly about Irish folklore and mythology in the nonfiction texts *Mother Ireland* (1976), *Some Irish Loving: A Selection* (1979), and *Tales for the Telling: Irish Folk and Fairy Tales* (1986), but her fiction is also saturated with references and allusions to this body of knowledge. Alicia Ostriker, in her discussion of women's revisionist mythmaking, emphasizes the way in which in women's versions of myths, the "earth means creative imagination instead of passive generativeness,"[13] a distinguishing characteristic of O'Brien's handling of the natural world, as outlined in chapter 3, and also of her approach to the supernatural, the focus of this chapter. O'Brien is sensitive to the abiding stereotypes of the Irish that include seeing them as childishly inarticulate, a childishness that explains, for example, their credulous devotion to fairy and folklore.[14] However, as Angela Bourke has demonstrated, fairy and folklore in Ireland historically have been put to sophisticated social uses. O'Brien's narratives often include characters who intuit and exploit the thinness of the membrane that separates categories of the natural and supernatural in Irish cultural tradition, though just as often her characters are so inhibited by regimes of discipline and surveillance as to be either blind to the possibilities of flexible and open modes of subjectivity or incapacitated by insecurity and anxiety when confronted with the idea of such alternatives. In discussing the appearance of fairy and folk tales in contemporary feminist fiction and poetry, Bourke has observed that such narratives, in both their traditional and adapted forms, "carry the potential to express profound truths and intense emotions" and "are particularly well-suited to the expression of ambivalence and ambiguity."[15] In O'Brien's fiction, mythology, fairy tales, and folklore offer powerful alternative systems for organizing knowledge while simultaneously testifying to the ingrained nature of binarized thinking and hierarchical, taxonomic impulses.

For example, Queen Maeve, an ancient Irish warrior, according to legend, both feared and honored by her subjects and enemies, is a figure frequently recruited by Irish feminists, beginning in the nineteenth century, including writers and artists such as Alice Milligan, Eva Gore-Booth, and Constance Markievicz. Early Irish feminists resisted the deployment of Irish legend for exclusively masculinist ends, especially violent ones, such as when, in *Down by the River*, Mary's father, while on a fishing trip with his daughter, a pretext for getting her to an isolated place in order to rape her, evokes "Finn Mac Caomhill," the mythological warrior, "who ate the salmon of knowledge."[16] In *Mother Ireland*, O'Brien recalls the way in which Queen Maeve's power, her strategic dominance, cunning, and strength, were not presented as inspiring qualities for young women but sources of shame, having caused her "tribe" to follow "the rump of a misguiding woman."[17] Identification with the women of Irish myth is not necessarily complimentary for O'Brien's characters. In *Time and Tide*, Nell is described as "Cathleen ni Houlihan or Deirdre of the Sorrows,"[18] avatars of mythic Irish womanliness that should suggest dignity if not strength but that are used jokingly to denigrate Nell, recalling Peggy O'Brien's infamous condemnation of Edna O'Brien, accusing the novelist of repeatedly transforming "the searing story of Deirdre into a maudlin melodramatic tale of woman's woe." Peggy O'Brien claims to find no indication of an "authorial awareness of how her penny-romance summary robs a great tragedy of passion."[19] On the contrary, however, the novelist is demonstrably aware of legendary Irish queens, referenced in many of her texts, including the novels *Time and Tide, Night* (1972), *The High Road* (1988), *House of Splendid Isolation* (1994), and *Wild Decembers* (1999), as well as in numerous short stories. The self-conscious irony of O'Brien's juxtaposition of these fabled queens with contemporary characters deliberately underscores the humiliating narratives of damage, including physical abuse, endured by women under patriarchy, "tragedies of passion" experienced at an intimate level of no apparent significance to Peggy O'Brien.

In *Some Irish Loving* (1979), a selection of Irish texts ranging from mythological cycle legends to contemporary work, in the introduction to "The Female" section, O'Brien only half humorously remarks, "considering their background I am surprised that all Irish women are not lying down on railway tracks uttering and wailing ejaculations for the coming train."[20] That background includes the early myths of "devouring women," which she realizes are "not peculiar to the Irish race, although those early queens Deirdre, Gráinne and Maeve merrily wrought treason, crime, havoc and disaster in the wake of their wilful lovings.... Woman as temple and sewer is true for all male thinking and her roles as sorceress, sow, enchantress, and she-devil is well and fulsomely propagated."[21] Rebecca Pelan observes that when not chaotic and threatening, "the prevailing female image, associated with the sacrificial myth, has been that of the less powerful and significantly more passive mother figure whose role is that of a breeder of sons for sacrifice in the name of Ireland or, alternatively, as supporters and nurturers of men who are fighting for Irish freedom."[22] The equivocal charge of being aligned with the supernatural and/or mythic is implicit when the reviewer Thomas Cahill, after arguing that O'Brien's prose "has the sound of something prehistoric" (as reported in chapter 3), links her primitive style to writing "with the sureness and conviction of a priestess or a prophetess, one of a long succession of prophetic Irish women."[23] Cahill casts O'Brien in the role of savage avatar emerging from the mists of prehistory, speaking as a medium for the gods, an inspired oracle, rather than an originator. Ailbhe Smyth has observed that in

Ireland, "women's experiences, visions, voices are fated to be submerged by the relentless flow of patriarchal myth and history, of politics and economics.... To tell our stories, we must write over the images and myths that overshadow us."[24] O'Brien makes a similar argument in a 1983 interview in *The Guardian*: "Women have been distanced from power by history, male collusion, and their own divided selves. Goddesses abound in myth but they are subsidiary to the ultimate decree of the gods. Power is not only grasped and sustained by men it is also something women—albeit unconsciously—are ambivalent about. We have not been breast fed on the idea that we are entitled to it. We have in our lexicon the words witch succubi nightmare—all female totems, but totems whose sovereignty is not political, merely carnal and intuitive." In the case of the mythic woman, her animal lusts and instincts are emphasized rather than her status as respected ruler or feared warrior. O'Brien concludes that the "biggest fallacy is that opposite to power is powerlessness—often the chimera of greatness."[25]

The destructive effects of dichotomizing structures of power and powerlessness, from family to church to state to culture, are evident in one of O'Brien's most controversial novels, *In the Forest* (2002). The novel was met in Ireland with something close to the outraged response incited by *The Country Girls* (1960) decades earlier. *In the Forest* was based on the murder of a young woman, Imelda Riney; her son, Liam; and a priest, Father Joe Walshe, in East Clare in 1994, and it was claimed that the victims' families had asked that O'Brien not write the novel.[26] On its publication, the author was excoriated in the press, expected to account for her (unwomanly) heartlessness as well as for her sympathetic portrayal of the fictional killer, inspired by the troubled Brendan O'Donnell, as a victim of abuse.[27] In an interview about the book with *The Observer*, O'Brien was asked whether she suffered any doubts or regrets, to which she replied in the negative. Of the novel itself, she said, "Ostensibly it's about a triple murder in a forest, but I believe that the novelist is the psychic and moral historian of his or her society. So it's about that part of Ireland I happen to know very well. It's about that part of Ireland, and the darkness that prevails."[28] The darkness in which the text's most violent events take place is the shadowed depths of fictional Cloosh Wood, based on Cregg Wood, where the real-life murders occurred. The violent climax of the narrative is a particularly dramatic manifestation of a long story of darkness, of abuse—psychic, social, physical, and ecological—of individual and collective grief, both inflicted and inherited, and of personal and historical madness.

Beginning with the title, which evokes a space of lurking dangers, the novel, more than any other in O'Brien's oeuvre, draws on fairy-tale and mythological imagery. A historical figure of mythic significance in Irish lore, who figures implicitly in *In the Forest*, is King Sweeney. His legend, "The Frenzy of Mad Sweeney," or *Buile Suibhne Geilt*, is based on a Northern Irish chieftain of the seventh century, whose "frenzy," or madness, drives him into the woods. The Sweeney legend is generally understood to be an instance of the ancient Celtic "Wild Man of the Woods."[29] The figure is explicitly evoked in O'Brien's *House of Splendid Isolation* when the fugitive IRA gunman hiding in the trees is compared to "Mad Sweeney in the poem,"[30] who believed he was a bird and attempted to live like one in the forest. The emotionally and mentally disturbed young killer Michen O'Kane of *In the Forest* regularly makes similar retreats to the trees. Writing about the Celtic tradition of the Wild Man, Neil Thomas tracks the influence of Christianity on the various legends. Mad Sweeney, in particular, is transformed from a soldier driven mad by the carnage of war who finds refuge in the "saner" realm of the natural world to a sinner who is cursed by a holy man, Ronan, because Sweeney has assaulted the saint and murdered one of his clerics. The later version of the legend concludes with Sweeney's repentance and redemption. Thomas's analysis makes frequent reference to the Christian doctrine of "contemptus mundi," which he translates as contempt for the world and worldly concerns. A modern iteration of such an attitude, ostensibly secular but grounded in Judeo-Christian tradition, has been identified by ecocritics as "ecophobia," which Simon Estok describes as "an irrational and groundless hatred of the natural world . . . present and subtle in our daily lives."[31] The frenzy of the psychotic O'Kane, who identifies with the natural world from a young age, an association that subjects him to abuse from his peers, is a tragedy that arises from the universally contemptuous treatment of a friendless, motherless child. Such contempt is mirrored in the community's dread of and hatred for the natural world. Both the dwindling woodland on the edge of the town and O'Kane stand as reproaches to a society that is increasingly tempted by the appeals of "progress," consumerism, and anonymity.

The novel opens with a description of a threatening woodland:

> A drowsy corpus of green, broken only where the odd pine has struck up on its own, spindly, freakish, the stray twigs on either side branched, cruciform-wise. In the interior the trapped wind gives off the rustle of a distant sea and the tall slender trunks of the spruces are so close together that the barks are a sable-brown, the light becoming darker and darker into the chamber of non-light. At the farthest entrance under the sweep of the brooding mountain there is a wooden hut choked with briars and brambles where a dead goat decomposed and stank during those frightened, suspended, and sorrowing days. It was then the wood lost its old name and its old innocence in the hearts of the people.[32]

O'Kane's triple murder administers a coup de grâce to the community's already tenuous relationship to the wood, described by novel's end as "marked by its violation."[33] The economic boom was at its height in 2002, and the novel's village, boasting new housing estates and footpaths extending into reclaimed "waste-land," as well as a modest share of "new Irish" (nonnative) inhabitants, has abandoned the wood, now associated with the past, with individual childhoods, as well as with a lost time once communally shared, a kind of reservoir of innocence left behind. At once mourned and feared, it also signifies a deeper past of savagery. The villagers are described by Shirley Peterson as entering "an increasingly globalized new century . . . drag[ging] with them a long traumatic history."[34] This largely ignored woodland, used most frequently as a rubbish dump or as a place for illicit, usually teenage, activities, shares qualities with what Paul Farley and Michael Symons Roberts refer to as "edgelands," the disregarded, untamed fringes of urban and suburban developments. These edgelands become "a place of forgetting," function as a "zone of inattention."[35] Cloosh Wood harbors the willfully forgotten and disavowed even as it retains an aura of enchantment, of a lost connection to the land and its legends, a tension embodied to catastrophic effect in the returned former villager, O'Kane, "true son of the forest," deranged rapist and killer.

As noted, a terrifying dream establishes the novel's terrain from the outset. Dreams and fairy tales are everywhere in the text, but it is the dark side of the fairy tale that dominates this novel of poisoned childhood and desecrated nature. Enchantment, lore, and fairy tales are *solitary* nightmares, not sources of social cohesion for a local populace in an increasingly anonymous, suburbanizing village that is no longer connected to a traditional sense of place. Fairy-tale and fairy-lore imagery and references range from James Stephen's *The Crock of Gold* to Brian Merriman's *Midnight Court* to Goldilocks and the Three Bears, Snow White, and Sleeping Beauty. A German immigrant to the village gives O'Kane a nickname, the evocative "Kinderschreck," meaning "child-frightener" or bogeyman, recalling the gruesome and gory fairy tales of nineteenth-century German literature, like those of the Grimm Brothers or Heinrich Hoffmann's *Der Struwwelpeter* (sometimes translated as "Shock-Headed Peter"), cautionary tales that mete out excessively violent punishments to children, including dismemberment and death, for crimes as trivial as thumb-sucking. O'Kane's childhood was spent enduring excessively violent punishment, initially for no ostensible crime, other than being poor and motherless. However, by the age of ten, already toughened by years in state care, he is described as having begun "his hoodlum times."[36] A local yet also an outsider from a young age, he is repeatedly identified in the text as a "country boy," a denomination that implicitly renders him simple-minded if not suspiciously reactionary, as well as insufficiently civilized.

As a very young child, O'Kane regularly fled the family home in terror, hiding in the wood whenever he witnessed his father beating his mother, traumatic events that left her with horrific injuries. After his mother's death, he again retreated to the woods, hoping to live a wild and independent existence. He decided that "he would give himself a secret name, Caoilte, the name of the forest," in memory of his mother, who, in an attempt to turn his terrified flight from violence into a heroic adventure, called him "a true son of the forest."[37] Caoilte evokes a legendary, glorious warrior past, recorded in the mythological Fenian Cycle. Nephew of Fionn Mac Cumhaill, Caoilte was known for his swiftness and was one of the Fianna, representatives in post-Independence Ireland of the ideal of Irish masculinity. O'Kane's fanciful plan does not succeed, and instead, he is shuttled through a series of Irish religious institutions and suffers relentless physical and sexual abuse, meted out by other boys as well as priests. Once he is too old for industrial school, he leaves for England and, after a series of petty crimes, spends time in prison, where he is subjected to further brutal institution-alization. He returns to the rural village of his childhood, where no one will claim him and yet where he is allowed to terrorize its inhabitants. Nothing is done about the fact that he briefly abducts a young girl in her own car, commits various acts of vandalism, including burning a car, and several robberies, most alarmingly, the theft of a gun. The local residents practice a kind of willful blind-ness to him, neither drawing him in nor driving him away. They leave food out for him as if, as he says himself, he were a dog but never invite him into their homes. They can neither reject nor accept him; to do either would require they accept their share of responsibility for the man he has become. In a passage that echoes the rising up of the neglected wood in the vengeful nightmare of the text's opening chapter, a character says of O'Kane late in the novel, "deep down we believe he has been sent by god as a punishment upon us."[38] He retreats once more to the woods and attempts to reinhabit an abandoned cottage he had once used as a refuge, but the cottage is now being lived in by the bohemian "blow in" Eily Ryan and her four-year-old son, Maddie, doomed to be O'Kane's first mur-der victims.

Eily is unaware not only of O'Kane's imagined prior claims to the house but also of the scandal her unconventional appearance and behavior are causing among established members of the local community, who will, as a result, be slow to raise the alarm when she is seen in O'Kane's company and then goes missing. Eily's "deviancies" include being an unmarried mother, carrying on an affair with a much-younger man, posing nude for a painter, drinking on her own in the pub, and holding theatrical, mock-pagan rituals deep into the night. Unconventional and independent, Eily is also naïve and impractical, unprepared for the idealized life in the woods she is attempting to lead. Her domesticating attempt at creating a wood path of chips, for example, wastes money and effort, as the muddy forest floor swallows the chips almost immediately. She claims she can feel the "harmony" of the woods, though just as this observation is made, a pack of hounds burst from the woods, "chasing their leader, who had a hunk of raw dripping meat hanging from his mouth,"[39] belying any notion of peaceful coexistence. Eily dabbles in Buddhism and entertains a quasi-mystical trust in blessings and luck, as evinced in her description of her new home: "Apple Tree

House was waiting for me, or so Billy [the auctioneer] said. He had it on his books for nearly a year, but kept it for someone special, and that someone turned out to be me. He had to bring a slash hook to fight his way through the briars and the brambles across the field, the house itself and the chimneys smothered in ivy and different trees. He put a crowbar to the door and pushed it in, and as it heaved and creaked back, a startled bird flew out at us, a blackbird."[40] Not only does the image of a bird make oblique reference to the "Mad Sweeney" character O'Kane, who will fly at Eily and her son with murderous intent later in the novel, but the blackbird is also significant in Irish and world folklore; it can bring good fortune but can also be seen as a bad omen.[41] Birds act as equivocal portents in several O'Brien texts, including *Night*, *Johnny I Hardly Knew You*, *Wild Decembers*, and *House of Splendid Isolation*. The devil takes the form of a blackbird in the story of Saint Benedict, who jumped into a thorn bush to counter the lustful thoughts that the blackbird/demon put into his head. The ambivalently totemic creature, possibly associated with "unorthodox" sexual desires, emerges from a house that Eily has invested with romance, perhaps unconsciously evoking in her description of it the traditional presentation of Sleeping Beauty's palace as surrounded by a near-impenetrable wilderness of brambles and thorns. Sleeping Beauty is the fairy tale most often evoked in the novel, hinted at from the opening paragraph's reference to "a wooden hut choked with briars and brambles," an image of the natural world reclaiming space, impeding the too-easy realization of the "happily ever after" conclusion of conventional heterosexual romance.

Amanda Greenwood uses the phrase "negative romance" to describe the "Brothers Grimm" side of the marital fairy tale experienced by women in O'Brien's fiction, the reality of what follows "happily ever after."[42] But all fairy tales, as Susan Brownmiller has observed, "are full of a vague dread, a catastrophe that only seems to befall little girls."[43] Many bleak ironies attend the appearance in the novel of references to tales happily resolved with the reanimation of a beautiful woman suspended between death and life. In another moment blending dreams and fairy tales, the man who discovers the bodies says, "It was like I dreamed it. It was like I'll dream it all my life."[44] He claims unique knowledge of the woods, some kind of extra sense that leads him to the "lifelike" corpse of Eily first: "The wood was fairly dark and I had to crawl along under the low branches and under the trees that had fallen athwart. Strands of dead moss dipped from their branches. I sensed something in the Instant before I saw it. . . . I knew she was dead, the smell alone told me that. She looked so remarkably lifelike that a person might be forgiven for thinking she could be brought back to life with a touch."[45] The Sleeping Beauty motif is explicitly invoked by O'Kane's grandmother, whom he visits after he has committed the murders but before anyone knows about the crime. He is bragging to her about a girlfriend. She asks to meet this girlfriend, but O'Kane says she sleeps all day. The grandmother responds,

"Oh, a Sleeping Beauty," and this prompts a memory that also evokes Snow White, another woman awaiting reanimation. The grandmother "recount[s] that day in the morgue when his poor mother died and it was snowing outside and him sliding down the bannister and out into the grounds to bring back a snow-ball to run over his mother's face, to give her the kiss of life."[46] The young O'Kane indulges in magical thinking, often the response to grief, believing he can revive his mother with a kiss like Prince Charming. As a child, he had also feared his grandmother would die next because he dreamt that she will. He had dreamt often of his mother's death before the event and worries afterward that he has the power to kill with his thoughts. Deprived of the means to develop beyond the trauma of his loss, he makes real this dreaded power.

The connection between the death of O'Kane's mother and Snow White is established early in the narrative:

> They said she was dead, but she wasn't; they buried her alive, suffocated her. They brought him up flights of stone stairs and into a cold room to show her lying on a slab with no colour in her cheeks and no breath. It was snowing outside. It was the snow that made her white and made the world white. She was not dead. . . . They put her in a coffin and buried her. He stole out at night and went and talked to her, and she talked back. . . . He scraped the earth back and made a hole where he could talk to his mother and where she could hear. She promised to come back and save him when she was less tired.[47]

In her classic diatribe against, inter alia, patriarchal mythmaking, Mary Daly argues that the Snow White tale is itself a "poisonous apple," "vain and illusory," which not only nurtures "woman hating" but also, by extension, is "fatal for the future of this planet."[48] O'Kane will come to see Eily as alternately a fairy prin-cess and a witch. As Jack Zipes observes of modern European fairy tales, they have "caused nothing but trouble for the female object of male desire and have also reflected the crippling aspect of male desire itself."[49] O'Kane pushes his community's sexist dismissal and disapproval of Eily to its limits when he describes her as having "stepped out of her own world into his, into his trans-mogrified dream of her, all-mothering, all-sinning, she-devil."[50]

O'Kane lives and has lived in a fantasy "transmogrified dream" world from a young age. He hears voices, has visions—not all of them violent or even malevolent—but so do other putatively "sane" characters in the novel. O'Kane's psychosis is not just a product of the conditions and abuses he endured in his home village growing up, as well as elsewhere, but a reflection of a larger social sickness, characterized by isolation and disaffection. As O'Brien says in the *Observer* interview, "Tragedy makes people mad, whether it's Ireland or the West Bank."[51] Tragedy and madness are not confined to the individual or even the community; they emerge from a much-broader context. Nor is it only the subject who is marginalized by sex or class that is compromised and even threatened under the ideological conditions consistently described by O'Brien but the larger matrix of which we are part. Jane Bennett has described our "fantasies of a human uniqueness" as enabling "earth-destroying fantasies of conquest and consumption."[52] In an earlier O'Brien novel, *The High Road* (1988), the narrator believes that "since Chernobyl the thrushes of the world had been contaminated,"[53] an offhand-seeming reference to the global significance of the intimate losses not only figured by but inextricably bound up in the fates of animals and the natural world at large, victimized by "earth-destroying fantasies of conquest and consumption." In O'Brien's late fiction, in a post-Chernobyl world, degradation and depredation of the natural world augur unique sorrows for *men*, an especially remarkable feature of her recent novels, most of which have been controversial, at least partly—and ironically—because of her *sympathetic* portrayals of violent, damaged men after a career-long reputation (not entirely deserved) for creating uniformly *unsympathetic* male characters who functioned only as villains and despoilers, as discussed in chapter 3. This sympathy or sensitivity, often conveyed through a relationship with animals and nature, as well as other aspects of the nonhuman world, is extended even to the irremediably savage O'Kane, an example of another natural resource, a child, being exploited and ultimately destroyed.

Before O'Kane discovers that "his" house is now occupied, while he is still trying to find a way into the life of the village, he first encounters Eily in town. He is attempting to frighten and intimidate people into giving him money and/or food, when she buys him a scone. He is entranced by her good looks as well as by her unexpected kindness, which marks her as an outsider like himself. He discovers where she works, entertaining children at her son's preschool, a job that does not make sense to him as real labor, contributing to the unreality of his image of Eily. From there, he "followed her and when he saw where she lived, he went wild. It was his house, his lair that summer before he went to England. He had slept upstairs in the attic room; he knew the foxes that came around there. . . . He loved sleeping there. Left an old mattress and things: an axe; souvenirs of his mother, her hairbrush and a pink bed jacket. His hidey-hole."[54] This home, this dwelling he worked to make for himself and especially the things in it, objects he preserves with care and even reverence, are all that connect O'Kane to any sort of shared reality. In "Dwelling Building Thinking," Martin Heidegger speaks of dwelling as "saving the earth," sparing and preserving, taking under care: "Dwelling itself is always a staying with things. Dwelling, as preserving, keeps the fourfold [the earth, the sky, the gods, our own mortality] in that with which mortals stay: in things."[55] O'Brien's own detailed attention to things and their vital, multiple significances has been discussed in chapter 2. As in Edmund Husserl's concept of the "lifeworld," which "denotes the way the members of one or more social groups . . . structure the world into objects,"[56] in O'Brien's fiction, relationships to objects are often indices of psychological health or otherwise, though perhaps not in the way one might predict. O'Kane's paradoxically egocentric inability to achieve a lifewordly, fully rounded self-image means he has limited capacity to experience empathy, which relies on an acknowledgment that people are objects among other objects in a the world, an acknowledgment that female characters feel compelled to accept.

The confused and mortified rage ignited in motherless O'Kane by the sight of mothers and children signifies the everyday psychic damage done by the larger global crime of what Greenwood has discussed in O'Brien's fiction as "cultural matricide."[57] Jennifer Slivka, narrowing the effects responsible for O'Kane's psychosis to Irish cultural formation, has identified O'Kane as one of O'Brien's "hypermasculine Gaels" angered by "their exclusion from the mother-child dyad."[58] The necessary contradictions attendant on male identity formation are exaggerated in the traumatized, deeply damaged O'Kane, who can torture and kill animals with no apparent feeling and yet dream of a beloved pet fox, with whom he imagines being reunited in the next world. O'Kane oscillates between these extremes of tenderness and cruelty toward animals, the latter a characteristic conventionally associated with socio- and psychopaths. O'Kane identifies with helpless, abject animals too powerfully to treat them objectively or rationally. He often refers to himself explicitly as an animal, for example, considering the abandoned cottage his "lair," and so does nearly everyone in the village.[59] He manifests the same ambivalence toward objects, which he cherishes or wantonly destroys, as in the scene of discovery that his "home" has been usurped. Following the catalogue of beloved things lost to him thanks to the unwelcome appearance of Eily and Maddie, "a sadness came over him, then rage and the thought of hurling stones through the windows, but a voice said, 'All you've got to do is make friends with her, son.' It was a good voice and his heart leapt to it, and he felt something like hope, he felt he was coming home for her."[60] From this point, O'Kane dwells imaginatively in this space, spying on the movements of the small family and indulging in an Oedipal fantasy of becoming the son/lover of Eily once he has removed Maddie: "in his daydreams there was no child, there was only him and her."[61] O'Kane lets himself into the house when mother and son are away and leaves gifts for Eily, more talismanic objects—a bracelet, a carved stone, chopped wood. Eily accepts these things in an unquestioning kind of distracted half belief in the "army of sprits" that she jokingly claims are protecting her anytime anyone expresses concern about her living in such isolation or alarm about her refusal to get a phone. This is a dangerous mutual delusion. O'Kane convinces himself that "it was as if with some subtle, unspoken signal she had let him in."[62]

The silver bracelet is "hidden" in the coal shuttle in the house, symbol of the hearth, of warmth. Husserl uses coal as an example of the way in which we populate our world with meaningful "entities" that are significant in intersubjective processes, processes that have gone terribly wrong or perhaps were never given a chance to develop at all in the broken O'Kane. Husserl's personalistic attitude is "the attitude we are always in when we live with one another, talk to one another, shake hands with one another in greeting, or are related to one another in love and aversion, in disposition and action, in discourse and discussion."[63] The entities involved in this process are not only human beings, but they are nonetheless meaningful and have a role in human consciousness. This is a truth about the vitality of things grasped by children and by the fairy tales written for them, usually peopled by "animated" objects. Karen Barad presses this idea a bit further in her "agential realist account," in which "all bodies, not merely human bodies, come to matter through the world's performativity—its iterative inter-activity. Matter is not configured as a mere effect or product of discursive practices, but rather as an agentive factor in its iterative materialization, and identity and difference are radically reworked."[64] "Empirical claims," Barad goes on to say, "do not refer to individually existing determinate entities, but to phenomena-in-their-becoming, where becoming is not tied to a temporality of futurity, but rather a radically open relatingness of the world worlding itself."[65] There is no relating or relatedness in the village of O'Kane's childhood, except in fantasies resulting from trauma or psychosis, and while the atomization and alienation described, or the "darkness," to bring back O'Brien's word, always prevailed, the sense of estrangement has only increased with the forces of capital that have, among other things, paved over places where O'Kane played as a child. There is no shared "lifeworld" or "homeworld" here, no common language. This is established in the novel's early dream of being unable to communicate; the dreaming woman cannot be heard by the search party, nor can she, even when awake, scream the scream that had been growing in her.

After the death of O'Kane's mother, he is haunted by the memory of the jeering reception that met his earlier claims to be "a true son of the forest," when his classmates called him, instead, "a mammy's boy, a patsy, a pandy, a sissy, and a ninny." Ironically, his years spent ridding himself of all traces of weakness or effeminacy have meant further dehumanization, rendering him both a man and "a monster,"[66] as he says of himself when he first appears back in his home place. As noted, O'Kane terrorizes his native village, and like the murderer on whom he is loosely based, he entertains fantasies about being a member of the IRA. "The terrorist is the contemporary incarnation of the beast," Michael Marder asserts, "within the nexus formed by the anthropocentric/colonial discourse of the human and the empire."[67] The East Clare villagers of the novel, including O'Kane, are trapped between an older nature-based tradition that endures, but only barely, in a landscape that is being rapidly despoiled and a more modern iteration of the values of their former colonial masters though which they see their earlier selves as animalistic savages. A deep feeling of shame persists that we are always in danger of disqualification from the ranks of the civilized, and these shames and fears are projected onto the monstrous other, especially the murdering terrorist, who may really be ourselves. The wood stands as a remnant of a shameful, uncivilized past, as does O'Kane, who hides himself within. Zipes has observed, discussing the gender politics of the fairy tale, in which innocent little girls are potential witches and fairies, that an "encounter in the woods . . . is an asocial act."[68] The woods are where falls the shadow of the ambivalence of male desire, "the natural setting for the fulfilment of desire . . . where the self can explore its possibilities."[69] The fulfillment of male desire will not be denied, and O'Kane's imposition of his will over Eily is total. Before killing Eily, he rapes her. He has absorbed his culture's lesson, that if a woman willingly enters the woods, she "incriminates herself in [the] act."[70]

The novel ends with a fantasy about a little lost boy, who may be a projection of the murderer O'Kane but who also could be Maddie, with whom the troubled O'Kane identified in his own twisted way. O'Kane tells the authorities that he decided to kill Maddie only because Maddie's mother was dead, and he did not want the little boy to grow up motherless, as he had. The source of the fantasy in the final chapter—is it someone's dream?—is not made clear. Perhaps it is a dream of O'Kane's, a re-creation of his first night in the forest, which is here remembered not as a terrified flight from violence (the horror of his mother being beaten by his father) but as a prelapsarian fantasy of unity with the natural world culminating with a comically Freudian scene of wandering through a "forest" made up of the legs of kindly, maternal cows: "They were far taller than he was, their coats were silky, and they had big soft pink diddies."[71] The boy is discovered by a farmer, who calls him a "scalawag." It is intended as a gentle rebuke, but it names a kind of separateness. For O'Kane, who can never develop a mature and fully rounded sense of self or others, the only world he inhabits is one he has attempted to build on his own, shared by speaking animals, the reanimated dead, and disembodied voices. Before this final dream or fantasy closes the narrative, Dr. Macready, the psychiatrist who had attended the mad O'Kane before his court hearing, follows some unconscious desire, or enchantment, and "accidentally" comes upon Cloosh Wood. He enters a scene featuring animated, speaking objects, like something from a fairy tale:

> His absentmindedness had brought him there. . . . The path was easy to follow, mementos all along the way like stations to a sepulchre. There were bits of mirror, broken rosaries, seashells all whispering their whisper: "This way, this way, ladies and gentlemen."
>
> When he got there, he found . . . it was obviously where the woman and child were slain, quite different from the rest of the forest. A garden had been planted . . .

and their little belongings—a gnome, a tortoiseshell comb, a vintage toy car, and a nailbrush with the likeness of a frog on its handle. Two tiny white crosses with their names painted on them seemed so childlike and belonged not to death but to moonlight and enchantment.[72]

For O'Kane, who has spent his life suffering "homesickness for a place that exists only in fantasy,"[73] trapped in an unregenerate state of childhood, enchantment can only be madness, an inescapable nightmare. The recalcitrant wood reflects his arrested state, resistant at its core to masculinist, adult rationality. Its ludic, savage force affects even the sanest representative of patriarchal adulthood, a professional "city man," a medical expert. Drawn helplessly to the depths of the forest, whispered to by shards of the civilized world that have been transformed by the green wood, Dr. Macready is ushered into the garden of death, an irresistible sight but one that few in the novel can bear to contemplate. If sober, logical Dr. Macready could fall under the spell of the eldritch wood, then Eily, for all her receptive witchiness, who hosted dramatic fairy-tale re-creations and dressed up as a goddess, stood little chance of resisting the attractions of the forest's appearance of innocence, plenitude, and harmony, unaware as she was of the depths of personal destruction and communal trauma, disavowed and repressed, lurking in the bosky "chamber of non-light."

5 · MYTH AND MUTATION

In mythology, anything could become anything else.

The brutally dehumanized figure of Michen O'Kane of *In the Forest* can only be understood by others as a monster, half man and half donkey or half wolf or dog, never entirely inhabiting either side of the purported divide between human and nonhuman animal. The figure of metamorphosis calls necessary attention to embodiment, potentially threatening to traditional notions of the masculine as transcendent of the bodily, always somehow "feminine." Defiance of categorization, like enchantment, like myth, does not emerge in O'Brien's fiction as simply empowering or assuasive, reductively or unambiguously liberatory. The urge to categorization is sometimes frustrated in O'Brien's work by the trope of metamorphosis, a conception of the body as without stable borders, subject to mutation. However, the trope can conversely enforce duality when metamorphosis represents an impasse, expressing, as Irving Massey has suggested, "a choice between difficult alternatives, a desperate choice."[1] As discussed in previous chapters, O'Brien's characters seek transformation, escape, and solace through attachments to the nonhuman world. The figure of shape-shifting in the fiction is similarly rooted in a desire to produce meaning from unresolved trauma, as well as an admission of the pain and struggle that attend any act of creative production.

Instances of shape-shifting and human-animal hybrids in O'Brien's fiction are figurations that can effect a kind of autoethnography, an ironic exoticizing of not just Irishness but also Irish femininity, both categories subject to being animalized. Rather than reject association with the animal and accept the categories of exclusion that define the association as derogatory, Irish women writers of the twentieth century, including O'Brien, through the transvaluation of nationalist, masculinized versions of myth, retrieve an ancient order of respect for and even veneration of the natural world and thereby resacralize women's embodied participation in nature's regenerative powers. Frances Devlin-Glass suggests that late-twentieth-century translations of Irish mythological cycles "reveal a body of narratives that are surprisingly rich for feminist deconstructive purposes and indeed have gender-political implications not just for women but for men's and women's understandings of how the sexual contract might be reconfigured."[2] Mythology and folklore are nonmodern motifs available to Irish writers, a store of imagery and narrative that links many contemporary writers and that has become a distinguishing feature of texts produced by Irish women in particular. This material not only addresses Ireland's oblique and fragmented accession to the modern but also offers multiple possibilities for cultural negotiations. Fairy lore and folklore, like the figure of the animal they revolve around, give voice to those outside the operations of power; but these are potentially ambivalent sites of enunciation, and Irish women writers struggle with the rebarbative equivocacies of such imagery. In an Irish context the distinctions between nature and culture, between the human and the nonhuman, seem especially nebulous, as evinced in the folklore and its many tales of shape-shifting, an ability attributed to the devious and deviant Irish since the twelfth century, by writers and observers including Edmund Spenser.[3]

As noted in chapter 4, for all of the liberatory potential of fairy tales, myth, and legend, they function ambiguously in women's writing. They can enchant women into unrealistic expectations and complicity in the perpetuation of their subordination but can also represent, as Catherine Kelly argues, a "more lateral way of thinking which takes into account different ways of 'knowing' such as through story,"[4] an oblique angle often enabled in folk tales by the presence of animals, which are often humans or deities, including goddesses, in disguise. This easy communication between realms, however, carries as much potential to provoke and even sanction patriarchal violence as it does the power to expose the violence that is sometimes veiled in narratives of romance and fantasy. Eileen Morgan's analysis of O'Brien's "de-mythologizing" of the "romantic nationalist tradition's gendered images and myths" in Ireland argues that "her more complex engagement with nationalist mythology . . . has been her exploration of Irish women's responses to the romantic myths of Irish womanhood and male chivalry that persist in post-colonial Ireland."[5] O'Brien's fiction attends to chivalry's role in rendering patriarchal inequalities seductive. For example, a beast disguised as "chivalrous" male appears in *The Little Red Chairs* (2015). The opening scene features a bearded man, dressed menacingly in a "long dark coat and white gloves," slouching through a lyrically rendered bucolic setting.[6] The first appearance in the environs of the quiet Irish village by this stranger, known in his homeland as Vuk, or "wolf," will later be reported in mystical, folkloric terms, as having summoned the "Pooka Man" amid thunder and "dogs barking crazily."[7] This fairy-tale "big bad wolf" in sheep's clothing is Vladimir Dragan, a fugitive war criminal known as the "Beast of Bosnia," an echo of the historical figure on whom the character is based, Radovan Karadzic, the Serbian political leader known as the "Butcher of Bosnia," who was eventually convicted of genocide and other crimes against humanity. Karadzic used the alias Dr. Dragan Dabíc in his decade as a fugitive, and, like him, O'Brien's Dragan passes himself off as an alternative healer dealing in folk remedies and non-Western medicine. A self-styled poet and mystic who "walks in the footsteps of the druids,"[8] his old-world charm captivates many in the small rural village.

As discussed in chapter 4, fairy-tale motifs, which consistently feature in O'Brien's fiction,[9] tap the primal dread at the heart of folk and fairy lore, which so often comprises violence against the vulnerable: women, children, the elderly. The bloodthirsty wolf or werewolf stalks many of O'Brien's characters, like the romantically disappointed librarian in "Send My Roots Rain," who dreams of her "true self" as a "she-wolf," drinking "the hot blood that spurted from the throat of a wounded animal."[10] Similarly, an abandoned wife in "The House of My Dreams" is haunted by "a sniff as of blood freshly drawn. . . . A wolf she thought. It made people laugh. 'A wolf,' they said, 'the proverbial big bad wolf.'"[11] Historical commentators on Ireland, including Gerald of Wales in the twelfth century and Spenser in the sixteenth, recorded the "facts" of the lycanthropic Irish; Gerald claimed that the Irish turned into wolves every seven years, while Spenser maintained it was an annual occurrence.[12] The wolf is associated with an eminent figure of metamorphosis in the Western imagination, Dracula, the creation of another Irish writer, Bram Stoker. Evoked by Dragan's name, Dracula, who can both command wolves and transform into one, has featured in O'Brien's writing since *The Country Girls*, regularly lurking in the background as a romantic figure, thrilling but evil, a shadow thrown by male characters in the foreground ready to consume and destroy unwary young girls and women. In a 1972 interview, O'Brien identified her "three loves of childhood" as Jesus, Dracula, and Heathcliff.[13] In her works of memoir, Dracula is remembered as a romantic figure from her youth, promising not only forbidden sexual intoxication and seduction but also the equally forbidden temptations of imagination and literature. In the memoir *Country Girl* (2012), O'Brien recalls the traveling players who came to her childhood town twice a year, bringing with them "the lure of drama." Their unchanging, quaintly nineteenth-century repertoire consisted of "*East Lynne, Murder in the Old Red Barn*, and *Dracula*." *Dracula*, in particular, "was too terrible to behold and also riveting. As living theatre it was matchless."[14] Young Edna was so enthralled with this annual event that she wrote her own play, *Dracula's Daughter*, which she summoned the courage one year to present to the actor who played Dracula.[15] (When she also offered to run away with the actor, his wife dismissed her.) These same three plays are listed as examples of "thrilling" dramas by Emma, the narrator's sister, in *A Pagan Place* (1970), when her mother discovers Emma's diary, enumerating various assignations with men. Emma explains that she is "trying her hand at being a playwright," and the sensational content her mother has discovered is material for a work of fiction.[16] As discussed in chapter 3, Emma measures her self-worth by her sexual desirability for men and, when she becomes pregnant as a result, only barely escapes being institutionalized by church and state. Emma's having been doubly victimized by the Victorian ideas about heterosexual "romance" that Dracula embodies and that persisted well into the twentieth century in Ireland—that sex is dangerous, forbidden, rarely consensual, and, therefore, necessarily predatory—makes her reference to the figure particularly apt as well as poignant.

Dracula, like Heathcliff, personifies the masculine romantic ideal as both protean and violently threatening, a perverse source of his appeal. About O'Brien's own infatuation with Dracula, she confessed, "When I think of it in retrospect, obviously it was complete romantic masochism."[17] In *Mother Ireland* (1976), among the terrifying male figures O'Brien recalls from childhood is a "madman who lived in a hut," armed with a razor, always prepared to meet the devil, a state of readiness not entirely mad to the young Edna: "always and in the background the Devil himself horned and black, most often seen at night, oftenest of all at dusk, and annually on stage a most bewitching personification of him, in the person of Count Dracula.... You dreamed of going with him ..., [to] be his stand-in maiden on whom he rehearsed the procedure of blood-sucking. Yes Dracula and you would go away and you would revive the saintly side of him."[18] The fairy-tale narrative of beauty taming and bringing about one final metamorphosis of the "bewitching" beast ambushes many of O'Brien's women. In *Time and Tide* (1992), Nell runs away with Walter, a Heathcliff type of whom she is afraid even as she is attracted to him. Years later, when she finally rebels against his obsessive domination of her and their children by refusing to hand over a substantial amount of money she has earned, Walter's Dracula persona emerges. He throws her on the bed and clamps "his hand like a vice on her throat."[19] Suspecting her of planning to leave, he threatens that if she does, "'Your life won't be worth living,' ... he laughed as his fingers ground into her throat. Ridiculously, she thought of Dracula. She also felt the breath being squeezed out of her,"[20] recalling Eugene, Kate's life-draining husband in *Girls in Their Married Bliss* (1964), who "sucked every thought and breath of her waking moments."[21]

Walter has his own vampiric minion, the devoted housemaid Rita, who, spying on Nell, "burst into the room, curlers in her hair and an eggshell mask on her face making her look like a ghoul."[22] After the divorce is finalized and Nell is granted custody of her children, Rita appears again at the courthouse, shouting that Nell is a bad woman, transforming her into the animal most readily identified with Dracula: "Then she ran back helter-skelter, as if the malediction had to be put somewhere safely, and she herself, batlike in her black attire, the custodian of this spurious curse." Patricia Coughlan's analysis of the figure of the bat in O'Brien's fiction reads the animal as, inter alia, symbolic of the "otherness" of the independent woman, an aspiration inassimilable to Irish ideals of womanliness.[23] Abused and disappointed women in O'Brien's work struggle to break the curse of traditional expectations for heterosexual romance, to forsake their belief in male saviors who will secure the happily-ever-after ending. Just as Nell fled her father's oppression by eloping with Walter, after subsequent exploitative relationships, she continues to believe "even then, even then, . . . that deliverance would come."[24] Her last, most destructive affair is with "Dr Rat," a man whom she knows to be untrustworthy, but "not once did she admit that what she sought was her own ruin."[25] When Nell takes LSD, the doctor metamorphoses before her eyes: "he had become a rat, . . . his bristles bristling rhythmically, the face however still human, the white features like a papier mâché mask above the furry tuxedo."[26] They are joined by other hybrid creatures, part human and part animal, in "a hell, the flames fluctuating between flames and blood,"[27] more terrifying versions of Walter's Rita.

The unilateral discourse of power informs the violence of the shape-shifters Dracula and Dr. Rat, in their roles as controlling (would-be) lovers, exploiting the human-nonhuman connection for the purposes of domination. According to Massey, metamorphosis is the product of fear, rather than pleasure.[28] Significantly for a discussion of O'Brien, Massey's analysis of metamorphosis in literature identifies marriage as the impossible social construct critiqued in classic tales of shape-shifting. Marriage, according to Massey, "leaves out the crucial knowledge that there is a nonlanguage which expresses the only important part of our nature; what it expresses is of a totally private kind; it is not of a quality to be shared. In fact, it is in direct contradiction to any possible marriage."[29] The appeal of metamorphosis, of escaping into "voiceless" animality, is an embodiment of the unknowable self, anathema to "romantic" ideals of total "possession" of and by the other. The heterosexist imperative to marry and procreate, an especially powerful force in Irish culture, is one of patriarchy's mechanisms of control and surveillance. Marriage in its traditional form of "couverture" potentially granted a husband implicit rights to, if not outright ownership of his wife's inner and outer lives, her private and public selves. Metamorphosis, by denying "the primacy of language," allows for an independence of the physical, freedom to mutate and grow, an individual experience of change outside of the translating operations conducted via the linguistic, which relies on the insupportable fiction of transparency.[30]

At once attractive and frightening, metamorphosis in this account shares qualities with the Dracula of O'Brien's childhood memories, especially as a trope for the transfiguring act of imagination itself. The "only important part of our nature," the body, the material self we share with animals, is prior to language, as Judith Butler has pointed out,[31] and is the ultimate source of creativity, imagining otherness, inhabiting different experiences. The anthropologist Mary Douglas has suggested that the connection between art and receptivity to the other, in every form, can be found as far back as Paleolithic cave paintings: "I risk the idea that if [Paleolithic man] painted animals at all it signifies something positive about his openness to commerce with his fellows. When he painted human beings with antlers or animal masks it might say even more about his friendly relations with fellow human beings of other groups. To see blasphemy in the idea of a baboon god or a goat-footed one, or in the deification of bulls or cows, is to reject other people's certainty that gods in animal form are proper objects of adoration. It also rejects an attitude towards foreign human beings."[32] Exchanging qualities with the nonhuman as acknowledgment of the kinship and relationality among all bodies, in figures of metamorphosis and hybridity, emerges as a critical figurative praxis in the work of O'Brien and other twentieth-century Irish women writers who draw on myth and folklore. According to Alicia Ostriker, myth, like metamorphosis in Massey's discussion, "is quintessentially intimate material, the stuff of dream life, forbidden desire, inexplicable motivation—everything in the psyche that to rational consciousness is unreal, crazed or abominable," despite its official status as product of classic, "high" culture, "handed 'down' the ages through religious, literary, and educational authority."[33] This is what Ostriker identifies as myth's "double power," to enable speech that is simultaneously private and public.[34] The modern reshaping of myth restores the irrational to its archaic status as providing valuable access to alternative and valuable forms of knowing, including knowing through the haptic, the bodily, capable of transformation and extension beyond the limits of propriety or the patriarchal self.

As discussed, for O'Brien, and for other writers, the figure of the animal indicates the impossibility of transparent, singular communication, the dangerous fantasy of human language's ascendancy, its power to manage and determine meaning. As Massey observes, in his discussion of literary metamorphosis, "Our easy language teaches us to forget the horror of the living fact."[35] At the same time, the figure can be associated with the dangerous, violent silencing of the powerless. Critics have noticed the way in which, in O'Brien's late fiction especially, she has borrowed from the story of Philomela. O'Brien's interest in Greek myths, especially their dramatization, is well documented, evinced in her own interpretation of Euripides' *Iphigenia in Aulis*, in her 2003 play *Iphigenia*. In the Greek myth of Philomela, included in Ovid's *Metamorphoses*, Philomela is raped by her brother-in-law, who tears out her tongue so that she cannot report his crime. She tells the story in a tapestry, a revenge that incites further violence, which she escapes by being transformed into a nightingale. Elizabeth Jane Dougherty discusses the appearance of resonances of the Philomela narrative in *Down by the River* (1998), while Marguerite Quintelli-Neary locates references to the myth in *House of Splendid Isolation* (1994). In both novels, a girl or young woman is doomed by her beauty to be sexually abused and, most explicitly in *Down by the River*, is unable to use her voice to defend herself or tell her story. In *Down by the River*, according to Dougherty, "Mary undergoes a symbolic metamorphosis from girl to bird," a transformation that "marks her passage from childhood to adulthood."[36] The novel's last reference to her metamorphosis into a bird, when she sings to a crowd in the final scene, "points to the disjunction between language and female experience,"[37] a theme throughout the work, as discussed in chapter 3. In the case of the appearance of Philomela in the fiction, according to Dougherty, the metamorphosed woman becomes a "symbol for male aesthetic inspiration," rather than a mode of artistic expression for the female artist.[38]

Other female and nonheteronormative metamorphoses in O'Brien can, however, function at an oblique angle to the official, binarized conception of volition and (in)dependence that enables the oppositions of "power" and "powerlessness," and of the human and nonhuman, though such resistance does not escape punishment. O'Brien's female shape-shifters are the kind of "metamorphic characters" that Massey describes as "refugees from comparison, from the binary. They seek to rejoin the peace and unity of the non-oppositional world."[39] One such shape-shifter is Catalina, from O'Brien's 1988 novel *The High Road*. As discussed in chapter 1, the novel's potentially transformative love between Anna and Catalina leads to the murder of the younger, native, working woman. Catalina's Spanish island village practices a pagan version of Catholicism. The older, privileged Anna follows the Stations of the Cross to the church, which is also "the seat of the Iberian moon goddess," an object of worship not easily distinguished from the Virgin Mary, to whom prayers are offered there in a "subhuman" drone.[40] According to Helen Thompson, "the Catholic litany to the Virgin Mother Anna hears in the church could also be a chanting ritual in honor of the moon goddess, because religion and mysticism are conflated here, thus creating an environment that may facilitate woman-centered desire."[41] The realm of dream and archaic myth unselfconsciously merges with the younger myth of Catholicism's virgin queen.[42] As discussed, woman-centered desire in O'Brien is often indexed to a rejection of understandings of subjectivity as something singular, bounded, and independent. In O'Brien, true connection, like that between Catalina and Anna, destabilizes the assumed integrity of both the human and the nonhuman, especially in relation to each other. Karen Barad argues that the "queerness" of identity itself resides in the noncoincidence of human subjectivity necessarily predicated on the nonhuman, when she maintains, in her essay on nature's "queer performativity," that "identity is not an individual affair. Identity is multiple within itself."[43] Catalina, an avowed devotee of Gaia, tells Anna that she loves the sea's constant state of becoming and change, its potential to effect "the most terrible transmutations."[44] Catalina is herself a constantly transforming creature who can look like a boy or a girl or an androgynous hybrid of both. Her hybridity even extends to half-animal transformation when she appears to Anna as a "mermaid being carried away towards the patches of blue."[45] Catalina joyfully relinquishes constructs of the inviolable self, relishes immersion in the rhythms of nonhuman forces, and occupies the rich in-between of relationality.

The significance of Catalina's cross-dressing was discussed in chapter 1, but she is not the only instance of transvestism in O'Brien's fiction. Similar to

Massey's figure of metamorphosis or Douglas's Paleolithic art, transvestism for Marjorie Garber is a source of meaning and creativity outside of language that is nevertheless constitutive of it, a "compelling force . . . in literature and culture" because it is an "instatement of metaphor itself, not as that for which a literal meaning must be found, but precisely as that without which there would be no such thing as meaning in the first place."[46] The transvestite is not always legible to O'Brien's characters, however, if they are themselves invested in conforming to heterosexist norms and particularly when they are insecure about their own gender performance. In *August Is a Wicked Month* (1965), the Joycean free indirect mode of narration, linked to the perceptions of the protagonist, Ellen, initially describes a drag artist in animal terms: "She wore heels so high that she looked like some kind of bird perched on long, thin legs."[47] An animal skin helps effect the transformation that Ellen witnesses: "When the girl was naked except for the petals over her breasts and her kerchief lower down, she took a natural-colour fox fur and began to draw it back and forth, slowly, between her legs."[48] Ellen, who considers herself "curiously unfinished,"[49] has been anxiously, and ultimately disastrously, attempting to prove her attractiveness to men after her divorce, through heavy drinking, wild partying, and indiscriminate sex. Just as she is told that the performer is a man, the narration uses a potentially confusing, nonpersonal modifier, "the" instead of "her" or "his," to describe both the performer and the fur, blurring the difference between them: "*The* natural-colour fox was black between *the* legs."[50] The unbearable revelation about gender identity as—literally—disarticulable performance makes Ellen feel "sick" and "disgusted," "cheated" by "a man who has perfectly mimicked all the coquette of a woman."[51] Her own terrifyingly "unfinished" state seems to be mocked by the figure onstage, adorned by an ironically "natural-coloured" disembodied animal with which she shares disturbingly indistinct and unstable contours.

The figure of the shape-shifting transvestite also appears in O'Brien's *House of Splendid Isolation*, about an IRA gunman, McGreevy, on the run in the Republic, who seeks shelter in what he has mistakenly been told is a safe house, the home of the elderly widow Josie, whom he initially takes hostage but with whom he develops a more complex relationship. Various versions of patriotic Irish masculinity compete for dominance in the text, especially between the guards (police), symbols and enforcers of custodial as well as disciplinary patriarchy, and the figure of the terrorist, if not exactly McGreevy himself, who becomes increasingly disenchanted with the macho codes of warfare, sacrificial brotherhood, and individualistic stoicism over the course of the narrative. When first on the move and successfully evading the authorities, McGreevy temporarily dons a disguise, including a wig, discovered by local twin girls. Their mother, shop owner Ma Hinchey, "pulls it down over her head clownishly" and is seen by her first customer of the morning, "the new young Guard," Flynn, whose expected flirtation with the shopkeeper follows a kind of predetermined script ("It's an understanding between them"). Hinchey places the wig on the counter, where it "looks different. It looks sinister and as if it might move of its own accord."[52] The twins are suddenly afraid of it, aware of the magic that inheres in transformation, saying it belongs to a witch and should be burned. Other people enter the shop, and speculations as to the source of the uncanny object range from a "woman taken in adultery" to "theatre folk" to Flynn's suggestion, "Transvestites they call them. They look the spitting image of a woman."[53] In the course of these musings, a neighbor recalls that the terrorist currently on the run broke into a Limerick hairdresser's and stole a wig. The officer, whose authority has been undermined, is "rattled with himself for not having thought of it." Embarrassed in front of the audience of women, he vents his frustration by "taking hold of the thing[;] he crushes and recrushes it as if it is an animal he must restrain."[54] McGreevy, who every day mocks Flynn and the entire police force by avoiding capture, flaunts his ascendancy over his bumbling pursuers with this symbol of his skillful elusiveness.

The liveliness and animality of the object is reaffirmed when Flynn brings the wig to the station, where another officer says it looks like a fox, a creature fabled for its slyness and cunning. "A human fox," replies Flynn, who attempts to reinstate his position as source of authoritative knowledge by quizzing the subordinate officer about the wig's possible origin. He further reassures himself by hinting at McGreevy's perversity and incomplete manliness, when he suggests McGreevy is a transvestite, one of those "half-and-half fellas."[55] The wig's supernatural qualities are evoked when Flynn claims, "Kids were playing pooka with it when I found it," [56] the pooka being a shape-shifting fairy that takes many forms in Irish lore, from hare to horse. As in *The High Road*, however, the release of forbidden desires and the embrace of disavowed connections across defining categories that metamorphosis promises are ultimately violently denied. Toward the end of the novel, the police surround Josie's house. She has come to feel sympathy and even a maternal tenderness for McGreevy, whom she fears the guards will shoot rather than capture alive when they discover his hiding place. As noted in chapter 4, McGreevy has escaped to the trees around the house, compared by the narrator to the shape-shifter "Mad Sweeny" of Irish legend, who became like a bird.[57] Josie approaches her door with the intention of pleading with the police, who see "a figure moving in the gloamy light of pre-dawn, a silhouette in a raincoat, with closely cropped hair," a figure they take for a man.[58] From her late husband's jealous friends, who in her youth called her "Queen of the Munster Fairies," to McGreevy's sneering dismissal of her at first meeting as someone who should "stick to [her] gracious living and folklore,"[59] folklore has been used to marginalize and disempower Josie. Her final, self-determined transformation leads to her death when the guards shoot someone they think is McGreevy. The guardians of the patriarchal state punish Josie's somehow-disloyal transvestism (she has not only abandoned her femininity but also betrayed her allegiance to the authorities who have determined McGreevy's criminality), just as the forces of the patriarchal family punish Catalina's boundary crossing.

The wig as indicator of unstable gender identification appears as well in *Time and Tide*, when Nell, while still living with her husband, receives from her neighbor the unusual gift of a wig made of the older woman's own hair. Return of the wig is demanded when Nell's sexual propriety comes into question. The novel also makes reference to the figure of the mermaid, an even more ambivalent presence here than in *The High Road*. *Time and Tide* opens with a prologue featuring fantastic creatures and a tale of metamorphosis. Nell, the narrator, refers to the "bottom of the Thames," where she imagines "the sea creatures and the sea monsters" are consuming the body of her drowned son, Paddy. Nell clings "to the little story he used to tell her about the souls of drowned bodies becoming seagulls, and in her river walks she looked for them, expecting one might seize her with a look that was not birdlike."[60] Throughout the novel, the River Thames figures significantly: the site of both Nell's reestablishment of a home after escaping an abusive marriage and the devastating tragedy of her grown son Paddy's death by drowning years later. The potency of water as symbol of the life-giving and death-dealing feminine is acknowledged in the prologue by an unattributed quotation from Carl Jung, a quotation described as "speaking itself," not originating from any of the characters: "In the morning of life, the son tears himself loose from the Mother. . . . He carries the enemy within himself, a deadly longing for the abyss, a longing to drown in his own source, to be sucked down into the realm of the Mothers."[61] There is no explanation offered for this oneiric, "illogical" irruption in the narrative, an appropriately weird moment in a novel about unbearable loss and trauma in which the figures of hybridity, metamorphosis, and folklore provide vehicles for expressing pain beyond language and the rational.

The human-nonhuman hybrid mermaid expresses Nell's ambivalent state of mind, even before the tragedy, when first appearing in the "small Victorian house" on the river that she has secured after winning custody of her sons. She allows herself the "luxury" of "a lamp with a milky glass stem, inside of which a mermaid was suspended."[62] Rather than simply symbolizing new freedoms, however, the mermaid also hints at the disabling terror of those potential freedoms, when Nell describes herself as "living in this frozen haze, like the mermaid in her sphere of glass."[63] Nell's ambivalence toward water recurs toward the end of the novel when she despairs of ever being able to bury her son, whose body has not been recovered: "Earth and not water was the kindest, meetest resting place. Why did she so fear water, water from whence he came, the waters of herself, her own being, as she in turn had come from her own mother, womb of waters, known and unknown, nourishing and leeching, giving and taking back.

She kept picturing earth, little slants of earth, little mounds, graveyards with things growing out of them, daisies, moss, anything."[64] There is some truth about herself and her own limitations that Nell wishes to bury with her son. The water is unfinished, unknown, not easily fitted into conventional, comforting pieties about death and birth. Nell is not the kind of heroic mermaid-explorer featured in Adrienne Rich's 1973 poem "Diving into the Wreck." Ostriker describes the mermaid-speaker's "watery descent" as an inversion of "the ascents and con-quests of male heroism," in a text that refuses the distinction between "real" and "mythic."[65] The speaker dives with mermen, with whom she merges in the lines "I am she: I am he / We are, I am, you are."[66] Ostriker notes the androgyny of the speaking voice and the significance of the fluidity of pronoun assignment.

As discussed in chapter 1, Rich and O'Brien were contemporaries who shared a number of common themes and preoccupations. O'Brien's own decentering pronominal indeterminacy was noted in chapter 3, and, as in the Rich poem, in O'Brien, the mermaid can function as an example of what Ostriker calls the "retrieved" mythic images "of what women have collectively and historically suf-fered; in some cases they are instructions for survival."[67] Examples include *Wild Decembers* (1999), set in a time-warped Irish rural community, unprepared for and unwelcoming of modernity, whether that is the latest tractor technology or immigrant neighbors. In a place shadowed by an unresolved history, the "curse" of "warring sons of warring sons," legends and fairy-tale characters inhabit the "profoundly pensive landscape," like the uncanny misfit known as "the Crock," referred to as a "goblin," and the witchy, spellbinding sisters Rita and Reena, characterized as "demonesses."[68] A comparison between the Fionnuala of Irish legend and the very ordinary mortal Breege suggests the tragedy awaiting the young woman, whose brother, Joseph, will murder Bugler, the Australian inter-loper, when Breege and Bugler are expecting a child. In the legend of the Children of Lír, Fionnula is cursed by her stepmother Aoife, who changes her and her brother into swans, doomed to wander the waterways of Ireland for nine hundred years, a narrative of intergenerational competition between women that would be familiar to O'Brien and her readers. The first encounter between Breege and Bugler begins hopefully in a suspended space of enchantment, the Christmas dance that transforms the local hotel into a "cave of colours" and ren-ders the locals fantastic, otherworldly beings, shifting from blue to magenta, with "heads of hair still wet with a mermaid's wetness."[69] The mermaid is a tenta-tively hopeful symbol in the final scene of another of O'Brien's state-of-the-nation novels, *Down by the River*. Mary, the adolescent incest victim whose attempt to obtain an abortion in England makes her a national cause, is reunited with Mona, a girl she first met in the English abortion clinic. As in *Wild Decem-bers*, they attend a Christmas celebration, in another "cave of colour."[70] Mona is onstage preparing to sing and undergoes a metamorphosis. She is "cool and bewitching," wearing "a pelt of lamé, magenta, the gleam of fish scale," and her hair is a "halo": "As the lights change so does Mona. She is a mermaid, necklaced in seaweed, one bare shoulder the melting fawn of fudge, the outstretched arms weaving, willing them to her."[71] The novel ends in a scene of joy and renewal that is unusual in O'Brien's work, as Mona sings "a paean of expectancy into the gaudy void," a "quiver of sound" that answers the "innermost cries" of her listeners' souls.[72] Here the retrieved image of the mermaid/siren offers an instance of Ostriker's "instructions for survival," but without resolving the figure's ambivalence. Like the frozen, suspended mermaid in *Time and Tide*, Mona's transfiguration can be read as continuing to sexualize her, keeping her suspended in the male gaze of the desiring audience.[73]

Another dryad-mermaid figure threatens Nell's fragile domestic harmony in *Time and Tide*, a contender for her son Paddy's love and attention, his shape-shifter girlfriend Emma, whose hybridity partakes of qualities both human and nonhuman: "a creature of the forest, in her dark green seersucker dress and eyes green and aqueous, like eyes loaned from the bottom of the sea, and yet her quality was that of a fern, still, absorbent, a venal thing."[74] This crossing over into the unnerving liveliness of the vegetable signals Nell's discomfort with her son being sexually active and recalls the parody of heterosexual reproduction and parenthood in *Night*, in which the narrator muses about experimenting with seminal emissions to create "a plant, a half-thing, a creature, nearly with animation, on the borders between animal and plant."[75] Nell's unhealthy possessiveness and competitive unpleasantness with Paddy's friends and girlfriends alienates her from both sons.[76] Her insecurity and depressive outlook seem to presage, if not determine, the forthcoming disaster. Her rigidity and constant desire to conform, her obsessive fear of punishment for having broken up her conventional family, conspire to make her view the young people around her sons like alien creatures: "They looked like night creatures, creatures of the forest, the sockets of their eyes ringed in dark arcs of ritual purple."[77] Young people in the novel are vagabond, mobile, open to an understanding of being and becoming that experiences identity as a fluid mingling and recombination of elements, an attitude as dystopian as it is celebratory. A dark, chaotic energy, a kind of animist sensibility that recalls the mythic, attaches to the formless, saturnalian partying of Paddy's friends, including Jock, whose eyes are "a hissing green, the colour [Nell] imagined a satyr's to be." This hybrid being seems magical, like a "Druid," when he takes "to the street, where three successive lots of traffic lights, weirdly biddable, glowed green to hasten his way."[78] All of Nell's mistrust of the mythic seems to be confirmed when Paddy is drowned in the river, along with other passengers in a pleasure boat. In her grief, she ironically personifies the river as a wolfish, possessive mother: "The inscrutable, voracious water, had taken him and others. Yes, death stalked the city that night, stalked the city like a great water wolf. The river—sheer, ruffled, grey, brown, black, and khaki—took them into her inhospitable bosom. Why? Why did the river want them?"[79]

Another wolf-like character in the novel is the "half-breed spaniel" Charlie, a stray with "something of the wolf" whom Nell minds for Paddy,[80] one of the dogs in O'Brien's fiction that takes on human and even supernatural qualities. O'Brien's fiction frequently associates dogs with death, an association in her work that crosses boundaries of the human and the nonhuman, as well as the mundane and the mystical.[81] In *The Country Girls*, for example, Cait cannot believe in the traumatic fact of her mother's death until she hears two grey-hounds moaning: "It was the moan of death. Suddenly I knew that I had to accept the fact that my mother was dead."[82] The indeterminate human-dog howl is also an uncanny medium of grief in the last lines of *A Pagan Place*: "the last thing you heard was a howl starting up, more ravenous than a dog's, more pierc-ing than a person's."[83] Charlie, in *Time and Tide*, makes his prehensile sympathy with Nell over Paddy's death known through his eerie howl. Nell describes her own crying as weeping "banshee tears."[84] When she returns home, "Charlie started up his own incantation, his own wake, his own subhuman howl night, . . . a howl that had a human plaint in it. Her own hysteria speaking back to her but animalized. Charlie knew."[85] Nell identifies Charlie later as sharing her "ban-shee" transformation.[86]

Patricia Lysaght's study of the banshee, the supernatural female "death-messenger" of Irish folklore, notes that "the howling of dogs, especially at night, is commonly considered to be a death-omen in Irish tradition."[87] The animalized voice of mourning evokes the Irish wake and the role of the keener (nearly always a woman), explicitly so in *Time and Tide*. David Lloyd, in his analysis of the "sound of a dog howling" in the opening of Sinéad O'Connor's song "Fam-ine" (from the album *Universal Mother*), described the sound as "uncanny for several reasons":[88]

> It is impossible to tell if the howl is of hunger, grief, or some condensation of the two; it is difficult to determine whether the sound we hear is actually a dog's howl or human imitation of the sound, a difficulty which in itself opens the uncanny domain where the human and the natural converge and mimic one another; this animal lament accentuates the absence or the silence of what properly should be the sound of human mourning: it as if the field of human society itself had been decimated to the extent that all remains of its domestic and affective fabric, for which the memory of the dead is an indispensable thread, is the anguish of the domestic animal on the verge of reverting to its wildness.[89]

The impossibility of distinguishing between the human and nonhuman unites the two in suffering, which reveals the tenuousness of the veneer of "civilization," the ever-present threat of animal "wildness," the fiction of human language and cul-ture's supremacy. Giorgio Agamben characterizes the connection between ani-mal cries and death as commemorative, in the same way that the constitutively animalistic keen functions in the wake: "The animal voice is the voice of death, . . . which preserves and recalls the living as dead, and it is, at the same time, an immediate trace and memory of death, pure negativity."[90] The blankness of loss resists human articulation.

Edmund Burke, the Irish parliamentarian and political thinker, included in his famous eighteenth-century text on the sublime and the beautiful a short section titled "The Cries of Animals," in which he argues for their expressive power: "Such sounds as imitate the natural inarticulate voices of men, or any animals in pain or danger, are capable of conveying great ideas."[91] Agamben and Burke both engage with the paradoxical expressivity of the "inarticulate" or "negative" implicit in animal sounds (and even humans' "natural" voice), an uncanny hovering between presence and absence, as in the eerily silent, though crowded, famine landscape in *Mother Ireland*, when O'Brien uses both the absence of "proper" voices and the reversion of dogs to a wolf-like state as figure for the final unraveling of the "domestic and affective fabric": "a vast silence, a creeping ruin over everything, an inability to curse because human passion had been quelled through starvation; children's eyes were senseless and wizened, work gangs who built walls and roads were voiceless like shadows, womanhood had ceased to be womanly, the birds carolled no more, the ravens dropped dead on the wing, and dogs hairless and with their vertebrae like the saw of a bone slunk into the ditch like wolves and the *anima mundi*, the soul of the land, was lying dim and dead."[92] The landscape of hunger and death, silenced like the landscapes that bear witness to sexual violence in O'Brien's fiction, as discussed in chapter 3, is not an anthropomorphized backdrop to human suffering but a participant. As "The Child" who narrates the prologue in *House of Splendid Isolation* observes, "History is everywhere. It seeps into the soil, the subsoil. Like rain, or hail, or snow, or blood. A house remembers. An outhouse remembers."[93]

According to Renate Lachman, memory, and especially memorialization, originates in myth, which stores cultural experience and knowledge and can offer strategies for communal acts of both forgetting and remembering.[94] The mythic figure of the banshee appears regularly in O'Brien's fiction, always associated with sexual danger, whether the imagined threat of women's sexuality or the consequences of sexuality suffered by women. In *Wild Decembers*, the haunted landscape already described is sometimes shrouded by a "white vapour, the white lady, that sometimes ran and danced on parts of the mountain, a dancing lady which drunk men believed was the banshee."[95] One of the lonely drunken men of the mountains, Crock, who despises and desires women, spitefully wishing to encourage Joseph's resentment of Bugler's relationship with Breege, compares the sound of Bugler's new tractor to a "banshee wail."[96] In *House of Splendid Isolation*, Josie recalls realizing that she is pregnant with a child she does not want, the product of marital rape: "A baby. It cried inside her. She could hear it at all hours. . . . It was not a normal child. In the mornings she searched the lavatory bowl for a sign and once roared with delight but it was a trick of the eye. What she thought was blood was a brown stain on the worn porcelain. It cried inside the walls of her womb. It was more like a banshee than a child."[97] Baba calls on the banshee to avenge such wrongs in the Epilogue to *The Country Girls Trilogy*. As Kristi Byron notes, O'Brien has Baba use "an Irish version of the monstrous feminine, the banshee, to convey her rage against the cultural codes imposed upon her generation,"[98] when she says of Kate, whose body Baba is bringing back to Ireland for burial, "I hope she rises up nightly like the banshee and does battle with her progenitors,"[99] an apt description of O'Brien's career of doing battle with the fathers. The figures O'Brien draws on from Irish and world mythologies and legend perform and invite transgression of multiple boundaries: those between the human and nonhuman, between the "real" and the "imaginary," and even between life and death. The journeys they promise are terrifying rather than reassuring, but they are potentially liberating and transformative.

6 · DISORDER, DIRT, AND DEATH

Dirt can be consoling and friendly in a strange place.

An unborn, never-to-be-born child torments the pregnant Josie in Edna O'Brien's *House of Splendid Isolation* (1994), a proleptic haunting that renders the fetus a kind of banshee, or death spirit. An unnamed "Child" is given the first and last words of the novel, identified in the epilogue as Josie's unborn baby, in possession of both ancient and timeless insights that emanate from the earth in which the child is buried: "So old and haunted, so hungry and replete. It talks. Things past and things yet to be."[1] Another of O'Brien's turn-of-the-century, state-of-Ireland novels, *Wild Decembers* (1999), opens similarly with a prologue describing an underground repository of the past that joins birth and death in cycles of violence. While the open-air fields are "more than life and more than death too," the site of "quickening" new life, under those fields, "fathoms deep the frail and rusted shards, the relics of battles of the long ago, and in the basins of limestone, quiet in death, the bone babes and the bone mothers, and the fathers too."[2] Thomas Laqueur argues that "the dead, like death itself, are of overwhelming consequence."[3] The dead body in O'Brien's fiction, as in Laqueur's discussion, is invested with meaning, "because, through it, the human past somehow speaks to us."[4] The dead provide "a powerful category for the imagination of the living" as well as a "temporal extension of our present, they are us— our symbolic world—as we imagine it in deep time."[5] Like the dead body, other forms of waste contribute to constructions of the self, provide representational structures and systems, "in the habits and embodied practices through which we decide what is connected to us and what isn't,"[6] a process theorized by Julia Kristeva as abjection. Kristeva's abject is a psychological process with gender implications, as it is rejection of the body, primarily the mother's body, as source of filth and otherness, on which identity formation is predicated. In O'Brien's work, this process of rejection is markedly incomplete, one source of the "extraordinarily frequent mentions of bodily scenes and of items eliciting disgust" that Patricia Coughlan has noted in O'Brien's work.[7] Dirt, death, and decay both determine and undermine the self in O'Brien's fiction and through this dynamic provide access to the liminality essential to creative imagination. Véronique Bragard suggests regarding waste "positively . . . as the sole type of matter that is independent of our intentionality," providing an opportunity to "rejoin what we perceive as refuse with the productive capacity inherent in matter."[8] As O'Brien told Susan Heller Anderson, writing for her is a kind of illness, an infection.[9] Confronting illness, decay, refuse, and death humbles the human, insists on our relationality, connects us to the rest of creation via the loss of our carefully guarded, inviolable self. The generation of life requires decay, is fertilized by rot and manure. Propagation and degeneration occupy the same continuum.

The categories of waste and dirt enable the imposition of ethics and order, forestalling what Gay Hawkins identifies as the "possibility of unnerving conflation between nature and culture, subject and object and what we call persons and what we call things."[10] One "object" that is also a subject, and thereby threatens this conflation, is the uncanny corpse, which wields allegorical power, according to Walter Benjamin: "Allegories are, in the realm of thoughts, what ruins are in the realm of things."[11] It is through the symbol of the corpse that literature engages with melancholy as a productive energy, according to both Benjamin and Kristeva. Kristeva acknowledges these dark, negative energies when discussing the connections between the abject and artistic production, arguing that literature is rooted in the borderland of the abject, the "fragile border" where identities do not exist,[12] a borderland especially apt for considering O'Brien's artistic production and the way in which the dead or unborn body figures as a fascinating object, even a source of wisdom (as in "The Child," discussed in chapter 3). It is at least as often the bodies of animals—considered to be disposable detritus more readily than is true for human corpses—that can speak meaningfully to O'Brien's characters, for example, in *The Country Girls* (1960), when Baba Brennan's father hits a rabbit while driving the girls home from their convent school from which they are longing to escape. Dr. Brennan throws the dead animal into the car where Cait Brady is seated, and she remembers, "I couldn't see it in the dark, but I knew how it looked and I knew there was blood everywhere on its soft dun-coloured fur."[13] An understanding of the temporary and illusory nature of Cait's feeling of freedom is conveyed here through sympathy with the heedlessly killed animal, a connection experienced somatically rather than intellectually. Similarly, the murderer Michen O'Kane of *In the Forest* (2002) has a troubled relationship to animals, as discussed in chapter 4. He is obsessed by them, visited by them in memories, dreams, and fantasies. He identifies with them and longs for their company but also hates them for their vulnerability, their abjectness, the victim status they share with him, and for this reason, he tortures and kills them; yet he can respond sensitively to the sight of a "dead animal in the road outstretched, its fur and its guts strewn there, a pitifulness, to it as if there was something that cat or fox badly needed to say."[14]

The dead urgently, vividly communicate in O'Brien's work, often, most poignantly, the bodies of beings not recognized as being capable of "speech" when alive, such as fetuses and animals. "The most haunting bird" is how Mary Hooligan, the narrator of O'Brien's novel *Night* (1972), describes an "unborn never-to-be born bird, two-dimensional, sketched on its own placenta, on a wood road that was soft and nobbled from acorns and the roots of various trees": "That bird was more of a bird than any that I have encountered."[15] Mary goes on to enumerate the birds she has seen in bushes, trees, cages, the sky, "dead on motorways," and even "cooked to a fine turn," but, she says, "none have left such an impression upon me as the one I saw on the roadside, two-dimensional, intact in its own placenta, fallen to its death before it actually became born. So near and yet so far."[16] The novel is an unbroken soliloquy delivered by Mary from a bed in a house that she is minding for absent friends. Her frequent musings about cows and birds are unsentimental, often scatological, as in the case of this recollection, prompted by noticing a circle of "birdshit" on the bedroom window, which she describes in detail. The remembered unborn bird troubles the meaning of birth, death, and representation, clears a space for yet-unthought possibilities. This is a "negative" image in more ways than one in its two-dimensionality: a kind of impress, a photonegative of a three-dimensional object, more real than its ideal fulfillment, a dubious original "sketch." Recalling Jack Halberstam's "shadow feminism," discussed in chapters 1 and 2,[17] the bird is an image of failed reproduction that everts the expected chronology, at once chicken and egg. It is sketched on itself, not a preliminary sketch of a future fully achieved, "finished," living bird. It is more than disturbing remains, more than what we can more comfortably define as a corpse, this unborn dead body.

The first appearance of this tiny animal body on soft, root-tangled ground is as rubbish, insignificant detritus. Patricia Yeager, writing about the aesthetics of garbage, sees "interest in detritus as a refusal of similar,"[18] including the self-similarity necessary to subject formation, always predicated on masculinity. This "never-to-be-born bird," described by what it is not, a figure of nonbeing and nondoing, is a kind of undoing, an act of discourse defined by the impossibility of definition. Jacques Derrida's "hauntology" describes this kind of presence that is neither alive nor dead and that both underlies and undermines what we think we know. Derrida's spectrality is not about actual belief in ghosts, as Fredric Jameson has explained, but an understanding that the past lives on and "that the living present is scarcely as self-sufficient as it claims to be."[19] This kind of humility about the limits of conventional subjectivity and human consciousness when confronting death and abjected otherness, even in its most "revolting" forms, including bodily waste, grants imaginative insight and freedom, however forbidden and improper. As mentioned in chapter 3, in *Casualties of Peace* (1966), Willa describes in a letter to her lover her first act of disobedience of her controlling, abusive husband by freeing a cow, who reacts to being released by defecating "contentedly over the new snow": "On its whiteness a treacle-coloured pat spread scutterishly over a big area. It made a crazy shape and liquid trickling out defiled still more snow. How I welcomed it: slime on the unlimited whiteness. A song. My first little rebellion."[20] The shapes of dark liquid on white snow are like notes in a musical score or the words on the blank page where Willa tells this story of communicating a message of defiance. This particularly deliquescent expression of emancipation also recalls the fantasy entertained by Willa's friend Patsy, as discussed in chapter 1, of escaping domestic drudgery by becoming a bird, flying away from "the irritation of fellow birds, eggs, repetitiveness," enjoying sexual freedom: "As the semen darted in her she would fly, letting it spill out in a wild jet of betrayal."[21] The narrator of *August Is a Wicked Month* (1965) expropriates and feminizes semen, conflating it with its female counterpart, while also alluding to O'Brien's prevalent casting of heterosexuality in terms of sadomasochism, as discussed in chapter 2: "She was thinking of egg white in its various stages of being whipped."[22] This image of semen as egg white also appears in unused manuscript pages of *Down by the River*, originally conceived of as a first-person narration, when Mary MacNamara describes being impregnated by her father: "I felt as if egg white was all over me, raw eggs being cracked all over me and the yolks dumped." She also describes her legs as "all slimy."[23]

As Ben Woodard has observed, "humans are well aware of the fact that our individual biological genes consist of the unceremonious mixtures of slimy biological components (sperm and egg); sexual procreation being an obvious example of the disgusting yet generative articulation of slime-as-life and life-as-slime." Despite our awareness, however, as in Kristeva's abject, according to Woodard, "slime remains something to be left behind and forgotten."[24] Unusually, then, the sliminess of embodiment and of sexual reproduction commands the attention of O'Brien and her characters, especially as represented by eggs, a recurring element across the work, identified most frequently with the mother and disgust. Everywhere in O'Brien's fiction, the bird, especially the domesticated hen, whether living or dead, figures as a nexus of concerns, beginning with female embodiment and sexuality, closely associated with the mother, who is the focus of longing and loss, the impetus, according to O'Brien, for her own creative production. The hardworking, oppressed, rural Irish mother of her fiction almost always has chicken meal on her hands and under her nails. She is devoted to the care of a traditional source of independent income for Irish women, "egg money." The mother's labor, on the farm and in the house, is conducted against the backdrop of a yard, a conduit between the interior and exterior spaces of rural women's work and an area distinguished by filth, decay, and rust. In *A Pagan Place* (1970), the yard features "a lodge of slime around the metal lid that concealed the manhole, repeated hen-droppings and chicken droppings."[25] This typical scene of domestic immiseration provides a rationale, both physical and psychological, for the ostensibly ironic aversion to the eating of eggs that is typical of the rural O'Brien mother, from *The Country Girls* to *Down by the River* (1997), a revulsion often passed down to daughters. In *The Country Girls*, Cait "develop[s] a disgust against all eggs,"[26] like her own mother and the mother in the short stories "Rose in the Heart" (1978) and "Paradise" (1968), as well as the mother in *A Pagan Place*, who "couldn't stand eggs although they were her liveli-hood."[27] The strongest expression of maternal disgust about eggs, a reaction tinged with sexual revulsion, occurs in *Down by the River*, when Mary's mother declares, "Never touched an egg. A gug. No not she. Dirty, that dirty bit of snout inside the yolk and the whites smeary, sticking to one."[28] Eggy sliminess expresses sexual and emotional disappointment in *House of Splendid Isolation*, when Josie, as a young woman, has an emotional affair with a priest, which he abruptly ends, crushing her hope of escaping an abusive marriage. Her feeling of hopelessness is experienced as an "awful depletingness, like a big goose-egg being skewered with a knitting needle, the juices leaking and dripping out of her and falling onto the toughened after-grass."[29]

The hen's egg in O'Brien's work can indicate a shared condition of marginal-ization and pain among women, especially when the egg is deformed, "unnatu-ral." The shell-less egg appears in *A Pagan Place*, *Time and Tide*, and *House of Splendid Isolation*,[30] as well as in *The Light of Evening*. In that latter novel, Elea-nora remembers her childhood as she attends the bedside of her mother, Dilly, who is dying of ovarian cancer, a disease related to the human egg (*ovarium* being the Latin for "egg-nut"), a fate that Dilly interprets as a punishment for being a woman. Eleanora recalls "of all things a shell-less egg, which was mushy in the hand and which our workman Shane called a Bugan," that is, an evil spirit.[31] In *Time and Tide* (1992), Nell writes a letter to her dead mother that pic-tures her gathering eggs, a wistful image of loss and regret: "There are moments in which you appear tender, like a snapshot melting, tinged with beauty and grace. . . . You would come down from the yard, your hands smeared with meal, a few eggs in a can, but never enough; they would be dunged and covered in meal and the one above all others that I remember is the shell-less egg, soft as any placenta, its bruisedness a resemblance of us. If only we could have imagined ourselves into each other's depths. If only!"[32] The shell-less egg, which elides the difference between the inside and the outside, evokes women's sexual role in its resemblance to a placenta, and the vulnerability inherent in that role, a "bruised-ness" that each woman feared to reveal to the other, a lost potential source of solidarity.[33] The egg is a potential medium of imagination, an access into the other's experience.

Dung and meal and unnerving sliminess, especially in the case of the shell-less egg, contribute to the perverse, oblique expressiveness for O'Brien of the egg and the hen, as well as all birds, domestic and wild, which feature so promi-nently and regularly in the fiction. Similar to the links found in O'Brien's work,

Hélène Cixous draws connections between the feminine, the bird, filth, and the figure of writing in her essay "Birds, Women, and Writing," in which she uses "women and birds as synonyms," both belonging to the biblical category of the unclean, or "abominable," an association that Cixous seeks to liberate into a condition of jouissance and creativity.[34] While the bird metaphor can promise liberation, it can also act as a figure for vulnerability. The references to placenta and bladder in descriptions of the incompletely formed shell-less egg emphasize the dangerously unstable border between inside and outside. As Mary Douglas has argued, "All margins are dangerous. . . . We should expect the orifices of the body to symbolize its especially vulnerable points. Matter issuing from them is marginal stuff of the most obvious kind. Spittle, blood, milk, urine, feces or tears by simply issuing forth have traversed the boundaries of the body."[35] As discussed in chapter 3, Jane Ussher notes the way in which the particularly leaky fertile female body "signifies association with the animal world, which reminds us of our mortality and fragility, and stands as the antithesis of the clean, contained, proper body."[36]

Parallels between the domestic woman's body and the domestic fowl's body are posited throughout the fiction. The problematic nature of the connection between recalcitrant human and nonhuman female bodies is suggested in O'Brien's story "The Return" (1981), when the child observer learns about a peacock hen who "contracted an ailment that kept her eggs embedded inside her, and though wanting to, she could not give lay. The mistress was childless too."[37] The unruly, withholding female body that fails to fulfill its expected function sometimes requires violent intervention by the mother herself, in her capacity as patriarchal gatekeeper. In A Pagan Place, among the self-mortifications the narrator entertains in expiation of an imagined sexual sin is one inspired by her mother: "you meant to put wire in your throat, the way she poked wire down young chickens when things got in their wind pipe."[38] This horrific image recurs in The Light of Evening when Eleanora looks forward to her first session with a female psychotherapist—clearly a mother substitute—after disappointing experiences with male doctors: "Maybe she could reach in and pull out all the tribulation and the mountainous bile. These thoughts often became fanciful and I pictured different methods, many surgical, then recalled my mother putting wire down the throttles of young chickens, to cure them of their pip. She would cure me of my pip, I thought."[39]

The "mountainous bile" contained in the female body constitutes a threat of contamination, even poison, in scenes of the rural mother preparing the domestic fowl for consumption. These scenes displace the tension between mother and daughter onto the body of the bird, which is often ruined, especially in the early fiction, in the distress of the moment, when the gallbladder is inadvertently burst, spoiling the meat with bile. In A Pagan Place, when a rumor reaches the narrator's parents that she has "seduced" the priest who sexually assaulted her, the mother confronts the daughter with these accusations while preparing a chicken: "The craw that she had been pulling at, burst. The brown tobacco-like content spilt all over the inside wall of the chicken. That was fatal, impaired the flavour, forever."[40] In a similar scene in *Time and Tide*, Nell fights with her mother, who disapproves of her impending divorce: "her mother flared up, poked savagely in the cavern of the bird, and broke the sac, letting the acrid stuff spill all over the pimply flesh."[41] The argument is an especially devastating one, "crammed" with "the unspent rows of many years." Nell recognizes the function of the chicken's body as vehicle for the unspeakable pain of the women's relationship: "if they could say everything, haul every single grievance out of their innards the way her mother had hauled out the chicken entrails, roughly and ferociously, then it might be alright, they might start afresh, poison or no poison."[42] Poison in these scenes gestures to the *pharmakon*, the Greek word for "poison" that also means its opposite, suggesting an unrealizable alternative, the possibility of healing.[43]

In the novel's last pages, Nell articulates the significance of that earlier moment, the destructive intergenerational jealousies inherited by women under patriarchy, when she acknowledges the "base emotion" and "fetid thoughts" aroused by the news that her son's girlfriend is pregnant: "Thinking it, she felt a poison course through her body, brown and off-brown, like water in a clogged ravine. She thought of a day, oh a distant day, years before, when her mother chastising her, no—no, not chastising her, consuming her—had in her wild assault burst a sac while gutting a chicken; the poison was the selfsame colour, tobacco colour, and the selfsame pervading stench. Thinking those things, she thought, too, what pretty names we give to the carniverousness that is called mother."[44] Women's insides are suspect, carnivorous, threatening, treacherous, especially the secret, rotting interior of the mother. Sunday evenings, mothers whisper "to each other about their wombs and their woes," in *Mother Ireland* (1976), assuming an equivalence beyond alliteration,[45] while, of the mother in "Rose in the Heart," the narrator says, "Her womb was sick unto death."[46] The narrator of *A Pagan Place* regards her sister Emma's pregnant body with revulsion and fear: "When you thought of her protrusion, your blood curdled and all of you hurt like you were being scraped inside with a razor."[47] Earlier, before Emma begins to show, when first trying to conceal her pregnancy from her parents, she leaves a doctor's appointment airily dismissing "what a nuisance it all was, one's insides, the inner paraphernalia of one." Her contention that "women's insides were a sea with shapes sliding and colliding, their fertility juices leaking away,"[48] echoes Ussher's observations about the uncontained, improper female body, while Ussher's association between the female body and mortality is echoed in *Time and Tide* by letters from Nell's mother, whose litany of woes, like those recalled in *Mother Ireland*, lead Nell to the conclusion that "cancer was rife, taking root in every woman's body, cancer which her mother referred to as growths, the word itself being too shocking to express. Even women who lived up the mountains suffered from these mysterious growths, women who ate wholesomely, never touched a drink, and slaved all their lives. So it was a woman's ailment."[49] The cultural construction of the female body as inherently pathological inspires a terrifying children's game of "operation" in "A Scandalous Woman" (1974). Nuala, wielding "a big black carving knife," focuses her surgical intentions on breasts, stomachs, and "lower down" and threatens her young patients "that there would be nothing but a shell by the time she had finished, and one wouldn't be able to have babies, or women's complaints ever."[50] The imagined medical interventions are at once punishment and reward, regressing the prepubescent girl to her egg state ("nothing but a shell"), a telling duality or perhaps ambivalence about the realities of female embodiment.

Nuala targets for excision those parts of the female body affected by puberty, the markers of female adulthood, "when childhood innocence may be swapped for the mantle of monstrosity with abject fecundity," as Ussher describes the onset of menarche: "The physical changes of puberty—breasts, pubic hair, curving hips and thighs, sweat, oily skin, and most significantly, menstrual blood—stand as signifiers of feminine excess, of the body as out of control."[51] Menstruation provokes shame, a way in which the female body is pathologized, connected to dirt, repulsion, and the wildness of the animal. A source of social stigma and disgust, traditionally considered "perilous—both magical and poisonous"—menstruation provides an "explanation" for a women's intrinsic state of disability and disorder.[52] Menstrual blood is a source of pollution, filth, an "abomination."[53] As the former political prisoner Brenda Murphy explains, the shame and silence around menstruation was especially intense in O'Brien's native country: "In Ireland you don't speak about your period. You don't even mention the word. My mother hardly ever mentioned it to us and we're a family of eight girls and one boy. You get your period, but you just don't talk about it. It's taboo."[54] However, it is the magical charge of menstrual blood's taboo status, especially the mother's menstrual blood, that makes it an object of fascination, if not veneration, for O'Brien's characters. In Kristevan terms, the typical O'Brien female subject resists the "proper" developmental movement from fascination to shame in treating the maternal body.[55] In the short story "Cords" (1964), Claire spends a tense, unhappy weekend with her disapproving Irish mother, who has traveled out of the country for the first time to visit her daughter in London, where Claire leads what her mother considers a life of dissipation. Distressed about the disastrous attempt at reconciliation, Claire has jumbled memories of forbidden sweets, hidden razor blades, her mother's blood, and the chapel sanctuary light, "a bowl of blood with a flame laid into it."[56] The image recurs in *Time and Tide* in a letter Nell writes to her mother reproaching her for not preparing her daughter for the onset of menses, despite the fact that, as Nell reports, she "had of course seen [her mother's] napkins in the bowls of water, put there to soak, the water blood red, like the oil in the sanctuary lamp, but otherwise carnal."[57] The unnamed protagonist of "Rose in the Heart" similarly blends the sacramental with maternal bleeding: "She was trying to start afresh to wipe out the previous life. She was staggered by the assaults of memory—a bowl with her mother's menstrual cloth soaking in it and her sacrilegious idea that if lit it could resemble the heart of Christ."[58] When the mother is an "illegitimate" one, not blessed by the church, the dirt of her body is more degrading. The narrator of *A Pagan Place* is witness to the developing crisis of her unmarried older sister Emma's pregnancy and shares Emma's obsessive policing of her body's emissions, regularly checking the toilet for blood. After Emma leaves the family home, the narrator and her mother ransack Emma's room for clues about her suspected condition. The narrator discovers a secret, "dirty" in more ways than one: "Under the pillow was the sanitary towel, stained, but not blood stained."[59]

The implicit connection between menstruation and animality colors the memory of the narrator's menarche in *A Pagan Place*: "blood flowed from you came upon you unsuspectingly when you were on a roadside where you had gone to sit and see horses and caravans and animals file past as the travelling circus came to town."[60] In another scene featuring performing animals, Anna, in *The High Road* (1988), recuperates and even sanctifies the connection between human and nonhuman embodiment evoked by menstruation, extending the connection to unite male and female, in her story of attending a bullfight in Madrid:

> It was my first bullfight and I was taken by some very smart people. . . . Afterward, they all gloated and discussed moves and the various passes, I agreed, like a sheep, except that I was bleeding, bleeding from the spectacle. I bled for an entire week, in sympathy, with either the bulls or the horses or the young picadors or the strutting matadors, or the whole ritual, which by its spectacle, its terror, and its gore brought to my mind too vividly Christ's bleeding wounds and the women I knew, including myself, as if Christ was woman and woman was Christ in the bloodied ventricles of herself. Man in woman and woman in man. The impossible.[61]

The "impossibly" sexed Christ here recalls the discussions in chapters 2 and 5, noting the frequency of the figures of transvestism and androgyny in O'Brien's fiction, their appearance at moments of anxiety that can at the same time potentially offer temporary, blessed release from social constraints and the limits of embodiment. Anna tells this bullfight story of fusion with the animal, a melding that also exceeds the boundaries of gender, to Catalina the morning after the two women first have sex and immediately after Catalina pours two bottles of water

over the lovers, "a baptism at once reckless and cleansing."[62] The liquid movement between identities enabled in this natural retreat is, as discussed in chapter 1, temporary, and their relationship is terminated by the violent reassertion of
patriarchal propriety and rights of property.

Anna viscerally empathizes with the painful bloody death of a trapped animal, "the paradigm of the victim,"[63] according to Jean-François Lyotard. The animal's ineluctable victimhood in the eyes of the human, according to Lyotard, is a
result of its inability to bear witness, a silence or silencing, an exclusion from
official forms of discourse shared with women, as discussed in previous chapters.
The slaughtered animal, sympathetically represented, frequently appears in
scenes of entrapment and violence against women, threatened or realized, in
O'Brien's fiction, most recently in *Girl* (2019). When the kidnapped schoolgirls
arrive in their jihadi captors' compound, they are given a uniform, and the
clothes and shoes they arrived in are burned in a ceremonial erasure of their former identities: "Our clothes were piled onto a heap and no sooner had she struck
the match and thrown some diesel in, that the flames shot up. . . . The stench of
the shoes lingered, because they took longer to burn. The smell recalled the skins
of different animals in the slaughterhouses next to the markets, hung up for
curing—pigs, yearlings, goats and sheep."[64] The uncanniness of slaughtered animal remains also affects Nell in *Time and Tide* as she begins to acknowledge the
self-defeating nature of her relationship with Duncan, a man whom she meets
after the end of her marriage and who strands her in Morocco, where the hotel
lobby is decorated with "ravelled skins with the ghosts of the animals they once
were immanent in them."[65] Duncan's tendencies to heedless manipulation and
exploitation are reflected in a scene later witnessed by Nell of men instrumental-
izing a feminized animal head, something to be bartered and handled with contempt: "she saw a young man bargaining for the dead head of a goat, a black severed
head with eyes which were brown, wide-open, and trusting, the jet-black hair
looked silken, girlish, yet the young man dangled it like a rag, waved and shook it at
the vendor, who was obviously asking too much, and dropped it with vehe-
mence."[66] The vulnerable, feminized animal, reduced to its parts, is disposable.

The yoking of women and animals in their function as commodity is important to Jamie, Josie's husband in *House of Splendid Isolation*. Tormented by self-
doubt, Jamie entertains contradictory fantasies of male domination, alternating
between imagining himself a revolutionary warrior and as lord of the Ascendancy manor, to which end he purchases a former Big House, develops upper-
class sporting interests, and marries a woman who is his social "superior" and
will incite jealousy, grace his elegant home, and establish his legacy by producing
sons. His conflicting desires and insecurity, however, drive him to confirm his
new wife's animalized subordination during a hunting trip from which Josie begs
to be excused, sickened by the growing pile of dead rabbits laid at her feet: "Jamie

would not hear of it. He decided to adorn her so two were laid on her shoulders like tippets, the fresh blood warm and simmery. They laughed, the men did, wild, sputtering, half-drunk laughs." Jamie then commands Josie to tell a story: "She refused to tell it, and in her refusal they stood testing one another.... Everything seems to be in waiting, the dead animals, the trees, the fields, and the mountains.... No, she would not tell. She arched her shoulder to ease off one of the animals, to show her sovereignty."[67] Josie's defiant stand among the bodies of slaughtered animals is punished later by a marital rape, performed "in mimicry of riding his favourite filly,"[68] as discussed in chapter 3. The link between male control, reassurance of masculine sovereignty, and hunting is also made in the earlier short story "Mrs Reinhardt" (1978), when the eponymous character recalls a hunting trip taken with her cruel, estranged husband: "The screeches of the dying hares and the dying stags pierced and then haunted her. They were so human. She cried ... when those over-human sounds reached her. He saw it but walked on. It was a man's world, a man's terrain, it was not the place for tears."[69]

Chapter 1 referred to a letter in which O'Brien referred to the "physical, sexual, emotional butchery" experienced in her childhood.[70] "Butchery" is a word and analogue frequently used in her fiction in connection with patriarchal mistreatment of women and girls, as when Maryam in *Girl* refers to the "butchery" being performed on her by her rapists.[71] When the narrator of *A Pagan Place*, a survivor of both sexual and domestic abuse, perpetrated, respectively, by priest and father, decides to join a religious order, she prepares for her retreat from the sensual and sexual world by mortifying her senses in various ways including standing "around the butcher's, watching them chop, chop, chop until the axe got right down to the fat and he had to give a few vital blows, watching the bluebottles, watching things you hated."[72] In the prevailing context of nonhuman animals' only "legitimate" relation to human animals being one of violent, murderous domination, the "animalization" associated with pregnancy can pose culturally specific terror. An extended, unused section of *Down by the River* enacts the full horror of inhabiting a body at the mercy of others. Mary MacNamara, pregnant victim of incestuous rape, is subject to further abusive control and coercion at the hands of religious antiabortion activists who have managed to get custody of her after her attempt to run away. Recalling chapter 3's discussion of the term "porker" to refer to an unborn baby, in the unpublished passage, which recounts Mary's panic about being essentially held captive, the adolescent girl thinks with dread of the "porker" inside her: "Imagining a little pig with pig's feet and the woman's cruelty and her mother's cruelty and now she had a porker, their own blood, a double disaster. Each time when she allowed herself to think on it, she began to feel the beginnings of toes or fingers scraping inside her and soon she became delirious and started to scream and consult mirrors to see her mad eyes like cat's eyes, eyes that registered two things, the imminence of suddenly killing someone or being killed."[73] As Mary and the fetus, engaged in an antagonistic struggle for survival, seem to undergo animal metamorphoses,[74] she desperately fantasizes about being killed "instantly by a stray bullet" so that she would be exonerated "in the eyes of everyone and the terrible thought of the thing in her—she called it the thing—being inside her forever and that made her more delirious so that she began to think of being dead and then being opened up and the thing taken out as she ran from room to room."[75] This new life she is being encouraged, if not bullied, to welcome and celebrate inspires instead thoughts and images of death, including, ironically, those featured on antiabortion literature: "she would come back to knowing that that the thing was in her and they [sic] were only two ways out of it and she could not take either way and there was no friend at all, just people, masses of people deciding different things because of wanting their own way, people shouting at each other, saying they knew what was right, pictures thrust in front of her oozing bloody foetuses."[76]

Pregnancy stages an encounter between life and death that is unique to women's experience. The maternal body creates a being that could destroy her, a monstrous other within, itself hovering on the unstable border between death and life throughout its gestation. Mary MacNamara is experiencing what Kristeva calls "motherhood's impossible syllogism,"[77] the experience of the splitting of the material self, the creation of another, intimate yet alien subjectivity. In the pregnant body, according to Kristeva, the "clean and proper" self becomes filthy, increasingly hybrid, impossible to delimit as singular and identical.[78] Pregnancy in O'Brien's work is a fraught condition that challenges fragile autonomy and reaffirms the problematic limitations of female embodiment under patriarchy. Most pregnancies in O'Brien's fiction are disasters, for rape victims like Mary in *Down by the River* or Maryam in *Girl*, for young unmarried women like Emma in *A Pagan Place* and Pandora in *Time and Tide*, as well as for wives. Maryam fantasizes about drowning her baby, while other women in O'Brien's work opt for abortions, like Josie in *House of Splendid Isolation*. Desperate to frustrate her rapist-husband's imperative that she reproduce, Josie undergoes an illegal, dangerous operation that causes her to bleed "like a pig,"[79] the paradigmatic unclean animal, as discussed in chapter 3. The liminal experiences of pregnancy, birth, and abortion all threaten pollution.[80] In *Time and Tide*, Pandora's experience of abortion emphasizes the uncanny persistence of life in death, which renders materiality a "gungy," gloppy slime, at once human and inhuman, familiar and foreign, present and absent: "But it was not blood and gore, it was it, something gone, a little thing, without trace. For some reason, she thought of it as mesh made liquid, like gunge in a liquidiser, her own blood which she had shed, but not blood alone, morels of flesh in it, the whole caboodle wrapped up in newspaper and put in an incinerator, but not gone, hovering. She could hear it at odd times, a little mewl, a little 'it's me.'"[81] Like "The Child" in *House of Splendid Isolation*, the aborted fetus "hovers" outside of categories of subject and object, appearing in Pandora's account like the unborn bird in *Night*, as formlessness, the quality Douglas ascribes to "the last phase of dirt," a symbol of creative potential. According to Douglas, the formlessness of "boundary transgression is power."[82]

In *Night*, the irreverent Mary Hooligan gleefully transgresses sexual and reproductive boundaries. Recalling one of many brief sexual encounters from her past, she satirizes the "domestic bliss" of conventional family-making by imagining a nonphysical process, mentioned in chapter 5, that emphasizes the monstrous weirdness of creating new life:

> Lately I'm thinking that if I'd kept some of these emissions instead of squandering them so, that if I'd put them in a little jar or a test tube, I could have done a bit of experimentation. . . . No knowing what might have emerged, a plant, gestation, a half-thing, a creature, nearly with animation, on the borders between animal and plant, no feet, moving by means of its cilia, always moving in the daylight, in the dusk, in the dark, with something of the phosphorescence of the glow worm of the ocean, a little wandering infusoria. I could have given it names, mused over names, the way expectant parents do, consulted a book. I forsook all that, the domestic bliss, spurned it.[83]

Throughout the novel, Mary's outrageous, playful oscillation between arousals of disgust and of desire recall Douglas's observation that pollution behaves "like an inverted form of humor," in that the "structure of its symbolism uses comparison and double meaning like the structure of a joke."[84] All life emerges from slime; humans develop from worm-like, footless fetuses, realities acknowledged here in this parody of science-fiction (and real-life) scenarios of creating life without women's troublesome bodies, a masculinist scenario that gained lasting nightmarish fame in Mary Shelley's *Frankenstein*. Denying the messiness and danger of reproduction only guarantees pain and disaster. Woodard maintains that there is "a central disgust to fungus, or plant life in general," because "creeping life is a life stripped down to its mechanisms, processes and breakdowns,"[85] that is, to its materiality, the mortality that women's bodies stand for, as Ussher explains, especially the powerful, threatening pregnant woman's body. Kristeva's interrogation of the "archaeology of impurity" suggests that this disgust is founded in fear of maternal power.[86] Rosi Braidotti similarly argues that traditional theories of monstrous conceptions, like the nonhuman-human hybrid imagined by Mary Hooligan, are "extreme versions of the deep-seated anxiety that surrounds the issue of women's maternal power of procreation in a patriarchal society."[87]

The terror of the mother, experienced culturally and individually, is simultaneously the terror of life, always necessarily moving toward destruction, paradoxical source of creativity and imagination, "the source of our wisdom, the quick of our pain," as Nell says in a letter to her mother. In the letter, Nell recounts her own terrifying first period, which came when cycling with her cousin: "I believed the blood was flowing, flowing wildly and weirdly out of me, and that if I moved, the flow would lead to death, my own death and a memory, oh yes, a memory-death of something long before that had to do with your blood, to do with you and me. It came to me then that you did not have the heart to bear me."[88] This is not the only instance of a woman in O'Brien's fiction projecting backward to her own possible or near abortion or miscarriage. In *The Light of Evening*, Eleanora believes, when pregnant herself, that her mother's "labour pains have got mixed up" with her own.[89] Later, as her mother is dying, Eleanora claims to remember her own conception and near abortion: "Human begetting raw raw raw. A scorching day, the smell of elderflower sickly, sickening. I was inside of you. Being banished. Wave after wave of it hour after hour. Your blood, your bloodshed, and my last stab at living. Between us, that blood feud, blood bond, blood memory. How can I know? I don't know. I do know. . . . I picture you walking back, the heaving desolation, blood running down your thighs, down your legs, jellied blobs of it, and the drops here and there spangling on the dry grass."[90] Merging with the mother, in O'Brien's fiction, is to merge with both life and death: "She the motherless mother, I, the motherless mother, the million, zillion motherless mothers, with all their skinless mysteries. . . . Death for her meant death for us both."[91] This terrifying, exhilarating merging is the source of creativity, as Eleanora recognizes—"Her mother came into everything she wrote"[92]—a kind of possession with implications for all spaces of creation, as comically observed by a male character: "Why, he asked her, did every woman he ever met have to bring her bloody mother into bed?"[93] For Nell in *Time and Tide*, the bloody site of birth and death brings the reality of her mother's death to her. When entering the dead woman's room, she sees her mother's stripped mattress: "She saw bloodstains, too—one huge bloodstain that had formed the shape of a fish, and lesser ones, spatters. She could taste blood, then, feel it going down her throat like a warm, rank cordial."[94] As usual in O'Brien's fiction, the daughter physically shares in her mother's suffering, a reunion with the mother in an ironic return to the oceanic oneness of infancy, mordantly "toasted" with an unusual "cordial." The loss of self in these moments is both terrible and exhilaratingly dangerous, a "put[ting] oneself at risk . . . to open oneself up to indeterminacy in moving towards what is to-come," and what is to-come is always death.[95]

The mother's death is at once momentous and ordinary, often linked with images of dirt, like Nell's confrontation with the soiled mattress, at other times with hen dirt, which assumes a comic poignancy. In *The Country Girls*, when Cait learns that the family home and farm will be sold after her mother's presumed death, she wanders through the house and yard, remembering her mother's sorrows and noting the neglected, ramshackle state of the place: "Mama was gone: the flag was white with hen-dirt and there were thistles and ragwort covering every inch of the front lawn."[96] In *Time and Tide*, Nell's mother dies "suddenly, . . . after feeding the chickens." Her funeral service is held in a "derelict" chapel, where Nell notices "an old crisscross bird's nest hanging askew from one of the rafters."[97] Connecting death to the natural world, as O'Brien so frequently does, recalls Braidotti's observations about the fragile border between life and death and the way in which human preoccupation with our sovereign individuality creates unnecessary fear of what is a natural and not necessarily terminal experience. Braidotti argues that death is the inhuman inside us: "Making friends with the impersonal necessity of death is an ethical way of installing oneself in life as a transient, slightly wounded visitor. We build our life on the crack, so to speak. . . . The proximity to death suspends life, not into transcendence, but rather into the radical immanence of 'just a life,' here and now, for as long as we can take."[98] Such "radical immanence" often characterizes O'Brien's representations of death as intimately caught up in life and natural cycles, a knowledge beyond logic and masculinist prerogatives of reason and language. She shares with her literary hero James Joyce a treatment of death that "disrupts fixed meanings and destabilizes narrative authority, opening the imaginative possibilities that are shut down by normative novelistic endings, ensuring that death functions as a point of reinvention or rebirth."[99] Death, dirt, and poison are all forms of writing beyond the singular authority of any individual.

According to Douglas, "consciousness of the knowledge we owe to our animal being is veiled by the purity rule."[100] Death in O'Brien's fiction is bodily, disorderly, animal, filthy, slimy, and also a source of renewal. In *House of Splendid Isolation*, a deer that is accidentally but seriously injured in a collision with a car is shot by one of the police sergeants in order to end the animal's suffering: "the quick delicate spatters of blood that come out seem not like the consequence of death at all but life-giving totem seeping back into the road that was ruddy from the mountainy rain."[101] In *Time and Tide*, Nell describes her own grief at the death of her young son as producing "reservoirs of tears that seemed hot and life-giving as blood. The blood of death as opposed to the blood of life."[102] The messiness of life and death run together in an impure admixture, and as Douglas has pointed out, "The final paradox of the search for purity is that it is an attempt to force experience into logical categories of non-contradiction. But experience is not amenable and those who make the attempt find themselves in contradiction."[103] The "logic" of separating life, birth, and death is not an organizing principle in O'Brien's fiction. As Spinoza observed, "The world, objects, bodies, my very soul are, at the moment of their birth in decline. This means, in the everyday sense, that they are mortal and bound for destruction. It also means that they form and arise. Nature declines and this is its act of birth."[104] More recently, Braidotti put this sentiment in a different way: "Death is overrated. The ultimate subtraction is after all only another phase in a generative process."[105]

O'Brien's uncompromising engagement with all that we fear and attempt to deny is one source of her power and endurance as a writer. Even the issues we think of as current preoccupations, like pollution and climate change, have been her concerns for decades. As noted in chapter 4, in *The High Road*, the narrator observes that "since Chernobyl the thrushes of the world had been contaminated,"[106] a reference to the global significance of the intimate losses not only figured by but inextricably bound up in the fates of animals and the natural world at large. Another marginal-seeming observation, appearing in a piece titled "Clothes," asserts, "We have botched the planet."[107] The zoonotic virus killing millions of people around the world at the time of this writing, the result of, among other disastrous exploitative practices, the heedless destruction of wild animal habitats, provides grim evidence not only of our inescapable embeddedness in the natural world but also of our willingness to damage that world and our place in it for capital gain, a reality that has always been legible to O'Brien. Despite her erstwhile reputation for writing disposable women's romance fiction, she has been serious from the first, involved since the 1960s in campaigns, for example, against the atom bomb, the Vietnam War, and the treatment of Republican prisoners during the Troubles in Northern Ireland. As she noted many years ago, with characteristically blunt and unsparing imagery, "We inhabit an obscene, declining capitalist society. To draw attention to obscenity in writing is to squeeze puss [*sic*] out of the already existing abscess."[108] She was once thought of as a "dirty" woman and writer, marginalized and pilloried. Douglas says of our "pollution behavior" that it is "the reaction which condemns any object or idea likely to confuse or contradict cherished classification"[109] O'Brien has been "trashed" for most of her career because she has consistently, bravely, resolutely contradicted "cherished classification." In her ninetieth year, O'Brien knows the real obscenity and the sources of the irredeemable filth of the world. She has survived years of abuse and prevailed. A scarred but unbent foremother, she will continue to be a source for generation and inspiration for however long we continue on this botched planet.

NOTES

INTRODUCTION

1. Michael Patrick Gillespie, "She Was Too Scrupulous Always: Edna O'Brien and the Comic Tradition," in *The Comic Tradition in Irish Women Writers*, ed. Theresa O'Connor (Gainesville: University Press of Florida, 1995), 111.

2. Edna O'Brien, *Mother Ireland* (New York: Plume, 1976), 28.

3. Quoted in Richard Woodward, "Edna O'Brien, Reveling in Heartbreak," *New York Times Book Review*, 12 March 1989, 42.

4. "2018 Nabokov Award: Edna O'Brien," February 2018. All references to this prize-giving ceremony quote the CSPAN recording: https://www.c-span.org/video/?c4716342/user-clip -2018-nabokov-award-edna-obrien.

5. For information on the publishing career of the nearly forgotten Ernest Gébler, see Michelle Woods, "Red, Un-Red and Edna: Ernest Gébler, and Edna O'Brien," in *Edna O'Brien: New Critical Perspectives*, ed. Kathryn Laing, Sinéad Mooney, and Maureen O'Connor (Dublin: Carysfort, 2006), 54–67. See also Carlo Gébler's recent book about his father's difficult young life and astonishing self-creation, *The Projectionist: The Story of Ernest Gébler* (Dublin: New Island Books, 2015).

6. Carlo Gébler provides a version of the marriage between these writers as well as information on his father's fascinating family background in *Father and I: A Memoir* (New York: Little, Brown, 2000).

7. Edna O'Brien, *Country Girl: A Memoir* (London: Faber and Faber, 2012), 6.

8. Ellen McWilliams notes that in Martin Amis's 1973 novel *The Rachel Papers*, the narrator sets up O'Brien's novels "as analogous to sex-technique handbooks." McWilliams, *Women and Exile in Contemporary Irish Fiction* (London: Palgrave Macmillan, 2013), 73.

9. Molly McQuade, "PW Interviews," *Publishers Weekly*, 18 May 1992, 48–49.

10. Sian Cain, "Irish Novelist Edna O'Brien Wins Lifetime Achievement Award," *The Guardian*, 26 November 2019, https://www.theguardian.com/books/2019/nov/26/irish-novelist -edna-obrien-wins-lifetime-achievement-award-country-girls-david-cohen-prize-nobel ?fbclid=IwAR2j_7d-IZgOPL2YRlQE5IekwX5kIEaetZEQwshoVPc2xHgIBqPXZoQT9Fg.

11. There is a tendency to overstate O'Briens' uniqueness in this regard. Both Maura Laverty and Mary Lavin wrote about the struggles of Irish Catholic women in rural Ireland in their fiction of the 1940s, though neither achieved the level of international recognition enjoyed by O'Brien. Contemporaries like Eilís Dillon and Una Troy, who also did not achieve the kind of international renown O'Brien did, wrote similarly about the oppression of Irish women and the sometimes brutal and punishing social pressures to conform to narrow sexual roles in a country essentially ruled by the church, but, in Dillon's case, from a different class perspective, or, as in Troy's fiction, using Dublin as a setting rather than rural Ireland.

12. O'Faolain goes on to describe O'Brien as a woman "from a recognisable landscape": "There are other landscapes to be described, and there is not, as far as I know, a woman writer in Ireland today who is willing to describe them for us, to accomplish a description of us." Nuala O'Faolain, *Irish Women and Writing in Modern Ireland* (1985), excerpted in *The Field Day Anthology of Irish Writing*, vol. 5 (Cork: Cork University Press, 2002), 1604–1605. Around this same time, O'Faolain argued that O'Brien "has had a more immediate and sustained

impact on her native audience than any other writer of the twentieth century." O'Faolain, "Edna O'Brien," *Ireland Today*, September 1983, 10.

13. Alix Coleman described O'Brien's performance in *The Hard Way* in terms of her "physical opulence" and delivering her lines with "a banshee wail." Coleman, "Edna O'Brien: Coming Out of Hiding," *TV Times*, 16–22 February 1980, 33.

14. Nick Hornby, "Death Nell," review of *Time and Tide*, *Times Literary Supplement*, 6 September 1992.

15. Anatole Broyard, review of *Arabian Days* for "Books of the Times," *New York Times*, 27 June 1978, http://movies2.nytimes.com/books/00/04/09/specials/obrien-arabian.html.

16. A 2019 *New Yorker* profile by Ian Parker, "Troubles" (14 October, 40–51), in which he represents O'Brien as a self-pitying charlatan determined to misrepresent her life and career, has unfortunately tarnished that decades-long relationship. There has been vigorous criticism of Parker's attack, beginning with Dawn Miranda Sherratt-Bado's 16 October 2019 piece for *The Irish Times*: "Edna O'Brien Profile Is Sexist and Cold Hearted," 6 October 2019, https://www.irishtimes.com/culture/books/the-new-yorker-s-edna-o-brien-profile-is-sexist-and-cold-hearted-1.4051169. After getting no response from the *New Yorker* about answering Parker's article in the magazine's pages, my reaction was published 1 April 2020 by the *Dublin Review of Books*: "A Gratuitous Assault," https://www.drb.ie/essays/a-gratuitous-assault, an article that was shared several thousand times on social media, a phenomenon reported on by Dalya Alberge for *The Observer*: "Scholars Hit Back over New Yorker 'Hatchet Job' on Edna O'Brien," 12 April 2020, https://www.theguardian.com/books/2020/apr/12/scholars-hit-back-over-new-yorker-hatchet-job-on-edna-obrien. When recently asked about the *New Yorker* profile, in a 9 May 2020 interview by John Self for *The Irish Times*, the Canadian author Richard Ford replied, "Well, it was crap. It was crap, is what it was. I think the poor writer was defensive, he was geared up to find someone who was formidable and beyond his ken, and he did find someone who was formidable and beyond his ken. And I think he just wasn't up to the task. I mean, to hold against her the things that he held against her, some little peevish indiscretions that he winkled out of her history. She's already written about all that stuff. Who cares?" "In America, No One Will Stay at Home," https://www.irishtimes.com/culture/books/richard-ford-in-america-no-one-will-stay-at-home-1.4239919?fbclid=IwAR1C_vZ4exyFccXVjURb6cZ_Vzn_VqVK4tNetgQGUQgnEDvTzAVQWWS2nHY.

17. Miller to O'Brien, 27 July 1977, Edna O'Brien Papers, Manuscript, Archives and Rare Book Library, Emory University, Series 1: Correspondence, 1939–2000; Subseries 1.1, Box 8, Folder 11.

18. Salinger to O'Brien, April 29, 1968, Edna O'Brien Papers, Manuscript, Archives and Rare Book Library, Emory University, Series 1: Correspondence, 1939–2000; Subseries 1.1, Box 11, Folder 3.

19. Dan O'Brien, "'A Harp in the Hallway': Edna O'Brien and Jewish-Irish Whiteness in *Zuckerman Unbound*," *Philip Roth Studies*, Fall 2016, 6–7.

20. Munro to O'Brien, 28 February 1991, Edna O'Brien Papers, Manuscript, Archives and Rare Book Library, Emory University, Series 1: Correspondence, 1939–2000; Subseries 1.1, Box 8, Folder 30.

21. Mary Gordon, "Risks of Loving," review of *A Rose in the Heart*, *Washington Post Book World*, 8 April 1979, L1, L4.

22. Before the novel's publication in April 1960, an excerpt was published in the British *Harper's Bazaar* in January of that year.

23. O'Brien, *Country Girl*, 135.

24. In one of history's ironies, Haughey would go on to found the Aosdána association.

25. Quoted by John Horgan, "An Irishman's Diary," *The Irish Times*, 1 October 2019, 15. My thanks to Tadhg Foley for alerting me to this piece.

26. Julia Carlson, *Banned in Ireland: Censorship and the Irish Writer* (Athens: University of Georgia Press, 1990), 72.

27. In a letter to O'Brien from her publisher Iain Hamilton, dated 4 May 1960, he pastes a clipping of Kennedy's review at the bottom of the page after closing, "Meanwhile, here is a copy for you of Maurice Kennedy's splendid review in *The Irish Times*." Edna O'Brien Papers, Manuscript, Archives and Rare Book Library, Emory University, Series 1: Correspondence, 1939–2000; Subseries 1.1, Box 5, Folder 7.

28. McAvoy to O'Brien, 21 June 1960, Edna O'Brien Papers, Manuscript, Archives and Rare Book Library, Emory University, Series 1: Correspondence, 1939–2000; Subseries 1.1, Box 30, Folder 81.

29. Dorothy Parker, review of *The Country Girls*, *Esquire*, August 1960, 16.

30. "New Fiction," *The Irish Times*, 15 December 1960.

31. Quoted on the cover of the 1962 Penguin edition of the novel.

32. V. S. Naipaul, "New Novels," *New Statesman*, 16 July 1960, 97.

33. This was possibly humorous hyperbole intended to ironicize his unusual level of enthusiasm for the book, as there is no evidence such a prize ever existed. The joking intention is further suggested by the fact that the only source I have found for the "prize" is a blurb on a Hutchinson's hard back 1961 edition of *The Country Girls*.

34. O'Brien's recent resurgence in popularity has encouraged the reissue of a number of novels that were long out of print, such as Picador's 2019 editions of *Lantern Slides*, *Time and Tide*, and *A Pagan Place*.

35. O'Brien's impression of this is different. Speaking to Miriam O'Callaghan in 2015, she argued, "[McGahern] was always popular in Leitrim. I was never popular in Scariff." "Miriam Meets," RTÉ Radio One, 15 November 2015.

36. Anne Enright, "Diary," *London Review of Books* 35, no. 6 (21 March 2013): 42–43.

37. Maggie Smith and Kate Nelligan have starred in productions of the play.

38. Virginia Woolf, *A Room of One's Own* (New York: Harcourt Brace Jovanovich, 1989), 67.

39. Little has changed. Joe Cleary dismisses O'Brien's work as being insufficiently politically engaged, failing to recognize the legitimacy of gender and sexual politics or even the political valence of family structure and challenges to it in the context of mid-twentieth-century Ireland. Cleary, *Outrageous Fortune: Capitalism and Culture in Modern Ireland* (Dublin: Field Day, 2007), 99–104.

40. Anne Fogarty, "Deliberately Personal? The Politics of Identity in Contemporary Irish Women's Writing," *Nordic Irish Studies* 1 (2002): 2.

41. Benedict Kiely, "Ireland," *Kenyon Review* 30, no. 4 (1968): 465. Recently Clair Wills has echoed and updated Kiely's observation: "It should not be surprising that the novels were burned and banned—they were accurately read as reflecting a new state of the nation, one in which the repression of the church, and its many related institutions, would be challenged." Wills, "Coda: Edna O'Brien and Eimear McBride," in *Ireland in Transition, 1980–2020*, ed. Eric Falci and Paige Reynolds (Cambridge: Cambridge University Press, 2020), 298.

42. Edna O'Brien, notes from an unidentified interview, Edna O'Brien Papers, Manuscript, Archives and Rare Book Library, Emory University, Series 6: Printed Material, 1958–1999; Subseries 6.2, Writings about O'Brien, Profiles and Interviews, Box 89, Folder 15.

43. Eithne Strong, review of *A Pagan Place*, *Irish Press*, 14 April 1973.

44. "Ernest and Edna, Living in Different Pasts," Londoner's Diary, *The Standard*, 22 April 1988.

45. Stan Gebler Davies, "The Trouble with Edna," review of *Time and Tide, London Evening Standard*, 19 October 1992.

46. Stan Gebler Davies, *Sunday Independent*, weekly column, 25 October 1992.

47. Though both writers, as Michael G. Cronin has observed, were "significant figures in the reform of literary censorship." Cronin, *Impure Thoughts: Sexuality, Catholicism, and Literature in Twentieth-Century Ireland* (Manchester: Manchester University Press, 2012), 177.

48. As O'Brien noted in a 2014 interview with Cole Morton, "I think I had to get old. I had to have my hip surgery before they would give me the credit." Morton, "Edna O'Brien: I Had to Grow Old before They'd Give Me Credit," *Sunday Independent*, 5 October 2014, https://www.independent.co.uk/news/people/edna-obrien-i-had-to-grow-old-before-theyd-give-me-credit-9774962.html.

49. Caleb Crain, "Edna O'Brien Investigates the Varieties of Murderous Experiences," review of *In the Forest, New York Times*, 7 April 2002, sec. 7, p. 11. Complaints in a similar vein include Paul Majkut's assessments of her novels, in an article providing summary reviews of new releases, including, in this case, *August Is a Wicked Month*, as "You read one, you read 'em all" *Bestsellers*, 15 June 1965, 135–136) and a review of *Night* that asks with apparent exasperation whether it is "possible that virtually nothing new can be thought or said about the emptiness of lives that are just plain empty?" Charles Lam Markmann, "Nothing above the Belt?," *The Nation*, 14 May 1973, 631.

50. Julia O'Faolain, review of *A Scandalous Woman, New York Times Book Review*, 22 February 1974, 3–4.

51. Nick Hornby, "Yearning and Canoodling," review of *Lantern Slides, Sunday Correspondent*, 3 June 1990, 39.

52. Sarah Hughes, "Déjà Vu in Dublin and New York," review of *The Light of Evening, The Observer*, 15 October 2006, https://www.theguardian.com/books/2006/oct/15/fiction.features.

53. Benedict Kiely, "The Whores on the Half-Doors," in *Conor Cruise O'Brien Introduces Ireland.*, ed. Owen Dudley Edwards (New York: McGraw Hill, 1969), 158.

54. The trilogy consists of *The Country Girls* (1960), *The Lonely Girl* (1962; reissued in 1964 as *Girl with Green Eyes*), and *Girls in Their Married Bliss* (1964).

55. The girls' predicament reflects reality, according to Cronin, for "the modern late twentieth-century subject," which is "a damaged one, trapped between old-fashioned bourgeois repressions and the empty stimuli of modern culture industries and commodified society" (*Impure Thoughts*, 194).

56. Cronin perceptively counters this too-common superficial reading of O'Brien's fiction, when he suggests that her "astringent and anaphrodisiac style of sexual writing offers a riposte to the delusionary exuberance provided by her literary antecedents" (ibid.).

57. David Streitfeld, "Edna O'Brien's Hard Edge of Heartbreak," *International Herald Tribune*, 31 July 1992.

58. Some examples include Bernard Bergonzi's review of *August is a Wicked Month*, which he calls a "sad, silly, unpleasant story," in *New York Review of Books*, 3 June 1965, 19; John Broderick, who describes O'Brien as a "silly and sloppy writer" in his review of *Mother Ireland, The Critic*, Winter 1976, 72; Robert Hogan who, in "Old Boys, Young Bucks, and New Women: The Contemporary Irish Short Story," his contribution to *The Irish Short Story: A Critical History*, ed James F Kilroy (Boston: Twayne, 1984), describes O'Brien's continuing "deterioration" as making her "a sillier and lesser writer than she could have been," 204; and, most infamously, Peggy O'Brien's essay, "The Silly and the Serious: An Assessment of Edna O'Brien," *Massachusetts Review* 28 (1987), *passim*.

59. Stuart Wavell, "Finding Company the Hard Way," *The Guardian*, 25 January 1980, 10.

60. Jan Moir, "Doing the Real Thing," *The Guardian*, 16 September 1992, 37. In a later 1990 interview with Julie Carlson, she complained, "If you happen to have your hair done, well then you can't be a serious writer" (*Banned in Ireland*, 73).

61. Rachel Cooke, interview of Edna O'Brien, *The Guardian*, 6 February 2011, https://www .theguardian.com/books/2011/feb/06/edna-obrien-ireland-interview; Mary Kenny, review of *Country Girl*, *Literary Review*, November 2012, https://literaryreview.co.uk/farewell-to -county-clare.

62. Kiely, "Whores on the Half-Doors," 159.

63. Bernard Bergonzi, "Total Recall," review of *Casualties of Peace*, *New York Review of Books*, 24 August 1967, 37.

64. John Mellors, review of *Johnny, I Hardly Knew You*, *The Listener* 98 (4 August 1977): 158. This is one of the typically outraged reviews of this novel, as will be noted in chapter 1.

65. Sean McMahon, "A Sex by Themselves: An Interim Report on the Novels of Edna O'Brien," *Éire-Ireland* 2, no. 1 (1967): 79.

66. Anatole Broyard, "The Rotten Luck of Kate and Baba," review of *Country Girls Trilogy*, *New York Times Review of Books*, 11 May 1986, 12. Derek Mahon, a career-long supporter, when writing about *A Pagan Place*, the last of her novels to be banned in Ireland, similarly speaks of O'Brien's "fierce feminism, her passionate love-hate for the place [that] rings bells of memory and self-recognition for a great number of people. . . . She is real and beautifully bannable." Mahon, "This Dump, This Dump—Derek Mahon Discusses Edna O'Brien's New Novel," review of *A Pagan Place*, *The Listener*, 23 April 1970.

67. J. O'Faolain, review of *A Scandalous Woman*.

68. Pearl K. Bell, "Women on Women," *New Leader*, 9 December 1974, 5.

69. Connery to O'Brien from Connery, 14 April 1967, Edna O'Brien Papers, Manuscript, Archives and Rare Book Library, Emory University, Series 1: Correspondence, 1939–2000; Subseries 1.1, Box 3, Folder 10. De Valera, one of the founders of the modern Irish state who served as the country's president and taoiseach (prime minister), was a notoriously conservative Roman Catholic.

70. Frank Packenham (Earl of Longford), *Pornography: The Longford Report* (London: Hodder and Stoughton, 1972), 65–66.

71. William Trevor, "Return to the Womb," *Manchester Guardian Weekly*, 13 June 1976, 21.

72. Derek Mahon, review of *A Pagan Place*, *New Statesman*, 4 June 1976, 747.

73. Quoted in Nicholas Wroe, "Country Matters," *The Guardian*, 2 October 1999, https:// www.theguardian.com/books/1999/oct/02/books.guardianreview8.

74. Declan Kiberd, citation on Edna O'Brien's receiving the award of the Ulysses Medal from University College Dublin, 15 June 2006, https://www.ucd.ie/news/jun06/060906_ulysses _medal_2.htm.

75. Clare Boylan, "Edna O'Brien as Others See Her," *Irish Independent*, 29 April 1989.

76. Anne Enright, review of *Country Girl: A Memoir*, *The Guardian*, 12 October 2012, https:// www.theguardian.com/books/2012/oct/12/country-girl-edna-obrien-review.

77. For details of the program, please see UCD School of English Drama Film, "'Infamous, Influential, Beloved': Irish Writers Celebrate Edna O'Brien," 17 September 2018, https://www .ucd.ie/englishdramafilm/newsandevents-archive/irishwriterscelebrateednaobrien/.

78. Quoted in Carlson, *Banned in Ireland*, 71.

79. Edna O'Brien, "Beckett at 80," *Sunday Times Magazine*, 6 April 1985, 53.

80. Myles McWeeney, "Welcome Home to a Not-So-Wicked Lady," *Irish Independent*, 27 April 1989, 8.

81. O'Brien, "Beckett at 80," 53.

82. Andrew Duncan, "The Andrew Duncan Interview," *The Guardian*, 2 October 1999, 6–7.

83. Richard Holmes, "Poetry International," *London Times*, 22 June 1972, 10.

84. Woodward, "Edna O'Brien," 42.

85. Barbara Rader, "Those Clear Eyes Hide a People Watcher," *New York Times*, 2 June 1965, 57.

86. Peggy O'Brien, 485, 474.

87. O'Brien vehemently objected to the characterization of relying heavily on autobiography in a 1985 interview, saying it is "a tag attached" to her. Miriam Gross, "The Pleasure and the Pain," *The Observer*, 14 April 1985.

88. Amanda Greenwood, *Edna O'Brien* (Devon, UK: Northcote House, 2003), 7.

89. O'Brien, *Mother Ireland*, 58.

90. Julia C. Obert, "Mothers and Others in Edna O'Brien's *The Country Girls*," *Irish Studies Review* 20, no. 3 (August 2012): 284. Mary Leland expressed similar sentiments about O'Brien's fiction: "Why must so many Irish readers cut her down to size by relating her only to the proportions and perspectives of her native country? These are often meagre proportions, perspectives foreshortened by lack of ambition or of courage." Leland, "Stories Which Transcend the Limits of Home," review of *Lantern Slides*, *Sunday Tribune*, 17 June 1990.

91. See Eileen Morgan, "Mapping Out a Landscape of Female Suffering: Edna O'Brien's Demythologizing Novels," *Women's Studies: An Interdisciplinary Journal* 29, no. 4 (2000): 449–476; Kristi Byron, "In the Name of the Mother . . . : The Epilogue of Edna O'Brien's *Country Girls Trilogy*," *Women's Studies: An Interdisciplinary Journal* 31, no. 4 (2002): 447–465; Rebecca Pelan, "Reflections on a Connemara Dietrich," in Laing, Mooney, and O'Connor, *Edna O'Brien*, 12–73; Greenwood, *Edna O'Brien*, 24, 51, 67; Bertrand Cardin, "Words Apart: Epigrams in Edna O'Brien's Novels," in Laing, Mooney, and O'Connor, *Edna O'Brien*, 54–67; Elizabeth Chase, "Re-writing Genre in the *Country Girls Trilogy*," *New Hibernia Review* 14, no. 3 (Autumn 2010): 91–105; Elizabeth Jane Dougherty, "'Never Tear the Linnet from the Leaf': The Feminist Intertextuality of Edna O'Brien's *Down by the River*," *Frontiers: A Journal of Women's Studies* 13, no. 3 (2010): 77–102.

92. Peter Stanford, "Stranger than Fiction," review of *In the Forest*, *The Independent*, 28 May 2002.

93. Mary Robinson, "A Life Well Lived, Well Told," review of *Country Girl*, *The Irish Times*, 29 September 2012, https://www.irishtimes.com/culture/books/a-life-well-lived-well-told-1.541231.

94. Penny Peyrick, "And Another Thing—Let's Have Lunch," *London Times*, 3 June 1985, 9.

95. Éilis Ní Dhuibhne, review of *The Little Red Chairs*, *The Irish Times*, 24 October 2015, https://www.irishtimes.com/culture/books/the-little-red-chairs-by-edna-o-brien-1.2403493.

96. As Dan O'Brien has noted, the late fiction "not only gives voice to the Irish diaspora, but also sets it in conversation with other mass displacements." O'Brien, *Fine Meshwork: Philip Roth, Edna O'Brien, and Jewish-Irish Literature* (Syracuse, NY: Syracuse University Press, 2020), 167.

97. Kirsty Lang, "Edna O'Brien on Her Novel *Girl*, Her First, *The Country Girls*, and Her Career in Between," BBC, 26 August 2019, https://www.bbc.co.uk/sounds/play/m0007wss.

98. As reported in the 2019 BBC One documentary *Edna O'Brien: Fearful . . . and Fearless*, https://www.bbc.co.uk/programmes/m0006pjj.

99. Alex Clark, "A Masterclass of Storytelling," review of *Girl*, *The Guardian*, 6 September 2019, https://www.theguardian.com/books/2019/sep/06/girl-edna-obrien-review.

100. Terence Rafferty, "O'Brien's Lonely Girls," review of *Girl*, *The Atlantic*, September 2019, 38.

101. Lynn Chancer, *Sadomasochism in Everyday Life: The Dynamics of Power and Powerlessness* (New Brunswick, NJ: Rutgers University Press, 1992).

102. Edna O'Brien, "A Reason of One's Own," Saturday Review, *Sunday Times*, 30 September 1970, 10.

103. Carlson, *Banned in Ireland*, 77.

104. Eimear McBride, introduction to *The Country Girls Trilogy* (London: Faber and Faber, 2017), ix–x.

105. Quoted in Emily Stokes, "Edna O'Brien Has Been Me-Too-ing for Fifty Years," *New Yorker*, 5 March 2018, https://www.newyorker.com/magazine/2018/03/05/edna-obrien-has -been-metoo-ing-for-fifty-years.

106. Anne Enright, "Murderous Loves," review of *The Light of Evening*, *The Guardian*, 14 October 2006, https://www.theguardian.com/books/2006/oct/14/featuresreviews.guardian review18.

107. Anne Enright, "A Bright Light amid Hearts of Darkness," review of *Girl*, *The Irish Times*, 7 September 2019, 20–21.

CHAPTER 1. ANTI-OEDIPAL DESIRES

1. BBC Archive, "1965: Panorama in Ireland: Irish Censorship," 5 April 2018, https://www .facebook.com/BBCArchive/videos/550571951982506/?v=550571951982506.

2. Letter to O'Brien from George Walsh, *Cosmopolitan* Managing Editor, 27 January 1967, quoting Gurley Brown: "I think Edna would be swell if she has feelings about being a daddy's girl. If she hasn't she might make it up, of course." O'Brien responds to Walsh in a letter dated 20 April 1967. Edna O'Brien Papers, Manuscript, Archives and Rare Book Library, Emory University, Series 1: Correspondence, 1939–2000; Subseries 1.1, Box 2, Folder 80.

3. Patricia Coughlan, "Killing the Bats: O'Brien, Abjection, and the Question of Agency," in *Edna O'Brien: New Critical Perspectives*, ed. Kathryn Laing, Sinéad Mooney, and Maureen O'Connor (Dublin: Carysfort, 2006), 177.

4. Edna O'Brien, "Parents," TS, Edna O'Brien Papers, Manuscript, Archives and Rare Book Library, Emory University, Series 3: Prose 1960–1999; Subseries 3.2, Box 31, Folder 10.

5. Ibid.

6. Ellen McWilliams has persuasively argued that this particular dynamic undergoes a change in O'Brien's 2006 novel, *The Light of Evening*, in which "the possibility of a more positive maternal influence emerges; the mother figure is shown to have her own finely honed artistic sensibility as well as having an active, productive—rather than simply censoring or repressive—influence." McWilliams, *Women and Exile in Contemporary Irish Fiction* (London: Palgrave Macmillan, 2013), 97.

7. For more on the institution of the Irish family, see, for example, Linda Connolly, ed., *The "Irish" Family* (London: Routledge, 2015); Gerardine Meaney, *Gender, Ireland and Cultural Change: Race, Sex and Nation* (London: Routledge, 2010); Clair Wills, "Women, Domesticity and the Family: Recent Feminist Work in Irish Cultural Studies," *Cultural Studies* 15, no. 1 (2001): 33–57; Michael G. Cronin, *Impure Thoughts: Sexuality, Catholicism, and Literature in Twentieth-Century Ireland* (Manchester: Manchester University Press, 2012).

8. Gerardine Meaney, *Sex and Nation: Women in Irish Culture and Politics* (Dublin: Attic, 1991), 191. Wills has similarly noted that in "this period of consolidation of the rural Catholic nationalist ideology, . . . the ideological construction of the familial sphere was intimately bound up with the public image of Ireland as a traditional rural society" ("Women, Domesticity and the Family," 35, 37).

9. Similar discoveries are expected in another mother and baby home in County Cork, Bessborough, run by the Congregation of the Sacred Hearts of Jesus and Mary, infamous even in the early twentieth century for its shocking death rate: Connall Ó Fátharta, "Burial Place of

Over 800 Children Who Died in Bessborough Unknown," *Irish Examiner*, 17 April 2019, https://www.irishexaminer.com/breakingnews/ireland/burial-place-of-over-800-children -who-died-in-bessborough-unknown-read-commissions-findings-on-mother-and-baby -homes-918325.html.

10. This practice was the subject of a recent expose by RTÉ Investigates. Aoife Hegarty, "Who Am I? The Story of Ireland's Illegal Adoptions," *RTÉ: Ireland's National Public Service Media*. 5 March 2021. https://www.rte.ie/news/investigations-unit/2021/0302/1200520-who -am-i-the-story-of-irelands-illegal-adoptions/.

11. Edna O'Brien, *Girls in Their Married Bliss* (London: Penguin, 1975), 115.

12. Edna O'Brien, *August Is a Wicked Month* (London: Penguin, 1967), 26–27.

13. Edna O'Brien, "House of My Dreams," in *A Scandalous Woman* (London: Penguin, 1974), 146. First published in the *New Yorker*, 12 August 1974.

14. Edna O'Brien, *A Pagan Place* (London: Penguin, 1971), 133–134.

15. For an insightful analysis of the challenge of the X case to dominant notions of Irish iden-tity and O'Brien's handling of the multiple crises instigated by the scandal, see Jane Elizabeth Dougherty, "From Invisible Child to Abject Maternal: Crises of Knowledge in Edna O'Brien's *Down by the River*," *Critique* 53 (2012): 393–409.

16. As reported by the author in an interview with Caroline Walsh, "Edna O'Brien: Miles from Melancholy," *The Irish Times*, 11 June 1986. In an earlier interview with Deirdre Purcell, the novelist also discussed the case of Ann Lovett, a fifteen-year-old who died giving birth in a grotto at the feet of a statue of the Virgin Mary. O'Brien notes that "it's like one of my sto-ries." Deirdre Purcell, "Edna O'Brien: Look, I Have Come Through," *The Sunday Tribune*, 22 July 1984.

17. Edna O'Brien, *The Country Girls* (London: Penguin, 1975), 171.

18. Edna O'Brien, "Rose in the Heart," in *Mrs Reinhardt and Other Stories* (London: Penguin, 1978), 109.

19. Edna O'Brien, *Time and Tide* TS [Excluded section] (1992), Edna O'Brien Papers, Manu-script, Archives and Rare Book Library, Emory University, Series 3: Prose 1960–1999; Sub-series 3.2, Box 40, Folder 1.

20. Helen Thompson, "Uncanny and Undomesticated: Lesbian Desire in Edna O'Brien's 'Sister Imelda' and *The High Road*," *Women's Studies: An Interdisciplinary Journal* 32, no. 21 (2003): 23.

21. Edna O'Brien, *Casualties of Peace* (London: Penguin, 1958), 27.

22. Edna O'Brien, *Night* (London: Penguin, 1974), 10.

23. Edna O'Brien, "Manhattan Medley," in *Saints and Sinners* (London: Faber and Faber, 2011), 137.

24. O'Brien, "House of My Dreams," 152.

25. Edna O'Brien, *Johnny I Hardly Knew You* (London: Penguin, 1986), 24.

26. Edna O'Brien, *The Light of Evening* (London: Weidenfeld and Nicolson, 2006), 22.

27. Edna O'Brien, *Country Girl: A Memoir* (London: Faber and Faber, 2012), 67.

28. Elaine Marks, "Lesbian Intertextuality," in *Homosexualities and French Literature: Cultural Contexts / Critical Texts*, ed. Elaine Marks and George Stambolian (Ithaca, NY: Cornell Uni-versity Press, 1979), 372.

29. Adrienne Rich, "Compulsory Heterosexuality and Lesbian Existence," *Signs* 5, no. 4 (Summer 1980): 650.

30. Nell Dunn, *Talking to Women* (London: Silver, 2018), 85.

31. Edna O'Brien, *The High Road* (London: Farrar, Straus and Giroux, 1988), 156.

32. Dunn, *Talking to Women*, 80.

33. Rich, "Compulsory Heterosexuality and Lesbian Existence," 648–649.

34. Ibid., 650.

35. Ibid., 637.

36. Nuala O'Faoilain, *Are You Somebody?* (Dublin: New Island Books, 1966), 58.

37. Caroline Moorehead, "Fresh as First Love," review of *The Country Girls, Girl with Green Eyes* and *Mrs Reinhardt and Other Stories, London Times,* 3 February 1980, 7.

38. O'Brien, *Country Girl,* 204.

39. Israel Shenker, "A Novelist Speaks of Work and Love," *New York Times,* 2 January 1973, 42.

40. Edward Pearce, "Words with No Wisdom," review of *House of Splendid Isolation, The Guardian,* 12 July 1994, 18.

41. Shusha Guppy, "The Art of Fiction No. 82: Interview with Edna O'Brien," *Paris Review* 92 (1984): 38.

42. O'Brien, *Country Girls,* 8.

43. Ibid., 6.

44. Heather Ingman, *Twentieth-Century Fiction by Irish Women: Nation and Gender* (Aldershot, UK: Ashgate, 2007), 115–116.

45. Julia Kristeva, "Stabat Mater," *Poetics Today* 6, nos. 1–2 (1985): 149.

46. For more on the connections and parallels to be drawn between exile from the mother country and withdrawal and alienation from the mother, see: Ellen McWilliams, "Making It Up with the Motherland: Revision and Reconciliation in Edna O'Brien's *The Light of Evening,*" *Women: A Cultural Review* 22, no 1 (2011): 50–68; and Tom Murray, "Edna O'Brien and Narrative Diaspora Space." *Irish Studies Review,* special issue "New Perspectives on Women and the Irish Diaspora" 21, no 1, (2013): 85–98.

47. Julie Wheelwright, "Edna O'Brien, The Mother of Invention," *The Independent,* 29 September 2006, https://www.independent.co.uk/arts-entertainment/books/features/edna-obrien-the-mother-of-invention-417886.html.

48. Edna O'Brien, *Mother Ireland* (New York: Plume, 1976), 15.

49. Sandra Manoogian Pearce, "An Interview with Edna O'Brien," *Canadian Journal of Irish Studies* 22, no. 2 (December 1996): 6.

50. O'Brien, *Mother Ireland,* 1.

51. Teresa de Lauretis, "Sexual Indifference and Lesbian Representation," *Theatre Journal* 40, no. 2 (May 1988): 158.

52. See, for example, essays by Coughlan, "Killing the Bats," 171–195; Mary Burke, "Famished: Alienation and Appetite in Edna O'Brien's Early Novels," 219–240; Shirley Peterson, "'Meaniacs' and Martyrs: Sadomasochistic Desire in Edna O'Brien's *The Country Girls* Trinity," 151–170; and Sinéad Mooney, "'Sacramental Sleeves': Fashioning the Female Subject in Edna O'Brien's Fiction," 196–218, all in Laing, Mooney, and O'Connor, *Edna O'Brien;* Wanda Balzano, "Godot Land and Its Ghosts: The Uncanny Genre and Gender of Edna O'Brien's 'Sister Imelda,'" 93–109; and Helen Thompson, "Hysterical Hooliganism: O'Brien, Freud, and Joyce," 31–57, both in *Wild Colonial Girl: Essays on Edna O'Brien,* ed. Lisa Colletta and Maureen O'Connor (Madison: University of Wisconsin Press, 2006).

53. Judith (Jack) Halberstam, *The Queer Art of Failure* (Durham, NC: Duke University Press, 2011), 123.

54. Ibid., 71.

55. Ibid.

56. Dunn, *Talking to Women,* 62.

57. Kristeva, "Stabat Mater," 149.

58. O'Brien, "Rose in the Heart," 111. The title was shortened when included in subsequent short story collections.

59. Ibid., 112.

60. O'Brien, *Country Girl*, 4.

61. Dunn, *Talking to Women*, 62.

62. Philip Roth, *Shop Talk: A Writer and His Colleagues and Their Work* (Boston: Houghton Mifflin, 2001), 111.

63. O'Brien to Carlo Gébler, n.d., Edna O'Brien Papers, Manuscript, Archives and Rare Book Library, Emory University, Series 1: Correspondence, 1939–2000; Subseries 1.2, Family Correspondence, Box 13, Folder 9.

64. Ingman, *Twentieth-Century Fiction*, 256.

65. Cheryl Herr, "The Erotics of Irishness," *Critical Inquiry* 17 (1990): 6.

66. Gilles Deleuze and Félix Guattari, *Kafka: Toward a Minor Literature*, trans. Dana Polan (Minneapolis: University of Minnesota Press, 1986), 64.

67. Pearl K. Bell, "Women on Women," *New Leader*, 9 December 1974, 5.

68. Anthony West, review of *Casualties of Peace, Vogue Books*, May 1967, 58.

69. Edna O'Brien Papers, Manuscript, Archives and Rare Book Library, Emory University, Series 7 audiovisual material, "Public Radio Book Show," 30 December 1990 (original: audio cassette; digital/digitized copy available in the Reading Room: id b7sq3), subseries 7.21 AV2.

70. O'Brien, *Country Girl*, 24.

71. For a detailed treatment of food and the body in O'Brien's work, see M. Burke, "Famished."

72. O'Brien, *Night*, 97.

73. Edna O'Brien, "Savages," in *A Fanatic Heart: Selected Stories* (New York: Plume, 1985), 75.

74. O'Brien, "Rose in the Heart," 125.

75. Edna O'Brien, "Over," in *A Scandalous Woman and Other Stories* (London: Penguin, 1976), 63.

76. Halberstam, *Queer Art*, 123.

77. Gébler used this fictional death—of a boy who shared the name of the couple's youngest child, Mark—as one of the signs of his ex-wife's unfitness as a mother when suing for sole custody of their sons.

78. O'Brien, *Johnny*, 17.

79. O'Brien, *The Light of Evening*, 33.

80. O'Brien, *Casualties of Peace*, 44.

81. Rich, "Compulsory Heterosexuality and Lesbian Existence," 650.

82. Edna O'Brien, *The Little Red Chairs* (London: Faber and Faber, 2015), 91.

83. Ibid., 96.

84. O'Brien, *Johnny*, 10.

85. Ibid., 59. The novel's unusually bitter tone might explain the intensely negative reviews. According to Susan Heller Anderson, "reactions to the book were divided by gender—the female reviewers appreciated it and the males did not." Anderson, "For Edna O'Brien, Writing Is a Kind of Illness," *New York Times*, 11 October 1977. Some examples: "A bad novel," was the blunt assessment of Anatole Broyard, "One Critic's Fiction," *New York Times Book Review*, 1 January 1978, 12. James Brockway found "the book, its prose, its situations . . . preposterous." Brockway, "Stories, Long, Short, and Tall," *Books and Bookmen*, April 1978, 51. Peter Ackroyd said of the novel that it had "all the resonance of an advertisement for mouthwash." Ackroyd, "Kiss Me!," *The Spectator*, 23 July 1977, 27.

86. O'Brien, *Johnny*, 94.

87. Ibid., 24.

88. Ibid., 8.

89. Elke D'Hoker, "Powerful Voices: Female Narrators and Unreliability in Three Irish Novels," *Études Irlandaises* 32, no. 1 (2007): 26.

90. O'Brien, *Johnny*, 69.

91. Edna O'Brien papers, Manuscript, Archives and Rare Book Library, Emory University. Series 3: Prose 1960–1999; Subseries 3.2, *Time and Tide* Notebooks (1992), Box 35, Folder 6.

92. "Nora," "Dora," and "Dina" (O'Brien's early nom de plume) all echo each other in oblique ways.

93. Bernice Schrank and Danine Farquharson, "Object of Love, Subject to Despair: Edna O'Brien's 'The Love Object' and Emotional Logic of Late Romanticism," *Canadian Journal of Irish Studies* 22, no. 2 (December 1996): 22.

94. O'Brien, *The High Road*, 82.

95. Ibid., 110.

96. St. John D. Seymour, "Three Medieval Poems from Kilkenny," *Proceedings of the Royal Irish Academy: Archaeology, Culture, History, Literature* 41 (1932–1934): 209.

97. O'Brien, *The High Road*, 160.

98. Heather Ingman, "Edna O'Brien: Stretching the Nation's Boundaries," *Irish Studies Review* 10, no. 3 (2002): 259.

99. Not to be confused with the 2013 collection of the same name comprising thirty-one stories from across O'Brien's career.

100. Schrank and Farquharson, "Object of Love, Subject to Despair," 35.

101. Ibid.

102. Kathryn Bond Stockton, "'God' between Their Lips: Desire between Women in Irigaray and Eliot," *NOVEL: A Forum on Fiction* 2, no. 3 (Spring 1992): 353.

103. O'Brien, *The High Road*, 79.

104. Ibid., 81.

105. Ibid., 83.

106. Ibid., 84.

107. Ibid., 85.

108. Ibid.

109. Marjorie Garber, *Vested Interests: Cross Dressing and Cultural Anxiety* (New York: Routledge, 1997), 71.

110. Ibid., 32.

111. Ibid., 283.

112. O'Brien, *The High Road*, 14–15.

113. It is worth noting that in an outline of the novel, O'Brien identifies Catalina, and not Anna, as the central character. Edna O'Brien Papers, Manuscript, Archives and Rare Book Library, Emory University, Series 3: Prose 1960–1999; Subseries 3.2, Box 33, Folder 9, *The High Road*, Notebooks.

114. Amanda Greenwood, *Edna O'Brien* (Devon, UK: Northcote House, 2003), 66.

115. O'Brien, *The High Road*, 87.

116. Ibid., 109.

117. Ibid., 157.

118. Bracha Ettinger, *The Matrixial Borderspace* (Minneapolis: University of Minnesota Press, 2006). My thanks to Moynagh Sullivan for introducing me to Ettinger's work.

119. O'Brien, *The High Road*, 117.

120. Ibid., 111.

121. Ibid., 180.

122. Christine Holmlund, "The Lesbian, the Mother, the Heterosexual Love: Irigaray's Decoding of Difference," *Feminist Studies* 17, no. 2 (Summer 1991): 298.

123. Ibid.

CHAPTER 2. THE LIBERATING SADOMASOCHISM OF THINGS

1. Edna O'Brien, *The High Road* (London: Farrar, Straus and Giroux, 1988), 180.

2. Ibid.

3. Edna O'Brien, *Girl* (London: Faber and Faber, 2019), 45.

4. Philip Roth, "A Conversation with Edna O'Brien: 'The Body Contains the Life Story,'" *New York Times*, 18 November 1984, 39.

5. Paul Scott, review of *The Love Object*, *London Times*, 6 June 1968.

6. Isobel Murray, "Irish Eyes," review of *A Scandalous Woman*, *Financial Times*, 12 September 1974.

7. Clare Boylan, "Pilgrimage to the Old Haunts," review of *Lantern Slides*, *Irish Times*, 16 June 1990.

8. Anne Enright, review of *Country Girl: A Memoir*, *The Guardian*, 12 October 2012, https://www.theguardian.com/books/2012/oct/12/country-girl-edna-obrien-review.

9. Éilis Ní Dhuibhne, review of *The Little Red Chairs*, *Irish Times*, 24 October 2015, https://www.irishtimes.com/culture/books/the-little-red-chairs-by-edna-o-brien-1.2403493.

10. Mary Gordon, "The Failure of True Love," review of *A Fanatic Heart*, *Los Angeles Times*, 18 November 1984, 37.

11. Nell Dunn, *Talking to Women* (London: Silver, 2018), 69–70.

12. Bill Brown, "Thing Theory," *Critical Inquiry* 28, no. 1 (Autumn 2001): 4.

13. Sinéad Mooney, "'Sacramental Sleeves': Fashioning the Female Subject in Edna O'Brien's Fiction," in *Edna O'Brien: New Critical Perspectives*, ed. Kathryn Laing, Sinéad Mooney, and Maureen O'Connor (Dublin: Carysfort, 2006), 197.

14. Enright, review of *Country Girl*.

15. Judith (Jack) Halberstam, *The Queer Art of Failure* (Durham, NC: Duke University Press, 2011), 131.

16. Shirley Peterson, "'Meaniacs' and Martyrs: Sadomasochistic Desire in Edna O'Brien's *The Country Girls* Trinity," in Laing, Mooney, and O'Connor, *Edna O'Brien*, 154.

17. Enright, review of *Country Girl*.

18. Amanda Greenwood, *Edna O'Brien* (Devon, UK: Northcote House, 2003), 106–107.

19. Ibid., 87.

20. "Places long associated with goddess worship in many European countries were frequently transformed into sacred Marian sites.... It was the Irish, however, who seemed to take to this idea with the greatest relish. In Ireland, 86 percent of all Christian shrines, including Our Lady of Knock, are based on wells once dedicated to the pagan goddess Brigid." Joelle Mellon, *The Virgin Mary in the Perception of Women: Mother, Protector and Queen* (Jefferson, NC: McFarland, 2008), 162.

21. Greenwood, *Edna O'Brien*, 107.

22. The "Big House" was the local representation of English occupation throughout the Irish countryside. These houses, not always significantly "big" in a physical sense, were occupied by landlords predominantly of the Protestant Anglo-Irish Ascendancy. For more on O'Brien and the "Big House," see, for example, Danine Farquharson and Bernice Schrank, "Blurring Boundaries, Intersecting Lives: History, Gender, and Violence in Edna O'Brien's *House of Splendid Isolation*," in *Wild Colonial Girl: Essays on Edna O'Brien*, ed. Lisa Colletta and Maureen O'Connor (Madison: University of Wisconsin Press, 2006), 110–142; and Michael Harris, "Outside History: Relocation and Dislocation in Edna O'Brien's *House of Splendid Isolation*," in Laing, Mooney, and O'Connor, *Edna O'Brien*, 122–137. For more on the Irish genre of Big House novel, see Claire Norris, "The Big House: Space, Place and Identity in Irish Fiction," *New Hibernia Review* 8, no. 1 (Spring 2004): 107–121; Jacqueline Genet, ed,. *The Big House in*

Ireland: Reality and Representation (Dingle: Brandon, 1991); Vera Kreilkamp, *The Anglo-Irish Novel and the Big House* (Syracuse, NY: Syracuse University Press, 1998).

23. See Aidan Beatty, *Masculinity and Power in Irish Nationalism, 1884–1938* (London: Palgrave Macmillan, 2016).

24. A significant exception to this blind spot is Farquharson and Schrank, "Blurring Boundaries, Intersecting Lives."

25. Edna O'Brien, *Country Girl: A Memoir* (London: Faber and Faber, 2012), 5.

26. Gerardine Meaney "Fiction, 1922–1960," in *A History of Modern Irish Women's Literature,* ed. Clíona Ó Gallchoir and Heather Ingman (Cambridge: Cambridge University Press, 2018), 192.

27. Maud Ellmann, "Shadowing Elizabeth Bowen," *New England Review* 24, no. 1 (Winter 2003): 149.

28. Shusha Guppy, "The Art of Fiction No. 82: Interview with Edna O'Brien," *Paris Review* 92 (1984): 38.

29. Edna O'Brien, "My Two Mothers," in *Saints and Sinners* (London: Faber and Faber, 2011), 179.

30. Ellmann, "Shadowing Elizabeth Bowen," 148.

31. David Lloyd, *Ireland after History* (Notre Dame, IN: Notre Dame University Press, 1999), 91.

32. Ibid., 91, 92.

33. For a consideration of the status and meaning of dirt and detritus in O'Brien's work as well as in Irish women's poetry, see Maureen O'Connor, "'The Most Haunting Bird': Unbeing and Illegibility in Contemporary Irish Women's Writing," *Women's Studies: An Interdisciplinary Journal* 44, no. 7 (September 2015): 940–955. Chapter 5 of this volume also discusses filth and pollution in O'Brien's work.

34. Alison Landsberg, *Prosthetic Memory: The Transformation of America* (New York: Columbia University Press, 2004).

35. Elizabeth Freeman, *Time Binds: Queer Temporalities, Queer Histories* (Durham, NC: Duke University Press, 2010), 161 (emphasis added).

36. Ibid., 160.

37. Peterson, "'Meaniacs' and Martyrs," 151.

38. Lynn Chancer, *Sadomasochism in Everyday Life: The Dynamics of Power and Powerlessness* (New Brunswick, NJ: Rutgers University Press, 1992), 16.

39. Peterson, "'Meaniacs' and Martyrs," 152.

40. Jane Bennett, *Vibrant Matter: A Political Ecology of Things* (Durham, NC: Duke University Press, 2010), 20.

41. Ibid., 21.

42. Halberstam, *Queer Art*, 11.

43. Ibid., 14

44. Ibid., 28.

45. Ibid., 131.

46. This statement is popularly credited to MacSwiney's inaugural speech upon being elected Lord Mayor of Cork: Robert Hume, "Terence MacSwiney: The Life and Times of a Cork Martyr," *Irish Examiner,* 27 March 2019, https://www.irishexaminer.com/breakingnews/lifestyle/features/terence-macswiney-the-life-and-times-of-a-cork-martyr-913766.html.

47. Rebecca Pelan, "Edna O'Brien's 'Love Objects,'" in Colletta and O'Connor, *Wild Colonial Girl,* 58–76. See also Bernice Schrank and Danine Farquharson, "Object of Love, Subject to Despair: Edna O'Brien's 'The Love Object' and Emotional Logic of Late Romanticism," *Canadian Journal of Irish Studies* 22, no. 2 (December 1996): 21–36.

48. Schrank and Farquharson, "Blurring Boundaries, Intersecting Lives," 22.

49. Enright, review of *Country Girl*.

50. Bennett, *Vibrant Matter*, 15.

51. Ibid., 20.

52. Edna O'Brien, *The Country Girls* (London: Penguin, 1975), 5.

53. Ibid., 7.

54. Ibid.

55. Ibid., 8.

56. Ibid., 31.

57. Edna O'Brien, "The Rug," in *The Love Object* (London: Penguin, 1972), 63–64. First published in the *New Yorker* in 1963.

58. Ibid., 66.

59. Ibid., 67.

60. Ibid., 72.

61. Ibid., 67.

62. Ibid., 72.

63. Edna O'Brien, "Green Georgette," in *Saints and Sinners*, 111.

64. Ibid., 112.

65. Ibid.

66. Ibid.

67. Ibid., 113.

68. Ibid., 116.

69. Ibid., 116–117.

70. Ibid. 118.

71. Ibid., 122.

72. Ibid., 124–125.

73. Ibid., 125.

74. O'Brien, *Country Girl*, 3–4.

75. Edna O'Brien, "Rose in the Heart," in *Mrs Reinhardt and Other Stories* (London: Penguin, 1978), 113, 114.

76. Ibid., 119. The black cat filled with sweets also appears in *A Pagan Place* (London: Penguin, 1971), where it is referred to as a "luxury" (64–65).

77. Brown, "Thing Theory," 5.

78. O'Brien, "Rose in the Heart," 108.

79. Ibid., 140.

80. Tim Inglold, *Perception of the Environment: Essay on Livelihood, Dwelling and Skill* (New York: Routledge, 2000), 189.

81. O'Brien, "Rose in the Heart," 139–140.

82. Freeman, *Time Binds*, 161.

83. O'Brien, *Country Girls*, 171.

84. Mooney, "Sacramental Sleeves," 200.

85. Edna O'Brien, "Inner Cowboy," in *Saints and Sinners*, 90.

86. My thanks to Tadhg Foley for this observation.

87. O'Brien, "Inner Cowboy," 92.

88. Ibid., 104.

89. Ibid., 93.

90. Brown, "Thing Theory," 4–5.

91. For a more developed discussion of toys in O'Brien's fiction, see O'Connor, "Most Haunting Bird."

92. O'Brien, "Inner Cowboy," 102.

93. Ibid., 105.

94. Bennett, *Vibrant Matter*, 121.

95. Ibid., 31.

96. Andrew Bennett has noted the "disturbing strangely intimate otherness of telephone communication," the way that the telephone "supplements and dissolves subjectivity," in his discussion of the instrument's role in Elizabeth Bowen's fiction, in which phones have "lives and minds and personalities of their own." Bennett, "Elizabeth Bowen on the Telephone, " in *Elizabeth Bowen: Theory, Thought and Things*, edited by Jessica Gildersleeve and Patricia Juliana Smith. (Edinburgh: Edinburgh University Press, 2019), 192, 188.

97. Edna O'Brien, "House of My Dreams," in *A Scandalous Woman* (London: Penguin, 1974), 136.

98. Edna O'Brien, *Time and Tide* (New York: Plume, 1992), 57, 145, 76.

99. Edna O'Brien, *House of Splendid Isolation* (New York: Plume, 1995), 69.

100. Edna O'Brien, "Manhattan Medley," in *Saints and Sinners*, 136.

101. See Maureen O'Connor, "Animals and the Irish Mouth in Edna O'Brien's Fiction," in "Irish Ecocriticism," special issue, *Journal of Ecocriticism* 5, no. 2 (September 2013), for a discussion of the object given voice in O'Brien's fiction.

102. O'Brien, "Inner Cowboy," 87.

CHAPTER 3. THE UNGRAMMATICAL SUBLIME

1. Jane Bennett, *Vibrant Matter: A Political Ecology of Things* (Durham, NC: Duke University Press, 2010), 118.

2. Edna O'Brien, "From the Ground Up," *The Writer*, October 1958, 15.

3. Edna O'Brien, "Inner Cowboy," in *Saints and Sinners* (London: Faber and Faber, 2011), 85.

4. A decontextualized and clichéd characterization that persists to the present moment, as in Clair Wills, "Coda: Edna O'Brien and Eimear McBride," in *Ireland in Transition, 1980–2020*, ed. Eric Falci and Paige Reynolds (Cambridge: Cambridge University Press, 2020), 297.

5. Val Plumwood, "The Concept of a Cultural Landscape: Nature, Culture, and Agency of the Land," *Ethics and the Environment* 11, no. 2 (2006): 117.

6. Catherine Nash, "Remapping and Renaming: New Cartographies of Identity, Gender, and Landscape in Ireland," *Feminist Review* 44 (Summer 1993): 47.

7. For a detailed account, see Rebecca Pelan, "Edna O'Brien's 'Love Objects,'" in *Wild Colonial Girl: Essays on Edna O'Brien*, ed. Lisa Colletta and Maureen O'Connor (Madison: University of Wisconsin Press, 2006), 58–76.

8. Edna O'Brien, *In the Forest* (Boston: Houghton Mifflin, 2002), 236–237.

9. Edna O'Brien, *Down by the River* (London: Phoenix, 2000), 61.

10. Charles Penwarden, "Of Word and Flesh—An Interview with Julia Kristeva," in *Rites of Passion: Arts for the End of the Century*, ed. Stuart Morgan and Frances Morris (London: Tate, 1995), 22.

11. Edna O'Brien, "Going Back to Clare" TS, Edna O'Brien Papers, Manuscript, Archives and Rare Book Library, Emory University, Series 3, Writings by O'Brien, ca. 1953–1999, Subseries 3.2, Prose 1960, 1999; NonFiction Essays and Short Pieces, Box 57, Folder 17.

12. Nash, "Remapping and Renaming," 41.

13. Based on a 1988 story, "Brothers and Sisters," that appeared in the *Transatlantic Review*, August 1988, 13–14; published as "Plunder," in *Saints and Sinners*, 77–84.

14. Edna O'Brien, *The Little Red Chairs* (London: Faber and Faber, 2015), 146.

15. Edna O'Brien, *Girl* (London: Faber and Faber, 2019), 3.

16. Ibid., 48.

17. Edna O'Brien, *Down by the River*, 5, 4.

18. Ibid., 2–3.

19. Ibid., 2.

20. Edna O'Brien, *Wild Decembers* (New York: Plume, 2001), 1.

21. Edna O'Brien, *House of Splendid Isolation* (New York: Plume, 1995), 3–4.

22. See Rebecca Pelan, "Reflections on a Connemara Dietrich," in *Edna O'Brien: New Critical Perspectives*, ed. Kathryn Laing, Sinéad Mooney, and Maureen O'Connor (Dublin: Carysfort, 2006), 14.

23. Mary Leland, "Stories Which Transcend the Limits of Home," review of *Lantern Slides*, *Sunday Tribune*, 17 June 1990, 85.

24. Dennis Schofield, "The Second Person: A Point of View?" *Colloquy* 1, no. 1 (1996): 70.

25. Kristi Byron, "In the Name of the Mother . . . : The Epilogue of Edna O'Brien's *Country Girls Trilogy*," *Women's Studies: An Interdisciplinary Journal* 31, no. 4 (2002): 455.

26. Elizabeth Chase, "Re-writing Genre in the *Country Girls Trilogy*," *New Hibernia Review* 14, no. 3 (Autumn 2010): 92–93.

27. Ibid., 102, 104.

28. Nicholas Wroe, "Country Matters," *The Guardian*, 2 October 1999, https://www.theguardian.com/books/1999/oct/02/books.guardianreview8.

29. Robert Nye, "Good Words for the Most Part in the Right Order," review of *Night*, *London Times*, 5 October 1972, 10.

30. Lorna Sage, *Women in the House of Fiction: Post-war Women Novelists* (London: Palgrave Macmillan, 1992), 83.

31. Patricia Coughlan on Spenser and the "prevailing image in England" of the Irish during the Cromwellian wars and the commonwealth as being "dominated by grotesque stereotypes [as] . . . . monsters of cruelty." Coughlan, "'Cheap and common animals': The English Anatomy of Ireland in the Seventeenth Century", in *Literature and the English Civil War*, edited by Thomas Healey and Jonathan Sawday (Cambridge: Cambridge University Press, 1990), 210.

32. For more on the political and ideological implications of characterizing the Irish in this way, see Tadhg Foley, *Death by Discourse? Political Economy and the Great Irish Famine* (Hamden, CT: Quinnipiac University Press, 2017).

33. For more on this subject, see Lionel Pilkington, *Theatre and the State in Twentieth-Century Ireland: Cultivating the People* (New York: Routledge, 2001), especially 191–223.

34. Edna O'Brien, *The Girl with Green Eyes* (London: Penguin, 1974), 172.

35. Lorna Sage, "Mother Ireland," review of *A Fanatic Heart*, *The Observer*, 21 April 1985, 22.

36. Edna O'Brien, *Country Girl: A Memoir* (London: Faber and Faber, 2012), 17–18.

37. Catherine Nash, "Reclaiming Vision: Looking at Landscape and the Body," *Gender, Place and Culture: A Journal of Feminist Geography* 3, no. 2 (1996): 166.

38. David Lloyd, *Ireland after History* (Notre Dame, IN: Notre Dame University Press, 1999), 76.

39. Annan, Gabriele, review of *Lantern Slides*, *The Spectator*, 9 June 1990, 40.

40. John Broderick, review of *Mother Ireland*, *The Critic*, Winter 1976, 72–73.

41. Sage, "Those Barren Leaves," 30. Sage also suggests in this review that "O'Brien does the queenly slattern to perfection."

42. Denis Donoghue, "Drums under the Window," review of *Mother Ireland*, *New York Review of Books*, 14 October 1976, 12.

43. Jan Moir, "Doing the Real Thing," *The Guardian*, 16 September 1992, 37.

44. Terence Rafferty, "A Fresh Start," review of *The High Road*, *New Yorker*, 30 January 1989, 94.

45. Thomas Cahill, review of *Lantern Slides*, *Los Angeles Times*, 11 April 1990.

46. Victoria Glendinning, "Elegiac and Life-Loving," review of *Rose in the Heart*, *New Yorker*, 11 February 1979.

47. Gerardine Meaney, *Sex and Nation: Women in Irish Culture and Politics* (Dublin: Attic, 1991), 22.

48. Anne Enright, "A Bright Light amid Hearts of Darkness," review of *Girl*, *Irish Times*, 7 September 2019, 20.

49. Karen Barad, "Posthumanist Performativity: Toward an Understanding of How Matter Comes to Matter," *Signs: Journal of Women in Culture and Society* 2, no. 3 (2003): 802.

50. Alicia Ostriker, "The Thieves of Language: Women Poets and Revisionist Mythmaking," *Signs* 8, no. 1 (Autumn 1982): 82.

51. "New Fiction," review of *August Is a Wicked Month*, *London Times*, 7 October 1965.

52. O'Brien, *Down by the River*, 1.

53. Hilary Mantel, review of *Down by the River*, *New York Times*, 25 May 1997, http://movies2.nytimes.com/books/97/05/25/reviews/970525.25mantelt.html.

54. O'Brien, *Down by the River* , 5.

55. Of Eimear McBride's 2013 novel *A Girl Is a Half-Formed Thing*, a text that McBride has acknowledged is indebted to O'Brien, Anne Fogarty has noted, "The feminine is a potent force on the grounds of its brokenness and the searing, unyielding poetry of girl's accusatory and self-nullifying monologue. The half-formed language of the girl is wielded by McBride to question every aspect of Irish reality, but particularly the ways in which adults wield social and sexual power over children whom they lastingly damage and misshape." Fogarty, "'It Was Like a Baby Crying': Representations of the Child in Contemporary Irish Fiction," *Journal of Irish Studies* 30 (October 2015): 24.

56. Mary Douglas, *Implicit Meanings: Selected Essays in Anthropology* (London: Routledge, 1975), 213.

57. Ibid., 217.

58. Ibid., 289.

59. O'Brien, *Country Girl*, 38.

60. Nash, "Remapping and Renaming," 52.

61. Bennett, *Vibrant Matter*, 114.

62. Gene Kerrigan, "They Knew about the Babies for 90 Years," *Sunday Independent*, 12 March 2017, https://www.independent.ie/opinion/columnists/gene-kerrigan/gene-kerrigan-they-knew-about-the-babies-for-90-years-35522685.html.

63. Dáil Éireann debate, Houses of the Oireachtas, 7 March 2017, https://www.oireachtas.ie/en/debates/debate/dail/2017-03-07/2/.

64. O'Brien, *Girl*, 15, 49.

65. Jane Ussher, *Managing the Monstrous Feminine: Regulating the Reproductive Body* (New York: Routledge 2006), 7.

66. Edna O'Brien, *The Country Girls* (London: Penguin, 1975), 98.

67. Ibid., 103.

68. Edna O'Brien, *Mother Ireland* (New York: Plume, 1976), 42.

69. Edna O'Brien, "A Scandalous Woman," in *A Scandalous Woman* (London: Penguin, 1976), 30.

70. O'Brien, *Down by the River*, 127. Later American editions change the wording from "noose of a trap" to "prongs of an iron trap."

71. O'Brien, *House of Splendid Isolation*, 47. The father in *A Pagan Place* (London: Penguin, 1971) also calls his wife "Mud, short for mother" (29).

72. Ussher, *Managing the Monstrous Feminine*, 19.

73. O'Brien, *House of Splendid Isolation*, 211.

74. Martin Shuttleworth described *Casualties of Peace* as "having as much shape as . . . pig's parts." Shuttleworth, review of *Casualties of Peace*, *Punch*, 9 November 1966, 717.

75. O'Brien, *Pagan Place*, 21.

76. Ibid., 22.

77. Ibid., 102.

78. Ibid., 103.

79. O'Brien, *The Country Girls*, 129.

80. O'Brien, *Mother Ireland*, 82–83

81. Sean McMahon, "A Sex by Themselves: An Interim Report on the Novels of Edna O'Brien," *Éire-Ireland* 2, no. 1 (1967): 79.

82. Edna O'Brien, *Casualties of Peace* (London: Penguin, 1958), 134.

83. Edna O'Brien, *August Is a Wicked Month* (London: Penguin, 1967), 72.

84. O'Brien, *Country Girl*, 83.

85. O'Brien, *Pagan Place*, 14.

86. Ibid., 15.

87. Nuala O'Faolain, "Devious Cool," review of *A Pagan Place*, *London Times*, 18 April 1970.

88. O'Brien, *Pagan Place*, 15.

89. Ibid., 18.

90. Clair Wills has recently made a similar observation about voice in the novel: "The entire narrative is spoken in the second person, making the girl's sexual shaming representative rather than, or as well as, unique." Wills, "Coda," 300.

91. Renate Lachmann, "Mnemonic and Intertextual Aspects of Literature," in *Cultural Memory Studies: An International and Interdisciplinary Handbook*, ed. Astrid Erll and Ansgar Nünning (Berlin: Walter de Gruyter, 2008), 302. My thanks to Ailbhe McDaid for drawing my attention to this text.

92. Gretchen Legler, "Ecofeminist Literary Criticism," in *Ecofeminism: Women, Culture, Nature*, ed. Karen J. Warren (Bloomington: Indiana University Press, 1997), 232.

93. O'Brien, *Pagan Place*, 51.

94. Ibid., 184.

95. Ibid., 185.

96. N. O'Faolain, "Devious Cool."

97. O'Brien, *Pagan Place*, 54.

98. Ibid., 185.

99. Ibid., 29.

100. Ibid., 84.

101. Ibid., 51–52.

102. Ibid., 165–166.

103. Ibid., 131.

104. Ibid., 94.

105. Ibid., 186.

106. Ibid., 187.

107. O'Brien, *House of Splendid Isolation*, 3–4.

108. Edna O'Brien, *Johnny I Hardly Knew You* (London: Penguin, 1986), 97.

109. O'Brien, *Mother Ireland*, 102.

110. Edna O'Brien, "In the Sacred Company of Trees: From My Window," *Irish Independent*, 2 June 1990, 32.

111. Seamus Heaney, "Morning Ireland," RTÉ Radio One, 7 May 2009.

112. Seamus Heaney, "Digging," in *Death of a Naturalist* (London: Faber and Faber, 1966), 14.

113. O'Brien, *Pagan Place*, 83.

CHAPTER 4. OTHERWORLDLY POSSESSIONS

1. David Haycock, "Edna O'Brien Talks to David Haycock about Her New Novel, *A Pagan Place*," *The Listener*, 7 May 1970, 616–617.

2. Edna O'Brien, "In the Sacred Company of Trees: From My Window," *Irish Independent*, 2 June 1990, 32.

3. Elke D'Hoker, *Irish Women Writers and the Modern Short Story* (London: Palgrave Macmillan, 2016), 154.

4. Jane Elizabeth Dougherty, "'Never Tear the Linnet from the Leaf': The Feminist Intertextuality of Edna O'Brien's *Down by the River*," *Frontiers: A Journal of Women Studies* 31, no. 3 (2010): 84.

5. Edna O'Brien Papers, Manuscript, Archives and Rare Book Library, Emory University, Series 7 audiovisual material, "Public Radio Book Show," 30 December 1990 (original: audio cassette; digital/digitized copy available in the Reading Room: id b7sq3), subseries 7.21 AV2

6. Edna O'Brien, *A Pagan Place* (London: Penguin, 1971), 18.

7. Mary Douglas, *Purity and Danger: An Analysis of the Concepts of Pollution and Taboo* (New York: Routledge, 1991), 94.

8. Edna O'Brien, "Shovel Kings," in *Saints and Sinners* (London: Faber and Faber, 2011), 28. For more about Biddy Early's magic bottle, see John Rainsford, "Feakle's Biddy Early: A Victim of Moral Panic?," *History Ireland* 1, no. 20 (January–February 2012), https://www.historyireland.com/18th-19th-century-history/feakles-biddy-early-a-victim-of-moral-panic/.

9. Insanity was historically linked to animality and femininity, especially in Ireland. See my *The Female and the Species: The Animal in Irish Women's Writing* (Bern: Peter Lang, 2010), 7–8. Leah Fisher Richards traces the "mythic madman" from ancient Celtic legend to Irish Literary Revival figures including W. B. Yeats, Austin Clarke, and Lady Gregory, to contemporary writers. Richards, "'No Nation Wanted It So Much': Mythic Insanity in the Development of a Modern Irish Literature," *Proceedings of the Harvard Celtic Colloquium* 18–19 (1998–1999): 385–395.

10. Edna O'Brien, *In the Forest* (Boston: Houghton Mifflin, 2002), 1–2.

11. Edna O'Brien, *Girl* (London: Faber and Faber, 2019), 30.

12. Clair Wills, "Women, Domesticity and the Family: Recent Feminist Work in Irish Cultural Studies," *Cultural Studies* 15, no. 1 (2001): 54.

13. Alicia Ostriker, "The Thieves of Language: Women Poets and Revisionist Mythmaking," *Signs* 8, no. 1 (Autumn 1982): 71.

14. For example, in *August Is a Wicked Month* (London: Penguin, 1967), Ellen tells someone she is from England because "saying one came from Ireland resulted in tedious stories about fairies and grandmothers" (41).

15. Angela Bourke, *The Burning of Bridget Cleary: A True Story* (London: Penguin, 1999), 200. Bourke identifies the rediscovery of "fairy-legends and fairy-places" in the work of contemporary Irish women writers whose "feminist fiction and drama use ideas about fairies to explore issues from housework to maternity hospitals" (206). Mary Douglas has similarly argued that "myth sits above and athwart the exigencies of social life. It is capable of presenting one picture and then its opposite." Douglas, *Implicit Meanings: Selected Essays in Anthropology* (London: Routledge, 975), 289.

16. Edna O'Brien, *Down by the River* (London Phoenix, 2000), 3.

17. Edna O'Brien, *Mother Ireland* (New York: Plume, 1976), 29.

18. Edna O'Brien, *Time and Tide* (London: Penguin, 1992). Marguerite Quintelli-Neary notes that O'Brien "tapped into the Irish Mythological Ulidian Cycle legend of Deirdre and Naoise" when writing *The Country Girls*. Quintelli-Neary, "Edna O'Brien's Metamorphoses: A New Voice for Ovid's Philomela," *Nordic Irish Studies* 12 (2013): 59.

19. Peggy O'Brien, "The Silly and the Serious: An Assessment of Edna O'Brien," *Massachusetts Review* 28 (1987): 475.

20. Edna O'Brien, *Some Irish Loving: A Selection* (London: Penguin, 1981), 148.

21. Ibid., 147.

22. Rebecca Pelan, "Undoing That Other Conquest," *Canadian Journal of Irish Studies* 25, nos. 1–2 (1999): 128–129.

23. Thomas Cahill, review of *Lantern Slides*, *Los Angeles Times*, 11 April 1990.

24. Ailbhe Smyth, introduction to *Wildish Things: Anthology of New Irish Women's Writing*, ed. Ailbhe Smyth (Dublin: Attic, 1989), 8, 7.

25. Edna O'Brien, "She Stoops but Fails to Conquer," *The Guardian*, 9 April 1995, 21.

26. Despite reports to the contrary, this did not happen, though a former partner of Riney's did ask O'Brien not to write the book. In an interview with the novelist in the *Irish Independent*, Eoghan Harris asked O'Brien whether she *would* have gone ahead with the book had the victims' close family members asked her not to. She responded, "Yes, I would." In this same interview and in others about the novel, O'Brien tells of being in Clare researching *Wild Decembers* when a local guard brought her to the memorial to the victims set up in Cregg Wood. She was deeply moved, struck by the thought, "I want to tell this woman's story." Eoghan Harris, "The Wood of the Whispering," review of *In the Forest*, *Irish Independent*, 10 March 2002, http://www.independent.ie/opinion/analysis/the-wood-of-the-whispering-26239781.html.

27. On the sexist media response to O'Brien's use of real-life crime as a basis for fiction, as opposed to the way other Irish novelists were treated, such as John Banville and Eoin Mac-Namee, who drew on similar sources, please see Rebecca Pelan, "Reflections on a Connemara Dietrich," in *Edna O'Brien: New Critical Perspectives*, ed. Kathryn Laing, Sinéad Mooney, and Maureen O'Connor (Dublin: Carysfort, 2006), 12–73.

28. Robert McCrum, "Deep Down in the Woods: Edna O'Brien's Account of a Triple Murder Has Touched a Raw Nerve at Home," *The Observer*, 28 April 2002, http://books.guardian.co.uk/departments/generalfiction/story/0,,706211,00.html.

29. See, for example, James Carney, "'Suibne Geilt' and 'The Children of Lir,'" in *Studies in Irish Literature and History* (Dublin: Dublin Institute for Advanced Studies, 1955); David J. Cohen, "Suibhne Geilt," *Celtica* 12 (1977): 113–124; Susan Shaw Sailor, "*Suibne Geilt*: Puzzles, Problems and Paradoxes," *Canadian Journal of Irish Studies* 24, no. 1 (1998): 115–131; and Neil Thomas, "The Celtic Wild Man Tradition and Geoffrey of Monmouth's *Vita Merlini*: Madness or *Contemptus Mundi*?," *Arthuriana* 10, no. 1 (2000): 27–42.

30. Edna O'Brien, *House of Splendid Isolation* (New York: Plume, 1995), 222.

31. Simon Estok, "Narrativizing Science: The Ecocritical Imagination and Ecophobia," *Configurations* 18, nos. 1–2 (2010): 144.

32. O'Brien, *In the Forest*, 1.

33. Ibid., 227.

34. Shirley Peterson, "Homeward Bound: Trauma, Homesickness, and Rough Beasts in O'Brien's *In the Forest* and McCabe's *Winterwood*," *New Hibernia Review* 13, no. 4 (2009): 41.

35. Paul Farley and Michael Symons Roberts, *Edgelands: Journeys into England's True Wilderness* (London: Vintage, 2012), 58, 103.

36. O'Brien, *In the Forest*, 3.

37. Ibid., 4.

38. Ibid., 180.

39. Ibid., 51.

40. Ibid., 26.

41. "In mythology," according to O'Brien, the black bird (if not the blackbird), "the crow or raven is the warning emblem of death." Patricia Harty, "Mother, Life Landscape, and the Connection," *Irish America*, February–March 2007, https://irishamerica.com/2007/02/mother -life-landscape-and-the-connection/.

42. Amanda Greenwood, *Edna O'Brien* (Devon, UK: Northcote House, 2003), 23.

43. Susan Brownmiller, *Against Our Will: Men, Women and Rape* (New York: Simon and Shuster, 1975), 43. Recent research has revealed the seventeenth-century art of the "fairy tale" in the French court by *conteuses*, women storytellers whose tales mounted critiques of patriarchy. "In the 19th century, when the Brothers Grimm began their project of collecting and publishing folktales, they dismissed the *conteuses* as inauthentic, as not representative of the common *volk*. But the Grimms' theory that fairytales had a linear relationship to folktales has been exposed by scholars as a nationalist—and masculinist, as the teller was usually an illiterate female—bias." Melissa Ashley, "The First Fairytales Were Feminist Critiques of Patriarchy. We Need to Revive Their Legacy," *The Guardian*, 11 November 2019, https://www.theguardian .com/books/2019/nov/11/the-first-fairytales-were-feminist-critiques-of-patriarchy-we-need-to -revive-their-legacy?CMP=share_btn_tw&fbclid=IwARofDukoTCBBzsCulni8RHnEYJUV -5QfKKhocSoAAnsxy2mlGeyEBod_ITo. (My thanks to Rebecca Pelan for drawing my attention to this article.)

44. O'Brien, *In the Forest*, 225.

45. Ibid., 225–226.

46. Ibid., 157.

47. Ibid., 4.

48. Mary Daly, *Gyn/Ecology: The Metaethics of Radical Feminism* (Boston: Beacon, 1978), 34, 46.

49. Jack Zipes, "A Second Gaze at Little Red Riding Hood's Trials and Tribulations," *Lion and the Unicorn* 7–8 (1983): 80.

50. O'Brien, *In the Forest*, 106.

51. McCrum, "Deep Down in the Woods."

52. Jane Bennett, *Vibrant Matter: A Political Ecology of Things* (Durham, NC: Duke University Press, 2010), ix.

53. Edna O'Brien, *The High Road* (New York: Farrar, Straus and Giroux, 1988), 86.

54. O'Brien, *In the Forest*, 71.

55. Martin Heidegger, "Building Dwelling Thinking," in *Poetry, Language, Thought*, trans. Albert Hofstadter (New York: Harper Colophon Books, 1971), 153.

56. "Edmund Husserl," *Stanford Encyclopedia of Philosophy*, 28 February 2003, http://plato .stanford.edu/entries/husserl/.

57. Greenwood, *Edna O'Brien*, 106–107.

58. Jennifer A. Slivka, "Irishness and Exile in Edna O'Brien's *Wild Decembers* and *In the Forest*," *New Hibernia Review* 17, no. 1 (2013): 116.

59. Just some of the animal terms used by other characters in reference to O'Kane include "half man, half donkey" (O'Brien, *In the Forest*, 8), "a wolfman" (178), "vermin" (200), "devil, all hooves and horns" (231), "pig" (237).

60. Ibid., 71.

61. Ibid., 72.

62. Ibid., 73.

63. "Edmund Husserl," quoting Husserl, *Husserliana*, vol. 4, 183.

64. Karen Barad, "Nature's Queer Performativity," *Kvinder Køn og forskning / Women, Gender and Research* 1–2 (2012): 32.

65. Ibid., 26.

66. O'Brien, *In the Forest*, 30.

67. Michael Marder, "Taming the Beast: The Other Tradition in Political Theory," *Mosaic* 39, no. 4 (2006): 54.

68. Zipes, "Second Gaze," 96.

69. Ibid., 93.

70. Ibid. As Zipes puts it more bluntly, in the traditional Red Riding Hood narrative, "it is the dumb girl who causes the 'near rape'" (101).

71. O'Brien, *In the Forest*, 262.

72. Ibid., 257.

73. Peterson, "Homeward Bound," 54.

CHAPTER 5. MYTH AND MUTATION

1. Irving Massey, *The Gaping Pig: Literature and Metamorphosis* (Berkeley: University of California Press, 1976), 2.

2. Frances Devlin-Glass, "The Sovereignty as Co-Lordship: A Contemporary Feminist Reading of the Female Sacred in the Ulster Cycle," in *Feminist Poetics of the Sacred: Creative Suspicions*, ed. Frances Devlin-Glass and Lynn McCreddon (Oxford: Oxford University Press, 2001), 106.

3. For a more detailed discussion of this history and its gendered implications, see Maureen O'Connor, *The Female and the Species: The Animal in Irish Women's Writing* (Bern: Peter Lang, 2010).

4. Catherine Kelly, "Breaking the Mould: Three Plays by Marina Carr," *Women's Studies Review* 8 (2002): 107.

5. Eileen Morgan, "Mapping Out a Landscape of Female Suffering: Edna O'Brien's Demythologizing Novels," *Women's Studies: An Interdisciplinary Journal* 29, no. 4 (2000): 449, 450. More recently, Emer Nolan, discussing iconic Irish women of the twentieth century, describes chivalry as "patriarchal nostalgia and condescension." Nolan, *Five Irish Women: The Second Republic, 1960–2016* (Manchester: Manchester University Press, 2019), 108.

6. Edna O'Brien, *The Little Red Chairs* (London: Faber and Faber, 2015), 3.

7. Ibid., 4.

8. Ibid., 57.

9. Julia O'Faolain acknowledges "the brisk and deadly pleasure of fairy tale" to be found in O'Brien's work. J. O'Faolain, review of *A Scandalous Woman*, *New York Times Book Review*, 22 February 1974.

10. Edna O'Brien, "Send My Roots Rain," in *Saints and Sinners* (London: Faber and Faber, 2011), 167.

11. Edna O'Brien, "House of My Dreams," in *A Scandalous Woman* (London: Penguin, 1974), 150.

12. Gerald of Wales (Geraldus Cambrensis), *The Topography of Ireland*, trans. Thomas Forester, ed. Thomas Wright (Cambridge, ON: In parentheses, 2000), 45–46, http://www.yorku.ca/inpar/topography_ireland.pdf; Edmund Spenser, *View of the Present State of Ireland* (London: Eric Partridge, 1934), 124.

13. Ludovic Kennedy, "Three Loves of Childhood—Irish Thoughts by Edna O'Brien," *The Listener*, 3 June 1976, 701–702.

14. Edna O'Brien, *Country Girl: A Memoir* (London: Faber and Faber, 2012), 60.

15. A typescript that appears to be a reworking of this early literary effort can be found in the Emory University archive, Series 3, Writings by O'Brien, ca. 1953–1999, Subseries 3.3, Scripts, 1962–1987, Box 70, Folder 6.

16. Edna O'Brien, *A Pagan Place* (London: Penguin, 1971), 104.

17. Susan O'Grady Fox, "Interview with Edna O'Brien," *Irish-America Magazine*, October–November 2005, http://www.irishabroad.com/irishworld/irishamericamag/octnov05/features/20-greatest-interviews.asp. Theatrical production was on O'Brien's mind in 2005, when her play *Family Butchers* was about to be produced in San Francisco, and in that same year, in another interview, she describes her memory of the village productions of Dracula as "vivid" but characterizes her romantic response to it more simply as "daft." Chad Jones, "Banned Books behind Her, O'Brien Tries the Stage," *Oakland Tribune*, 29 September 2005.

18. Edna O'Brien, *Mother Ireland* (New York: Plume, 1976), 34.

19. Edna O'Brien, *Time and Tide* (London: Penguin, 1992), 35.

20. Ibid., 35.

21. Edna O'Brien, *Girls in Their Married Bliss* (London: Penguin, 1975), 100.

22. O'Brien, *Time and Tide*, 49.

23. Ibid., 62. For more on the significance of the bat in O'Brien's writing, see Patricia Coughlan, "Killing the Bats: O'Brien, Abjection, and the Question of Agency," in *Edna O'Brien: New Critical Perspectives*, ed. Kathryn Laing, Sinéad Mooney, and Maureen O'Connor (Dublin: Carysfort, 2006), 171–195.

24. O'Brien, *Time and Tide*, 209.

25. Ibid., 142. A Dr. Rat character also appears in the earlier novel *Johnny I Hardly Knew You* (London: Penguin, 1986), first published in 1977. In both novels, Dr. Rat administers LSD to the protagonists. In *Johnny*, the doctor "assumed the properties of a rat" to Nora as she is "hurtled down, down, down, into the denisons of horror" (94).

26. O'Brien, *Time and Tide*, 142.

27. Ibid., 143.

28. Massey, *Gaping Pig*, 218.

29. Ibid., 110. Massey associates this contradiction with the figure of the vampire (105).

30. Ibid., 51.

31. Judith Butler, *Bodies That Matter: On the Discursive Limits of Sex* (New York: Routledge, 1993), 30.

32. Mary Douglas, *Implicit Meanings: Selected Essays in Anthropology* (London: Routledge, 1975), 312.

33. Alicia Ostriker, "The Thieves of Language: Women Poets and Revisionist Mythmaking," *Signs* 8, no. 1 (Autumn 1982): 72.

34. Ibid.

35. Massey, *Gaping Pig*, 110.

36. Jane Elizabeth Dougherty, "'Never Tear the Linnet from the Leaf': The Feminist Intertextuality of Edna O'Brien's *Down by the River*," *Frontiers: A Journal of Women Studies* 31, no. 3 (2010): 91.

37. Ibid., 94.

38. Ibid.

39. Massey, *Gaping Pig*, 185.

40. Edna O'Brien, *The High Road* (New York: Farrar, Straus and Giroux, 1988), 19, 20.

41. Helen Thompson, "Uncanny and Undomesticated: Lesbian Desire in Edna O'Brien's 'Sister Imelda' and *The High Road*," *Women's Studies: An Interdisciplinary Journal* 32, no. 1 (2003): 24–25.

42. O'Brien claimed to be "very committed to [her] mythology, which is Roman Catholic," in conversation with Bolivar Le Franc, "Committed to Mythology," *Books and Bookmen*, September 1968, 52–53.

43. Karen Barad, "Nature's Queer Performativity," *Kvinder Køn og Forskning / Women, Gender and Research* 1, no. 2 (2012): 32.

44. O'Brien, *The High Road*, 112.

45. Ibid., 108.

46. Marjorie Garber, *Vested Interests: Cross Dressing and Cultural Anxiety* (New York: Routledge, 1997), 390.

47. O'Brien, *August Is a Wicked Month* (London: Penguin, 1967), 65.

48. Ibid., 66.

49. Ibid., 110.

50. Ibid. (emphasis added).

51. Ibid., 67.

52. Edna O'Brien, *House of Splendid Isolation* (New York: Plume, 1995), 72.

53. Ibid., 73.

54. Ibid., 74.

55. Ibid., 75.

56. Ibid., 76.

57. Ibid., 222.

58. Ibid., 220–221.

59. Ibid., 67, 92.

60. O'Brien, *Time and Tide*, 5.

61. Ibid., 4.

62. Ibid., 65.

63. Ibid., 66.

64. Ibid., 276.

65. Ostriker, "Thieves of Language," 72.

66. Adrienne Rich, "Diving into the Wreck," in *Poems Selected and New, 1950–1974* (New York: Norton, 1974), 196–198.

67. Ostriker, "Thieves of Language," 73.

68. Edna O'Brien, *Wild Decembers* (New York: Plume, 2001), 2, 3.

69. Ibid., 28.

70. Edna O'Brien, *Down by the River* (London: Phoenix, 2000), 293.

71. Ibid., 294.

72. Ibid., 297, 298.

73. For a persuasive and powerful reading of this element of the text, see Dougherty, "Never Tear the Linnet from the Leaf," 405.

74. O'Brien, *Time and Tide*, 79.

75. Edna O'Brien, *Night* (London Penguin, 1974), 105.

76. O'Brien, however, objected to the copy on the proposed original Viking cover: "'Nell's passion for her boys' wreaks the kind of chummy banality that I am doing everything in my work to avoid." O'Brien to the literary agent Gillon Aitken, n.d., Edna O'Brien Papers, Manuscript, Archives and Rare Book Library, Emory University, Series 1: Correspondence, 1955–2000; Subseries 1.1, Alphabetical Correspondence, Box 1, Folder 10.

77. O'Brien, *Time and Tide*, 238.

78. Ibid.

79. Ibid., 265.

80. Ibid., 235.

81. Shep, in *Down by the River*, witnesses the brutal attempt of Mary's father to abort his daughter with a splintered broom handle. Shep is more of a "human" than Mary's father is: "Shep a few feet from her, like a person, feeling it all, sensing it all, prehensile, there for her. There" (106). The ascription of the adjective "prehensile," usually used to describe a mechanical grasping ability, to Shep's emotional sensitivity merges the physical and the affective, privileging canine insight. The sheep dog Bull's-Eye demonstrates similar capacities of insight and sympathy in O'Brien's first novel, *The Country Girls*. From the novel's first page, Bull's-Eye proves himself to be the most reliable informant regarding the whereabouts of Cait's drunken father. Bull's-Eye remains a sympathetic presence, a touchstone of Cait's lost childhood, as the narrative progresses. He is even credited with powers of expression by Cait's father, who tells her in a letter late in the text, "Bull's-Eye misses you and so do I." Edna O'Brien, *The Country Girls* (London: Penguin, 1975), 80.

82. O'Brien, *Country Girls*, 143.

83. O'Brien, *Pagan Place*, 203.

84. O'Brien, *Time and Tide*, 274.

85. Ibid., 281–282.

86. Ibid., 299.

87. Patricia Lysaght, *The Banshee: The Irish Supernatural Death Messenger* (Dublin: O'Brien, 1986), 73.

88. O'Brien has often expressed a desire to be a singer like Sinéad O'Connor.

89. David Lloyd, *Irish Culture and Colonial Modernity, 1800–2000: The Transformation of Oral Space* (Cambridge: Cambridge University Press, 2011), 49.

90. Giorgio Agamben, *Language and Death: The Place of Negativity*, trans. Karen E. Pinkus (Minneapolis: University of Minnesota Press, 1991), 43.

91. Edmund Burke, *Philosophical Enquiry into the Origin of Our Ideas of the Sublime and Beautiful* (Oxford: Oxford University Press, 1990), 77.

92. O'Brien, *Mother Ireland*, 60.

93. O'Brien, *House of Splendid Isolation*, 3.

94. Renate Lachmann, "Mnemonic and Intertextual Aspects of Literature," in *Cultural Memory Studies: An International and Interdisciplinary Handbook*, ed. Astrid Erll and Ansgar Nünning (Berlin: Walter de Gruyter, 2008), 301–310.

95. O'Brien, *Wild Decembers*, 19–20.

96. Ibid., 144.

97. O'Brien, *House of Splendid Isolation*, 49.

98. Kristi Byron, "In the Name of the Mother . . . : The Epilogue of Edna O'Brien's *Country Girls Trilogy*," *Women's Studies: An Interdisciplinary Journal* 31, no. 4 (2002): 459.

99. Edna O'Brien, *The Country Girls Trilogy and Epilogue* (New York: Farrar, Straus and Giroux, 1986), 523.

CHAPTER 6. DISORDER, DIRT, AND DEATH

1. Edna O'Brien, *House of Splendid Isolation* (New York: Plume, 1995), 3.

2. Edna O'Brien, *Wild Decembers* (Boston: Houghton Mifflin, 2001), 1.

3. Thomas Laqueur, *The Work of the Dead: A Cultural History of Mortal Remains* (Princeton, NJ: Princeton University Press, 2015), 106.

4. Ibid., 6.

5. Ibid., 79, 92.

6. Gay Hawkins, *Ethics of Waste: How We Relate to Rubbish* (Lanham, MD: Rowman and Littlefield, 2005), 4.

7. Patricia Coughlan, "Killing the Bats: O'Brien, Abjection, and the Question of Agency." In *Edna O'Brien: New Critical Perspectives*," edited by Kathryn Laing, Sinéad Mooney, and Maureen O'Connor (Dublin: Carysfort, 2006), 173.

8. Véronique Bragard, "Introduction: Languages of Waste: Matter and Form in Our Garbage" *Interdisciplinary Studies in Literature and Environment* 20, no. 3 (Summer 2013): 460, 461.

9. Susan Heller Anderson, "For Edna O'Brien, Writing Is a Kind of Illness," *New York Times*, 11 October 1977.

10. Hawkins, *Ethics of Waste*, 5.

11. Walter Benjamin, *The Origin of German Tragic Drama*, trans. John Osborne (New York: Verso, 1977), 177–178.

12. Julia Kristeva, *Powers of Horror: An Essay on Abjection*, trans. Leon S. Roudiez (New York: Columbia University Press, 1982), 12–13.

13. Edna O'Brien, *The Country Girls* (London: Penguin, 1975), 94.

14. Edna O'Brien, *In the Forest* (Boston: Houghton Mifflin, 2002), 23.

15. Edna O'Brien, *Night* (London: Penguin, 1974), 62–63.

16. Ibid., 63.

17. Judith (Jack) Halberstam, *The Queer Art of Failure* (Durham, NC: Duke University Press, 2011), 14, 28, 123, 131, and *passim*.

18. Patricia Yeager, "The Death of Nature and the Apotheosis of Trash; or, Rubbish Ecology," *Publication of the Modern Language Association* 123, no. 2 (March 20018): 336.

19. Fredric Jameson, "Marx's Purloined Letter," in *Ghostly Demarcations: A Symposium on Jacques Derrida's "Spectres de Marx,"* ed. Michael Sprinker (New York: Verso, 1999), 39. Derrida first articulated his influential theory of "hauntology" in *Specters of Marx: The State of the Debt, the Work of Mourning and the New International*, translated by Peggy Kamuf (London and New York: Routledge 1994).

20. Edna O'Brien *Casualties of Peace* (London: Penguin, 1958), 134.

21. Ibid., 44.

22. Edna O'Brien, *August Is a Wicked Month* (London: Penguin, 1967), 89.

23. Edna O'Brien, *Down by the River* MS (1996), Edna O'Brien Papers, Manuscript, Archives and Rare Book Library, Emory University, Series 3: Prose 1960–1999; Subseries 3.2, Novels, Box 51, Folder 5.

24. Ben Woodard, *Slime Dynamics: Generation, Mutation, and the Creep of Life* (Winchester, UK: Zero Books, 2012), 1.

25. Edna O'Brien, *A Pagan Place* (London: Penguin, 1971), 27.

26. O'Brien, *Country Girls*, 134.

27. O'Brien, *Pagan Place*, 62.

28. O'Brien, *Down by the River* (London: Phoenix, 2000), 134.

29. O'Brien, *House of Splendid Isolation* (New York: Plume 1995), 145.

30. "The eggs that had no shells were funny to hold. . . . It was like a bladder, the outside skin of the shell-less egg" (O'Brien, *Pagan Place*, 63). "The hen had something missing in her, calcium, hence the soft egg" (O'Brien, *House of Splendid Isolation*, 48).

31. Edna O'Brien, *The Light of Evening* (London: Weidenfeld and Nicolson, 2006), 212.

32. Edna O'Brien, *Time and Tide* (London: Penguin, 1992), 191.

33. The young second-person narrator of *A Pagan Place* confusedly construes her sister's alarming pregnancy as "something to do with the bladder" (97).

34. Hélène Cixous, "Birds, Women, and Writing," in *Animal Philosophy*, ed. Peter Atterton and Matthew Calarco (London: Continuum, 2004), 169.

35. Mary Douglas, *Purity and Danger: An Analysis of the Concepts of Pollution and Taboo* (New York: Routledge, 1991), 121.

36. Jane Ussher, *Managing the Monstrous Feminine: Regulating the Reproductive Body* (London: Routledge 2006), 7.

37. Edna O'Brien, "The Return," in *A Fanatic Heart: Selected Stories* (London: Penguin, 1984), 453.

38. O'Brien, *Pagan Place*, 184–185.

39. O'Brien, *Light of Evening*, 226.

40. O'Brien, *Pagan Place*, 180.

41. O'Brien, *Time and Tide*, 14.

42. Ibid., 15.

43. Jacques Derrida discusses the *pharmakon*, or medicine that is both remedy and poison, and relates it to the "alchemy" of writing itself, in "Plato's Pharmacy," in *Dissemination*, trans. Barbara Johnson (Chicago: University of Chicago Press, 1981), 63–171. Having trained in pharmacy, O'Brien would be aware of the dual potentialities of any medicine.

44. O'Brien, *Time and Tide*, 301.

45. Edna O'Brien, *Mother Ireland* (New York: Plume, 1976), 66.

46. Edna O'Brien, "Rose in the Heart," in *Mrs Reinhardt and Other Stories* (London: Penguin, 1978), 109.

47. O'Brien, *Pagan Place*, 135.

48. Ibid., 99.

49. O'Brien, *Time and Tide*, 66–67.

50. Edna O'Brien, "A Scandalous Woman," in *A Scandalous Woman* (London: Penguin, 1976), 11.

51. Ussher, *Managing the Monstrous Feminine*, 19.

52. Ingrid Johnston-Robledo and Joan Chrisler, "The Menstrual Mark: Menstruation as Social Stigma, *Sex Roles* 68 (2013): 10.

53. Ibid.

54. Quoted in Theresa O'Keefe, "Menstrual Blood as a Weapon of Resistance," *International Feminist Journal of Politics* 8, no. 4 (2006): 538. Johnston-Robledo and Chrisler note that stigmatizing silence around menstruation continues to be the norm in contemporary Western culture, in private and public discourse, not only in Ireland ("Menstrual Mark," 12).

55. Kristeva, *Powers of Horror*, 78.

56. Edna O'Brien, "Cords," in *The Love Object* (London: Penguin, 1970), 126. The story was first published as "Which of These Two Ladies Is He Married To?" in the *New Yorker*, 25 April 1964.

57. O'Brien, *Time and Tide*, 149.

58. O'Brien, "Rose in the Heart."

59. O'Brien, *Pagan Place*, 100.

60. Ibid., 93.

61. Edna O'Brien, *The High Road* (London: Farrar, Straus and Giroux, 1988), 157.

62. Ibid.

63. Lean-François Lyotard, *The Differend: Phases in Dispute*, trans. George Van den Abbeele (Manchester: Manchester University Press, 1988), 28.

64. Edna O'Brien, *Girl* (London: Faber and Faber, 2019), 9.

65. O'Brien, *Time and Tide*, 127.

66. Ibid., 130.

67. O'Brien, *House of Splendid Isolation*, 45.

68. Ibid., 47.

69. Edna O'Brien, "Mrs Reinhardt," in *Mrs Reinhardt and Other Stories* (London: Penguin, 1986), 201.

70. O'Brien to Carlo Gébler, n.d., Edna O'Brien Papers, Manuscript, Archives and Rare Book Library, Emory University, Series 1: Correspondence, 1939–2000; Subseries 1.2, Family Correspondence, Box 13, Folder 9.

71. O'Brien, *Girl*, 34.

72. O'Brien, *Pagan Place*, 197.

73. Edna O'Brien papers, Manuscript, Archives and Rare Book Library, Emory University. Series 3; Writings by O'Brien, ca.1953–2000, Subseries 3.2 Prose, 1960–1999, Novels, *Down by the River* (1996), Box 56 Folder 2. Labeled in handwriting, "Raw and unusable written in bleakest (non) time spring 95."

74. Recall that, according to Irving Massey, as discussed in chapter 5, metamorphosis is the product of fear, rather than pleasure. Massey, *The Gaping Pig: Literature and Metamorphosis* (Berkeley: University of California Press, 1976).

75. Edna O'Brien papers, Manuscript, Archives and Rare Book Library, Emory University. Series 3; Writings by O'Brien, ca.1953–2000, Subseries 3.2 Prose, 1960–1999, Novels, *Down by the River* (1996), Box 56 Folder 2.

76. Ibid.

77. Julia Kristeva, *Desire in Language: A Semiotic Approach to Literature and Art*, ed. Leon S. Rudiez, trans. Thomas Gorn (New York: Columbia University Press, 1980), 237.

78. Kristeva, *Powers of Horror*, 107.

79. O'Brien, *House of Splendid Isolation*, 211.

80. In the same unused manuscript pages of *Down by the River* in first person, referenced earlier, Mary MacNamara describes her pregnant body as "polluted." Edna O'Brien papers, Manuscript, Archives and Rare Book Library, Emory University. Series 3: Prose 1960–1999; Subseries 3.2, Novels, *Down by the River* (1996), Box 51, Folder 5.

81. O'Brien, *Time and Tide*, 294.

82. Douglas, *Purity and Danger*, 161.

83. O'Brien, *Night*, 105.

84. Douglas, *Purity and Danger*, 122.

85. Woodard, *Slime Dynamics*, 29.

86. Kristeva, *Powers of Horror*, 91.

87. Rosi Braidotti, "Signs of Wonder and Traces of Doubt: On Tetrology and Embedded Differences," in *Feminist Theory and the Body: A Reader*, ed. Janet Price and Magrit Shildrick (New York: Routledge, 1999), 291.

88. O'Brien, *Time and Tide*, 149.

89. O'Brien, *Light of Evening*, 134.

90. Ibid., 228.

91. Ibid., 209.

92. Ibid., 131.

93. Ibid., 202.

94. O'Brien, *Time and Tide*, 294.

95. Karen Barad, "Quantum Entanglements and Hauntological Relations of Inheritance: Dis/continuities, SpaceTime Enfoldings, and Justice-to-Come," *Derrida Today* 3, no. 2 (2010): 264.

96. O'Brien, *Country Girls*, 59.

97. O'Brien, *Time and Tide*, 16, 167.

98. Rosi Braidotti, *The Posthuman* (Cambridge, UK: Polity Books, 2013), 132.

99. Bridget English, *Laying Out the Bones: Death and Dying in the Modern Irish Novel* (Syracuse, NY: Syracuse University Press, 2017), 18. My thanks to Flicka Small for her presentation on this topic, "'Microbes, Germs, Bacteria;: Living Micro-organisms in James Joyce's *Ulysses*,"

delivered at the 2019 "Beastly Modernisms" conference at the University of Glasgow, and for the illuminating conversation afterward.

100. Douglas, *Implicit Meanings*, 216–217.

101. O'Brien, *House of Splendid Isolation*, 215.

102. O'Brien, *Time and Tide*, 274.

103. Douglas, *Purity and Danger*, 162.

104. Baruch Spinoza, *Ethics*, quoted in Jane Bennett, *Vibrant Matter: A Political Ecology of Things* (Durham, NC: Duke University Press, 2010), 154.

105. Rosi Braidotti, *Nomadic Theory: The Portable Rosi Braidotti* (New York: Columbia University Press, 2011), 333.

106. O'Brien, *The High Road*, 144.

107. Edna O'Brien, "Clothes" TS, Edna O'Brien Papers, Manuscript, Archives and Rare Book Library, Emory University, Series 3, Writings by O'Brien, ca. 1953–1999, Subseries 3.2, Prose 1960, 1999; NonFiction Essays and Short Pieces, Box 57, Folder 6.

108. Edna O'Brien, notes from an unidentified interview, Edna O'Brien Papers, Manuscript, Archives and Rare Book Library, Emory University, Series 6: Printed Material, 1958–1999; Subseries 6.2, Writings about O'Brien, Profiles and Interviews, Box 89, Folder 15.

109. Douglas, *Purity and Danger*, 36.

BIBLIOGRAPHY

PRIMARY SOURCES

O'Brien, Edna. *August Is a Wicked Month*. London: Penguin, 1967.

———. "Beckett at 80." *Sunday Times Magazine*, 6 April 1985, 51, 53.

———. *Casualties of Peace*. London: Penguin, 1958.

———. "Cords." In *The Love Object*, 115–130. London: Penguin, 1970.

———. *Country Girl: A Memoir*. London: Faber and Faber, 2012.

———. *The Country Girls*. London: Penguin, 1975.

———. *The Country Girls Trilogy and Epilogue*. London: Farrar, Straus and Giroux, 1986.

———. *Down by the River*. London: Phoenix, 2000.

———. "From the Ground Up." *The Writer*, October 1958, 13–15.

———. *Girl*. London: Faber and Faber, 2019.

———. *The Girl with Green Eyes*. London: Penguin, 1974.

———. *Girls in Their Married Bliss*. London: Penguin, 1975.

———. "Green Georgette." In *Saints and Sinners*, 111–125. London: Faber and Faber, 2011.

———. *The High Road*. London: Farrar, Straus and Giroux, 1988.

———. "House of My Dreams." In *A Scandalous Woman*, 135–159. London: Penguin, 1974.

———. *House of Splendid Isolation*. New York: Plume, 1995.

———. "Inner Cowboy." In *Saints and Sinners*, 85–109. London: Faber and Faber, 2011.

———. *In the Forest*. Boston: Houghton Mifflin, 2002.

———. "In the Sacred Company of Trees: From My Window," *Irish Independent*, 2 June 1990, 32.

———. *Johnny I Hardly Knew You*. London: Penguin, 1986.

———. *The Light of Evening*. London: Weidenfeld and Nicolson, 2006.

———. *The Little Red Chairs*. London: Faber and Faber, 2015.

———. "Manhattan Medley." In *Saints and Sinners*, 127–148. London: Faber and Faber, 2011.

———. *Mother Ireland*. New York: Plume, 1976.

———. "Mrs Reinhardt." In *Mrs Reinhardt and Other Stories*, 192–222. London: Penguin, 1986.

———. "My Two Mothers." In *Saints and Sinners*, 169–182. London: Faber and Faber, 2011.

———. *Night*. London: Penguin, 1974.

———. "Over." In *A Scandalous Woman and Other Stories*, 44–66. London: Penguin, 1976.

———. *A Pagan Place*. London: Penguin, 1971.

———. "Plunder." In *Saints and Sinners*, 77–84. London: Faber and Faber, 2010.

———. "A Reason of One's Own." Saturday Review, *Sunday Times*, 30 September 1970, 10.

———. "The Return." In *A Fanatic Heart: Selected Stories*, 453–461. London: Penguin, 1984.

———. "Rose in the Heart." In *Mrs Reinhardt and Other Stories*, 108–140. London: Penguin, 1978.

———. "The Rug." In *The Love Object*, 63–72. London: Penguin, 1972.

———. "Savages." In *A Fanatic Heart: Selected Stories*, 73–96. New York: Plume, 1985.

———. "A Scandalous Woman." In *A Scandalous Woman*, 9–43. London: Penguin, 1976.

———. "Send My Roots Rain." In *Saints and Sinners*, 149–168. London: Faber and Faber, 2011.

———. "She Stoops but Fails to Conquer." *The Guardian*, 9 April 1995, 21.

———. "Shovel Kings." In *Saints and Sinners*, 1–36. London: Faber and Faber, 2011.

———. *Some Irish Loving: A Selection*. London: Penguin, 1981.

———. *Time and Tide*. London: Penguin, 1992.

———. *Wild Decembers*. New York: Plume, 2001.

INTERVIEWS

Anderson, Susan Heller. "For Edna O'Brien, Writing Is a Kind of Illness." *New York Times*, 11 October 1977.

BBC Archive. "1965: Panorama in Ireland: Irish Censorship." 5 April 2018. https://www.facebook.com/BBCArchive/videos/550571951982506/?v=550571951982506.

Carlson, Julia. *Banned in Ireland: Censorship and the Irish Writer*. Athens: University of Georgia Press, 1990.

Coleman, Alix. "Edna O'Brien: Coming Out of Hiding." *TV Times*, 16–22 February1980, 33.

Cooke, Rachel. Interview of Edna O'Brien. *The Guardian*, 6 February 2011. https://www.theguardian.com/books/2011/feb/06/edna-obrien-ireland-interview.

Duncan, Andrew. "The Andrew Duncan Interview." *The Guardian*, 2 October 1999, 6–7.

Dunn, Nell. *Talking to Women*. London: Silver, 2018.

Edna O'Brien: Fearful ... and Fearless. BBC One documentary, 2019. https://www.bbc.co.uk/programmes/m0006pjj.

"Ernest and Edna, Living in Different Pasts." Londoner's Diary. *The Standard*, 22 April 1988.

Gross, Miriam. "The Pleasure and the Pain." *The Observer*, 14 April 1985.

Guppy, Shusha. 'The Art of Fiction No. 82: Interview with Edna O'Brien." *Paris Review* 92 (1984): 22–50.

Harty, Patricia. "Mother, Life, Landscape, and the Connection." *Irish America*, February–March 2007. https://irishamerica.com/2007/02/mother-life-landscape-and-the-connection/.

Haycock, David. "Edna O'Brien Talks to David Haycock about Her New Novel, *A Pagan Place*." *The Listener*, 7 May 1970, 616–617.

Heaney, Seamus. "Morning Ireland." RTÉ Radio One, 7 May 2009.

Kennedy, Ludovic. "Three Loves of Childhood—Irish Thoughts by Edna O'Brien." *The Listener*, 3 June 1976, 701–702.

Lang, Kirsty. "Edna O'Brien on Her Novel *Girl*, Her First, *The Country Girls*, and Her Career in Between." BBC, 26 August 2019. https://www.bbc.co.uk/sounds/play/m0007wss.

Le Franc, Bolivar. "Committed to Mythology." *Books and Bookmen*, September 1968, 52–53.

McCrum, Robert. "Deep Down in the Woods: Edna O'Brien's Account of a Triple Murder Has Touched a Raw Nerve at Home." *The Observer*, 28 April 2002. http://books.guardian.co.uk/departments/generalfiction/story/0,,706211,00.html.

McQuade, Molly. "PW Interviews." *Publishers Weekly*, 18 May 1992, 48–49.

McWeeney, Myles. "Welcome Home to a Not-So-Wicked Lady." *Irish Independent*, 27 April 1989, 8.

Moir, Jan. "Doing the Real Thing." *The Guardian*, 16 September 1992, 37.

Morton, Cole. "Edna O'Brien: I Had to Grow Old before They'd Give Me Credit." *Sunday Independent*, 5 October 2014. https://www.independent.co.uk/news/people/edna-obrien-i-had-to-grow-old-before-theyd-give-me-credit-9774962.html.

O'Callaghan, Miriam. "Miriam Meets." RTÉ Radio One, 15 November 2015.

O'Grady Fox, Susan. "Interview with Edna O'Brien." *Irish-America Magazine*, October–November 2005. http://www.irishabroad.com/irishworld/irishamericamag/octnov05/features/20-greatest-interviews.asp.

Parker, Ian. "Troubles." *New Yorker*, 14 October 2019, 40–51.

Pearce, Sandra Manoogian. "An Interview with Edna O'Brien." *Canadian Journal of Irish Studies* 22, no. 2 (December 1996): 5–8.

PEN/Nabokov Prize CSPAN recording. "2018 Nabokov Award: Edna O'Brien," February 2018. https://www.c-span.org/video/?c4716342/user-clip-2018-nabokov-award-edna-obrien

Peyrick, Penny. "And Another Thing—Let's Have Lunch." *London Times*, 3 June 1985, 9.

Purcell, Deirdre. "Edna O'Brien: Look, I Have Come Through." *The Sunday Tribune*, 22 July 1984.

Rader, Barbara. "Those Clear Eyes Hide a People Watcher." *New York Times*, 2 June 1965, 57.

Roth, Philip. "A Conversation with Edna O'Brien: 'The Body Contains the Life Story.'" *New York Times*, 18 November 1984, 39.

———. *Shop Talk: A Writer and His Colleagues and Their Work*. Boston: Houghton Mifflin, 2001.

Self, John. "In America, No One Will Stay at Home." Interview with Richard Ford. *The Irish Times*, 9 May 2020. https://www.irishtimes.com/culture/books/richard-ford-in-america -no-one-will-stay-at-home-1.4239919?fbclid=IwAR1C_vZ4exyFccXVjURb6cZ_Vzn_Vq VK4tNetgQGUQgnEDvTzAVQWWS2nHY.

Shenker, Israel. "A Novelist Speaks of Work and Love." *New York Times*, 2 January 1973, 42.

Stokes, Emily. "Edna O'Brien Has Been Me-Too-ing for Fifty Years." *New Yorker*, 5 March 2018. https://www.newyorker.com/magazine/2018/03/05/edna-obrien-has-been-metoo-ing -for-fifty-years.

Streitfeld, David. "Edna O'Brien's Hard Edge of Heartbreak." *International Herald Tribune*, 31 July 1992.

Wheelwright, Julie. "Edna O'Brien, The Mother of Invention." *The Independent*, 29 September 2006. https://www.independent.co.uk/arts-entertainment/books/features/edna-obrien -the-mother-of-invention-417886.html.

Woodward, Richard. "Edna O'Brien, Reveling in Heartbreak." *New York Times Book Review*, 12 March 1989, 42, 50–51.

Wroe, Nicholas. "Country Matters." *The Guardian*, 2 October 1999. https://www.theguardian .com/books/1999/oct/02/books.guardianreview8.

Walsh, Caroline. "Edna O'Brien: Miles from Melancholy." *The Irish Times*, 11 June 1986.

Wavell, Stuart. "Finding Company the Hard Way." *The Guardian*, 25 January 1980, 10.

REVIEWS

Ackroyd, Peter. "Kiss Me!" Review of *Johnny I Hardly Knew You*. *The Spectator*, 23 July 1977, 27.

Annan, Gabriele. Review of *Lantern Slides*. *The Spectator*, 9 June 1990, 40.

Bergonzi, Bernard. "Total Recall." Review of *Casualties of Peace*. *New York Review of Books*, 24 August 1967, 37.

———.Review of *August is a Wicked Month*, *New York Review of Books*, 3 June 1965, 19.

Bell, Pearl K. "Women on Women." *New Leader*, 9 December 1974, 5.

Boylan, Clare. "Edna O'Brien as Others See Her." *Irish Independent*, 29 April 1989.

———. "Pilgrimage to the Old Haunts." Review of *Lantern Slides*. *The Irish Times*, 16 June 1990.

Brockway, James. "Stories, Long, Short, and Tall." *Books and Bookmen*, April 1978, 51.

Broderick John. Review of *Mother Ireland*. *The Critic*, Winter 1976, 72–73.

Broyard, Anatole. "One Critic's Fiction." *New York Times Book Review*, 1 January 1978, 12.

———. Review of *Arabian Days* for "Books of the Times." *New York Times*, 27 June 1978. http://movies2.nytimes.com/books/00/04/09/specials/obrien-arabian.html.

———. "The Rotten Luck of Kate and Baba." Review of *Country Girls Trilogy*. *New York Times Review of Books*, 11 May 1986, 12.

Cahill, Thomas. Review of *Lantern Slides*. *Los Angeles Times*, 11 April 1990.

Cain, Sian. "Irish Novelist Edna O'Brien Wins Lifetime Achievement Award." *The Guardian*, 26 November 2019. https://www.theguardian.com/books/2019/nov/26/irish-novelist-edna -obrien-wins-lifetime-achievement-award-country-girls-david-cohen-prize-nobel?fbclid =IwAR2j_7d-IZgOPL2YRlQE5IekwX5kIEaetZEQwsh0VPc2xHgIBqPXZ0QT9Fg.

Clark, Alex. "A Masterclass of Storytelling." Review of *Girl. The Guardian*, 6 September 2019. https://www.theguardian.com/books/2019/sep/06/girl-edna-obrien-review.

Crain, Caleb. "Edna O'Brien Investigates the Varieties of Murderous Experiences." Review of *In the Forest. New York Times*, 7 April 2002, sec. 7, p. 11.

Donoghue, Denis. "Drums under the Window." Review of *Mother Ireland. New York Review of Books*, 14 October 1976, 12–15.

Enright, Anne. "A Bright Light amid Hearts of Darkness." Review of *Girl. The Irish Times*, 7 September 2019, 20–21.

———. "Murderous Loves." Review of *The Light of Evening. The Guardian*, 14 October 2006. https://www.theguardian.com/books/2006/oct/14/featuresreviews.guardianreview18.

———. Review of *Country Girl: A Memoir. The Guardian*, 12 October 2012. https://www.theguardian.com/books/2012/oct/12/country-girl-edna-obrien-review.

Gebler Davies, Stan. "The Trouble with Edna." Review of *Time and Tide. London Evening Standard*, 19 October 1992.

Glendinning, Victoria. "Elegiac and Life-Loving." Review of *Rose in the Heart. New Yorker*, 11 February 1979.

Gordon, Mary. "The Failure of True Love." Review of *A Fanatic Heart. Los Angeles Times*, 18 November 1984, 37.

———. "Risks of Loving." Review of *A Rose in the Heart. Washington Post Book World*, 8 April 1979, L1, L4.

Harris, Eoghan. "The Wood of the Whispering." Review of *In the Forest. Irish Independent*, 10 March 2002. http://www.independent.ie/opinion/analysis/the-wood-of-the-whispering-26239781.html.

Hornby, Nick. "Death Nell." Review of *Time and Tide. Times Literary Supplement*, 6 September 1992.

———. "Yearning and Canoodling." Review of *Lantern Slides. Sunday Correspondent*, 3 June 1990, 39.

Hughes, Sarah. "Déjà Vu in Dublin and New York." Review of *The Light of Evening. The Observer*, 15 October 2006. https://www.theguardian.com/books/2006/oct/15/fiction.features.

Jones, Chad. "Banned Books behind Her, O'Brien Tries the Stage." *Oakland Tribune*, 29 September 2005.

Kenny, Mary. Review of *Country Girl: A Memoir. Literary Review*, November 2012. https://literaryreview.co.uk/farewell-to-county-clare.

Leland, Mary. "Stories Which Transcend the Limits of Home." Review of *Lantern Slides. Sunday Tribune*, 17 June 1990, 85.

Mahon, Derek. "This Dump, This Dump—Derek Mahon Discusses Edna O'Brien's New Novel." Review of *A Pagan Place. The Listener*, 23 April 1970.

Majkut, Paul. *Bestsellers*, 15 June 1965, 135–136.

Mantel, Hilary. Review of *Down by the River. New York Times*, 25 May 1997. http://movies2.nytimes.com/books/97/05/25/reviews/970525.25mantelt.html.

Markmann, Charles Lam. "Nothing above the Belt?" Review of *Night. The Nation*, May 14 1973, 631.

McMahon, Sean. "A Sex by Themselves: An Interim Report on the Novels of Edna O'Brien." *Éire-Ireland* 2, no. 1 (1967): 79–87.

Mellors, John. Review of *Johnny, I Hardly Knew You. The Listener* 98, 4 August 1977: 158.

Moorehead, Caroline. "Fresh as First Love." Review of *The Country Girls, Girl with Green Eyes* and *Mrs Reinhardt and Other Stories. London Times*, 3 February 1980, 7.

Murray, Isobel. "Irish Eyes." Review of *A Scandalous Woman*. *Financial Times*, 12 September 1974.

Naipaul, V. S. "New Novels." *New Statesman*, 16 July 1960, 97.

"New Fiction." *The Irish Times*, 15 December 1960.

"New Fiction." Review of *August Is a Wicked Month*. *London Times*, 7 October 1965.

Ní Dhuibhne, Éilis. Review of *The Little Red Chairs*. *The Irish Times*, 24 October 2015. https://www.irishtimes.com/culture/books/the-little-red-chairs-by-edna-o-brien-1.2403493.

Nye, Robert. "Good Words for the Most Part in the Right Order." Review of *Night*. *London Times*, 5 October 1972, 10.

O'Connor, Maureen. "Girl Trouble." Review essay of *The Country Girls*. *Dublin Review of Books* 55, 5 May 2014. http://www.drb.ie/essays/girl-trouble.

———. "Not Telling." Review of *Country Girl: A Memoir*. *Dublin Review of Books* 34, 6 May 2013. http://www.drb.ie/essays/not-telling.

O'Faolain, Julia. Review of *A Scandalous Woman*. *New York Times Book Review*, 22 February 1974, 3–4.

O'Faolain, Nuala. "Devious Cool." Review of *A Pagan Place*. *London Times*, 18 April 1970.

Parker, Dorothy. Review of *The Country Girls*. *Esquire*, August 1960, 16.

Pearce, Edward. "Words with No Wisdom." Review of *House of Splendid Isolation*. *The Guardian*, 12 July 1994, 18.

Rafferty Terence. "A Fresh Start." Review of *The High Road*. *New Yorker*, 30 January 1989, 92–94.

———. "O'Brien's Lonely Girls." Review of *Girl*. *The Atlantic*, September 2019, 36–38.

Robinson, Mary. "A Life Well Lived, Well Told." Review of *Country Girl*. *The Irish Times*, 29 September 2012. https://www.irishtimes.com/culture/books/a-life-well-lived-well-told-1.541231.

Sage, Lorna. "Mother Ireland." Review of *A Fanatic Heart*, *The Observer*, 21 April 1985, 22.

———. "Those Barren Leaves." Review of *Mrs Reinhardt and Other Stories*. *The Observer*, 4 June 1978, 30.

Scott, Paul. Review of *The Love Object*. *London Times*, 6 June 1968.

Shuttleworth, Martin. Review of *Casualties of Peace*. *Punch*, 9 November 1966, 717.

Stanford, Peter. "Stranger than Fiction." Review of *In the Forest*. *The Independent*, 28 May 2002.

Strong, Eithne. Review of *A Pagan Place*. *Irish Press*, 14 April 1973.

Trevor, William. "Return to the Womb." *Manchester Guardian Weekly*, 13 June 1976, 21.

West, Anthony. Review of *Casualties of Peace*, *Vogue Books*, May 1967, 58.

SECONDARY SOURCES

Agamben, Giorgio. *Language and Death: The Place of Negativity*. Translated by Karen E. Pinkus. Minneapolis: University of Minnesota Press, 1991.

Alberge, Dalya. "Scholars Hit Back over New Yorker 'Hatchet Job' on Edna O'Brien." *The Observer*, 12 April 2020. https://www.theguardian.com/books/2020/apr/12/scholars-hit-back-over-new-yorker-hatchet-job-on-edna-obrien.

Ashley, Melissa. "The First Fairy Tales Were Feminist Critiques of Patriarchy. We Need to Revive Their Legacy." *The Guardian*, 11 November 2019, https://www.theguardian.com/books/2019/nov/11/the-first-fairytales-were-feminist-critiques-of-patriarchy-we-need-to-revive-their-legacy?CMP=share_btn_tw&fbclid=IwARofDukoTCBBzsCulni8RHnEYJUV-5QfKKhocSoAAnsxy2mlGeyEBod_ITo.

Balzano, Wanda. "Godot Land and Its Ghosts: The Uncanny Genre and Gender of Edna O'Brien's 'Sister Imelda.'" In *Wild Colonial Girl: Essays on Edna O'Brien*, edited by Lisa Colletta and Maureen O'Connor, 93–109. Madison: University of Wisconsin Press, 2006.

Barad, Karen. "Nature's Queer Performativity." *Kvinder Køn og Forskning / Women, Gender and Research* 1, no. 2 (2012): 25–53.

———. "Posthumanist Performativity: Toward an Understanding of How Matter Comes to Matter." *Signs: Journal of Women in Culture and Society* 2, no. 3 (2003): 801–831.

———. "Quantum Entanglements and Hauntological Relations of Inheritance: Dis/continuities, SpaceTime Enfoldings, and Justice-to-Come." *Derrida Today* 3, no. 2 (2010): 240–268.

Beatty, Aidan. *Masculinity and Power in Irish Nationalism, 1884–1938*. London: Palgrave Macmillan, 2016.

Benjamin, Walter. *The Origin of German Tragic Drama*. Translated by John Osborne. New York: Verso, 1977.

Bennett, Andrew. "Elizabeth Bowen on the Telephone." In *Elizabeth Bowen: Theory, Thought and Things*, edited by Jessica Gildersleeve and Patricia Juliana Smith, 182–198. Edinburgh: Edinburgh University Press, 2019.

Bennett, Jane. *Vibrant Matter: A Political Ecology of Things*. Durham, NC: Duke University Press, 2010.

Bourke, Angela. *The Burning of Bridget Cleary: A True Story*. London: Penguin, 1999.

Bragard, Véronique. "Introduction: Languages of Waste: Matter and Form in Our Garbage." *Interdisciplinary Studies in Literature and Environment* 20, no. 3 (Summer 2013): 459–463.

Braidotti, Rosi. *Nomadic Theory: The Portable Rosi Braidotti*. New York: Columbia University Press, 2011.

———. *The Posthuman*. Cambridge, UK: Polity Books, 2013.

———. "Signs of Wonder and Traces of Doubt: On Tetrology and Embedded Differences." In *Feminist Theory and the Body: A Reader*, edited by Janet Price and Magrit Shildrick, 291–301. New York: Routledge, 1999.

Brown, Bill. "Thing Theory." *Critical Inquiry* 28, no. 1 (Autumn 2001): 1–16.

Brownmiller, Susan. *Against Our Will: Men, Women and Rape*. New York: Simon and Shuster, 1975.

Burke, Edmund. *Philosophical Enquiry into the Origin of Our Ideas of the Sublime and Beautiful*. Oxford: Oxford University Press, 1990.

Burke, Mary. "Famished: Alienation and Appetite in Edna O'Brien's Early Novels." In *Edna O'Brien: New Critical Perspectives*, edited by Kathryn Laing, Sinéad Mooney, and Maureen O'Connor, 219–240. Dublin: Carysfort, 2006.

Butler, Judith. *Bodies That Matter: On the Discursive Limits of Sex*. New York: Routledge, 1993.

Byron, Kristi. "In the Name of the Mother . . . : The Epilogue of Edna O'Brien's *Country Girls Trilogy*." *Women's Studies: An Interdisciplinary Journal* 31, no. 4 (2002): 447–465.

Cardin, Bertrand. "Words Apart: Epigrams in Edna O'Brien's Novels." In *Edna O'Brien: New Critical Perspectives*, edited by Kathryn Laing, Sinéad Mooney, and Maureen O'Connor, 54–67. Dublin: Carysfort, 2006.

Carney, James. *Studies in Irish Literature and History*. Dublin: Dublin Institute for Advanced Studies, 1955.

Chancer, Lynn. *Sadomasochism in Everyday Life: The Dynamics of Power and Powerlessness*. New Brunswick, NJ: Rutgers University Press, 1992.

Chase, Elizabeth. "Re-writing Genre in the *Country Girls Trilogy*." *New Hibernia Review* 14, no. 3 (Autumn 2010): 91–105.

Cixous, Hélène. "Birds, Women, and Writing." In *Animal Philosophy*, edited by Peter Atterton and Matthew Calarco, 167–173. London: Continuum, 2004.

Cleary, Joe. *Outrageous Fortune: Capitalism and Culture in Modern Ireland*. Dublin: Field Day, 2007.

Cohen, David J. "Suibhne Geilt." *Celtica* 12 (1977): 113–124.

Connolly, Linda, ed. *The "Irish" Family*. London: Routledge, 2015.

Coughlan, Patricia. "'Cheap and Common Animals': The English Anatomy of Ireland in the Seventeenth Century." In *Literature and the English Civil War,* edited by Thomas Healey and Jonathan Sawday, 205–23. Cambridge: Cambridge University Press, 1990.

———. "Killing the Bats: O'Brien, Abjection, and the Question of Agency." In *Edna O'Brien: New Critical Perspectives,* edited by Kathryn Laing, Sinéad Mooney, and Maureen O'Connor, 171–195. Dublin: Carysfort, 2006.

Cronin, Michael G. *Impure Thoughts: Sexuality, Catholicism and Literature in Twentieth-Century Ireland*. Manchester: Manchester University Press, 2012.

Dáil Éireann debate. Houses of the Oireachtas, 7 March 2017. https://www.oireachtas.ie/en /debates/debate/dail/2017-03-07/2/.

Daly, Mary. *Gyn/Ecology: The Metaethics of Radical Feminism*. Boston: Beacon, 1978.

de Lauretis, Teresa. "Sexual Indifference and Lesbian Representation." *Theatre Journal* 40, no. 2 (May 1988): 155–177.

Deleuze, Gilles, and Félix Guattari. *Kafka: Toward a Minor Literature*. Translated by Dana Polan. Minneapolis: University of Minnesota Press, 1986.

Derrida, Jacques. "Plato's Pharmacy." In *Dissemination*. Translated by Barbara Johnson, 63–171. Chicago: Chicago University Press, 1981.

———. Specters of Marx: The State of the Debt, the Work of Mourning and the New *International*. Translated by Peggy Kamuf. London and New York: Routledge, 1994.

Devlin-Glass, Frances. "The Sovereignty as Co-Lordship: A Contemporary Feminist Reading of the Female Sacred in the Ulster Cycle" In *Feminist Poetics of the Sacred: Creative Suspicions,* edited by Frances Devlin-Glass and Lynn McCreddon, 106–132. Oxford: Oxford University Press, 2001.

D'Hoker, Elke. *Irish Women Writers and the Modern Short Story*. London: Palgrave Macmillan, 2016.

———. "Powerful Voices: Female Narrators and Unreliability in Three Irish Novels." *Études Irlandaises* 32, no. 1 (2007): 21–31.

Dougherty, Jane Elizabeth. "From Invisible Child to Abject Maternal Body: Crises of Knowledge in Edna O'Brien's *Down by the River*." *Critique* 53 (2012): 393–409.

———. "'Never Tear the Linnet from the Leaf': The Feminist Intertextuality of Edna O'Brien's *Down by the River*." *Frontiers: A Journal of Women Studies* 31, no. 3 (2010): 77–102.

Douglas, Mary. *Implicit Meanings: Selected Essays in Anthropology*. London: Routledge, 1975.

———. *Purity and Danger: An Analysis of the Concepts of Pollution and Taboo*. New York: Routledge, 1991.

Ellmann, Maud. "Shadowing Elizabeth Bowen." *New England Review* 24, no. 1 (Winter 2003): 144–169.

English, Bridget. *Laying Out the Bones: Death and Dying in the Modern Irish Novel*. Syracuse, NY: Syracuse University Press, 2017.

Enright, Anne. "Diary." *London Review of Books* 35, no. 6 (21 March 2013): 42–43.

Estok, Simon. "Narrativizing Science: The Ecocritical Imagination and Ecophobia." *Configurations* 18, nos. 1–2 (2010): 141–159.

Ettinger, Bracha. *The Matrixial Borderspace*. Minneapolis: University of Minnesota Press, 2006.

Farley, Paul, and Michael Symons Roberts. *Edgelands: Journeys into England's True Wilderness*. London: Vintage, 2012.

Farquharson, Danine, and Bernice Schrank. "Blurring Boundaries, Intersecting Lives: History, Gender, and Violence in Edna O'Brien's *House of Splendid Isolation*." In *Wild Colonial*

Girl: Essays on Edna O'Brien, edited by Lisa Colletta and Maureen O'Connor, 110–142. Madison: University of Wisconsin Press, 2006.

Fogarty, Anne. "Deliberately Personal? The Politics of Identity in Contemporary Irish Women's Writing." *Nordic Irish Studies* 1 (2002): 1–17.

———. "'It Was Like a Baby Crying': Representations of the Child in Contemporary Irish Fiction." *Journal of Irish Studies* 30 (October 2015): 13–26.

Foley, Tadhg. *Death by Discourse? Political Economy and the Great Irish Famine*. Hamden, CT: Quinnipiac University Press, 2017.

Freeman, Elizabeth. *Time Binds: Queer Temporalities, Queer Histories*. Durham, NC: Duke University Press, 2010.

Garber, Marjorie. *Vested Interests: Cross Dressing and Cultural Anxiety*. New York: Routledge, 1997.

Gébler, Carlo. *Father and I: A Memoir*. New York: Little, Brown, 2000.

———. *The Projectionist: The Story of Ernest Gébler*. Dublin: New Island Books, 2015.

Gebler Davies, Stan. *Sunday Independent* weekly column, 25 October 1992.

Genet, Jacqueline, ed. *The Big House in Ireland: Reality and Representation*. Dingle: Brandon, 1991.

Gerald of Wales (Geraldus Cambrensis). *The Topography of Ireland*. Translated by Thomas Forester. Edited by Thomas Wright. Cambridge, ON: In Parentheses, 2000. http://www.yorku.ca/inpar/topography_ireland.pdf.

Gillespie, Michael Patrick. "She Was Too Scrupulous Always: Edna O'Brien and the Comic Tradition." In *The Comic Tradition in Irish Women Writers*, edited by Theresa O'Connor, 108–123. Gainesville: University Press of Florida, 1995.

Greenwood, Amanda. *Edna O'Brien*. Devon, UK: Northcote House, 2003.

Halberstam, Judith (Jack). *The Queer Art of Failure*. Durham, NC: Duke University Press, 2011.

Harris, Michael. "Outside History: Relocation and Dislocation in Edna O'Brien's *House of Splendid Isolation*." In *Edna O'Brien: New Critical Perspectives*, edited by Kathryn Laing, Sinéad Mooney, and Maureen O'Connor, 122–137. Dublin: Carysfort, 2006.

Hegarty, Aoife. "Who Am I? The Story of Ireland's Illegal Adoptions," *RTÉ: Ireland's National Public Service Media*. 5 March 2021. https://www.rte.ie/news/investigations-unit/2021/0302/1200520-who-am-i-the-story-of-irelands-illegal-adoptions/

Hawkins, Gay. *Ethics of Waste: How We Relate to Rubbish*. Lanham, MD: Rowman and Little-field, 2005.

Hayes, Joanna. *My Story*. Dublin: Brandon Books, 1985.

Heaney, Seamus. "Digging." In *Death of a Naturalist*. London: Faber and Faber, 1966, 13–14.

Heidegger, Martin. "Building Dwelling Thinking." In *Poetry, Language, Thought*. Translated by Albert Hofstadter, 143–161. New York: Harper Colophon Books, 1971.

Herr, Cheryl. "The Erotics of Irishness." *Critical Inquiry* 17 (1990): 1–34.

Hogan, Robert. "Old Boys, Young Bucks, and New Women: The Contemporary Irish Short Story." In *The Irish Short Story: A Critical History*, edited by James F Kilroy, 202–204. Boston: Twayne, 1984.

Holmes, Richard. "Poetry International." *London Times*, 22 June 1972, 10.

Holmlund, Christine. "The Lesbian, the Mother, the Heterosexual Love: Irigaray's Decoding of Difference." *Feminist Studies* 17, no. 2 (Summer 1991): 283–308.

Horgan, John. "An Irishman's Diary." *The Irish Times*, 1 October 2019, 15.

Hume, Robert. "Terence MacSwiney: The Life and Times of a Cork Martyr." *Irish Examiner*, 27 March 2019. https://www.irishexaminer.com/breakingnews/lifestyle/features/terence-macswiney-the-life-and-times-of-a-cork-martyr-913766.html.

"Husserl, Edmund." *Stanford Encyclopedia of Philosophy*. 28 February 2003. http://plato
.stanford.edu/entries/husserl/.

Inglold, Tim. *Perception of the Environment: Essay on Livelihood, Dwelling and Skill*. New York:
Routledge, 2000.

Ingman, Heather. "Edna O'Brien: Stretching the Nation's Boundaries." *Irish Studies Review*
10, no. 3 (2002): 253–265.

———. *Twentieth-Century Fiction by Irish Women: Nation and Gender*. Aldershot, UK: Ashgate, 2007.

Jameson, Fredric. "Marx's Purloined Letter." In *Ghostly Demarcations: A Symposium on
Jacques Derrida's "Spectres de Marx,"* edited by Michael Sprinker, 26–67. New York:
Verso, 1999.

Johnston-Robledo, Ingrid, and Joan Chrisler. "The Menstrual Mark: Menstruation as Social
Stigma." *Sex Roles* 68 (2013): 9–18.

Kelly, Catherine. "Breaking the Mould: Three Plays by Marina Carr." *Women's Studies Review*
8 (2002): 105–114.

Kerrigan, Gene. "They Knew about the Babies for 90 Years." *Sunday Independent*, 12 March 2017.
https://www.independent.ie/opinion/columnists/gene-kerrigan/gene-kerrigan-they
-knew-about-the-babies-for-90-years-35522685.html.

Kiberd, Declan. Citation on Edna O'Brien's receiving the award of the Ulysses Medal from
University College Dublin, 15 June 2006. https://www.ucd.ie/news/jun06/060906
_ulysses_medal_2.htm.

Kiely, Benedict. "Ireland." *Kenyon Review* 30, no. 4 (1968): 463–469.

———. "The Whores on the Half-Doors." In *Conor Cruise O'Brien Introduces Ireland*, edited
by Owen Dudley Edwards, 148–161. New York: McGraw Hill, 1969.

Kreilkamp, Vera. *The Anglo-Irish Novel and the Big House*. Syracuse, NY: Syracuse University
Press, 1998.

Kristeva, Julia. *Desire in Language: A Semiotic Approach to Literature and Art*. Edited by Leon S.
Rudiez. Translated by Thomas Gorn. New York: Columbia University Press, 1980.

———. *Powers of Horror: An Essay on Abjection*. Translated by Leon S. Roudiez. New York:
Columbia University Press, 1982.

———. "Stabat Mater." *Poetics Today* 6, nos. 1–2 (1985): 133–152.

Lachmann, Renate. "Mnemonic and Intertextual Aspects of Literature." In *Cultural Memory
Studies: An International and Interdisciplinary Handbook*, edited by Astrid Erll and Ansgar
Nünning, 301–310. Berlin: Walter de Gruyter, 2008.

Landsberg, Alison. *Prosthetic Memory: The Transformation of America*. New York: Columbia
University Press, 2004.

Laqueur, Thomas. *The Work of the Dead: A Cultural History of Mortal Remains*. Princeton, NJ:
Princeton University Press, 2015.

Legler, Gretchen. "Ecofeminist Literary Criticism." In *Ecofeminism: Women, Culture, Nature*,
edited by Karen J. Warren, 227–238. Bloomington: Indiana University Press, 1997.

Lloyd, David. *Ireland after History*. Notre Dame, IN: Notre Dame University Press, 1999.

———. *Irish Culture and Colonial Modernity, 1800–2000: The Transformation of Oral Space*.
Cambridge: Cambridge University Press, 2011.

Lyotard, Lean-François. *The Differend: Phases in Dispute*. Translated by George Van den
Abbeele. Manchester: Manchester University Press, 1988.

Lysaght, Patricia. *The Banshee: The Irish Supernatural Death Messenger*. Dublin: O'Brien, 1986.

Marder, Michael. "Taming the Beast: The Other Tradition in Political Theory." *Mosaic* 39,
no. 4 (2006): 47–60.

Marks, Elaine. "Lesbian Intertextuality." In *Homosexualities and French Literature: Cultural Contexts / Critical Texts,* edited by Elaine Marks and George Stambolian, 353–377. Ithaca, NY: Cornell University Press, 1979.

Massey, Irving. *The Gaping Pig: Literature and Metamorphosis.* Berkeley: University of California Press, 1976.

McBride, Eimear. Introduction to *The Country Girls Trilogy,* ix–xvii. London: Faber and Faber, 2017.

McWilliams, Ellen. "Making It Up with the Motherland: Revision and Reconciliation in Edna O'Brien's *The Light of Evening." Women: A Cultural Review* 22, no. 1 (2011): 50–68.

———. *Women and Exile in Contemporary Irish Fiction.* London: Palgrave Macmillan, 2013.

Meaney, Gerardine. "Fiction, 1922–1960." In *A History of Modern Irish Women's Literature,* edited by Clíona Ó Gallchoir and Heather Ingman, 187–203. Cambridge: Cambridge University Press, 2018.

———. *Gender, Ireland and Cultural Change: Race, Sex and Nation.* London: Routledge, 2010.

———. *Sex and Nation: Women in Irish Culture and Politics.* Dublin: Attic, 1991.

Mellon, Joelle. *The Virgin Mary in the Perception of Women: Mother, Protector and Queen.* Jefferson, NC: McFarland, 2008.

Mooney, Sinéad. "'Sacramental Sleeves': Fashioning the Female Subject in Edna O'Brien's Fiction." In *Edna O'Brien: New Critical Perspectives,* edited by Kathryn Laing, Sinéad Mooney, and Maureen O'Connor, 196–218. Dublin: Carysfort, 2006.

Morgan, Eileen. "Mapping Out a Landscape of Female Suffering: Edna O'Brien's Demythologizing Novels." *Women's Studies: An Interdisciplinary Journal* 29, no. 4 (2000): 449–476.

Murray, Tom. "Edna O'Brien and Narrative Diaspora Space." *Irish Studies Review,* special issue "New Perspectives on Women and the Irish Diaspora," 21, no. 1 (2013): 85–98.

Nash, Catherine. "Reclaiming Vision: Looking at Landscape and the Body." *Gender, Place and Culture: A Journal of Feminist Geography* 3, no. 2 (1996): 149–170.

———. "Remapping and Renaming: New Cartographies of Identity, Gender, and Landscape in Ireland." *Feminist Review* 44 (Summer 1993): 39–57.

Nolan, Emer. *Five Irish Women: The Second Republic, 1960–2016.* Manchester: Manchester University Press, 2019.

Norris, Claire. "The Big House: Space, Place and Identity in Irish Fiction." *New Hibernia Review* 8, no. 1 (Spring 2004): 107–121.

Obert, Julia C. "Mothers and Others in Edna O'Brien's *The Country Girls." Irish Studies Review* 20, no. 3 (August 2012): 283–297.

O'Brien, Dan. *Fine Meshwork: Philip Roth, Edna O'Brien, and Jewish-Irish Literature.* Syracuse, NY: Syracuse University Press, 2020.

———. "'A Harp in the Hallway': Edna O'Brien and Jewish-Irish Whiteness in *Zuckerman Unbound." Philip Roth Studies,* Fall 2016, 5–23.

O'Brien, Peggy. "The Silly and the Serious: An Assessment of Edna O'Brien." *Massachusetts Review* 28 (1987): 474–488.

O'Connor, Maureen. "Animals and the Irish Mouth in Edna O'Brien's Fiction." In "Irish Ecocriticism." Special issue. *Journal of Ecocriticism* 5, no. 2 (September 2013). http://ojs.unbc.ca/index.php/joe/issue/view/31.

———. *The Female and the Species: The Animal in Irish Women's Writing.* Bern: Peter Lang, 2010.

———. "A Gratuitous Assault." *Dublin Review of Books,* 1 April 2020. https://www.drb.ie/essays/a-gratuitous-assault.

———. "'The Most Haunting Bird': Unbeing and Illegibility in Contemporary Irish Women's Writing." *Women's Studies: An Interdisciplinary Journal* 44, no. 7 (September 2015): 940–955.

O'Faolain, Nuala. *Are You Somebody?* Dublin: New Island Books, 1966.

———. "Edna O'Brien." *Ireland Today*, September 1983, 10–13.

———. *Irish Women and Writing in Modern Ireland* (1985). Excerpted in *The Field Day Anthology of Irish Writing*, vol. 5, 1601–1605. Cork: Cork University Press, 2002.

Ó Fátharta, Connall. "Burial Place of Over 800 Children Who Died in Bessborough Unknown." *Irish Examiner*, 17 April 2019. https://www.irishexaminer.com/breakingnews /ireland/burial-place-of-over-800-children-who-died-in-bessborough-unknown-read -commissions-findings-on-mother-and-baby-homes-918325.html.

O'Keefe, Theresa. "Menstrual Blood as a Weapon of Resistance." *International Feminist Journal of Politics* 8, no. 4 (2006): 535–556.

Ostriker, Alicia. "The Thieves of Language: Women Poets and Revisionist Mythmaking." *Signs* 8, no. 1 (Autumn 1982): 68–90.

Packenham, Frank (Earl of Longford). *Pornography: The Longford Report*. London: Hodder and Stoughton, 1972.

Pelan, Rebecca. "Edna O'Brien's 'Love Objects.'" In *Wild Colonial Girl: Essays on Edna O'Brien*, edited by Lisa Colletta and Maureen O'Connor, 58–76. Madison: University of Wisconsin, Press, 2006.

———. "Reflections on a Connemara Dietrich." In *Edna O'Brien: New Critical Perspectives*, edited by Kathryn Laing, Sinéad Mooney, and Maureen O'Connor, 12–73. Dublin: Carysfort, 2006.

———. "Undoing That Other Conquest." *Canadian Journal of Irish Studies* 25, nos. 1–2 (1999): 126–146.

Penwarden, Charles. "Of Word and Flesh—An Interview with Julia Kristeva." In *Rites of Passion: Arts for the End of the Century*, edited by Stuart Morgan and Frances Morris, 21–27. London: Tate, 1995.

Peterson, Shirley. "Homeward Bound: Trauma, Homesickness, and Rough Beasts in O'Brien's *In the Forest* and McCabe's *Winterwood*." *New Hibernia Review* 13, no. 4 (2009): 40–58.

———. "'Meaniacs' and Martyrs: Sadomasochistic Desire in Edna O'Brien's *The Country Girls* Trinity." In *Edna O'Brien: New Critical Perspectives*, edited by Kathryn Laing, Sinéad Mooney, Maureen O'Connor, 151–170. Dublin: Carysfort, 2006.

Pilkington, Lionel. *Theatre and the State in Twentieth-Century Ireland: Cultivating the People*. New York: Routledge, 2001.

Plumwood, Val. "The Concept of a Cultural Landscape: Nature, Culture, and Agency of the Land." *Ethics and the Environment* 11, no. 2 (2006): 115–150.

Quintelli-Neary, Marguerite. "Edna O'Brien's Metamorphoses: A New Voice for Ovid's Philomela." *Nordic Irish Studies* 12 (2013): 59–77.

Rainsford, John. "Feakle's Biddy Early: A Victim of Moral Panic?" *History Ireland* 1, no. 20 (January–February 2012). https://www.historyireland.com/18th-19th-century-history /feakles-biddy-early-a-victim-of-moral-panic/.

Rich, Adrienne. "Compulsory Heterosexuality and Lesbian Existence." *Signs* 5, no. 4 (Summer 1980): 631–660.

———. "Diving into the Wreck." In *Poems Selected and New, 1950–1974*, 196–198. New York: Norton, 1974.

Richards, Leah Fisher. "'No Nation Wanted It So Much': Mythic Insanity in the Development of a Modern Irish Literature." *Proceedings of the Harvard Celtic Colloquium* 18–19 (1998–1999): 385–395.

Sage, Lorna. *Women in the House of Fiction: Post-war Women Novelists*. London: Palgrave Macmillan, 1992.

Schofield, Dennis. "The Second Person: A Point of View?" *Colloquy* 1, no. 1 (1996): 67–89.

Schrank, Bernice, and Danine Farquharson. "Object of Love, Subject to Despair: Edna O'Brien's 'The Love Object' and Emotional Logic of Late Romanticism." *Canadian Journal of Irish Studies* 22, no. 2 (December 1996): 21–36.

Seymour, St. John D. "Three Medieval Poems from Kilkenny." *Proceedings of the Royal Irish Academy: Archaeology, Culture, History, Literature* 41 (1932–1934): 205–209.

Shaw Sailor, Susan. "*Suibne Geilt*: Puzzles, Problems and Paradoxes." *Canadian Journal of Irish Studies* 24, no. 1 (1998): 115–131.

Sherratt-Bado, Dawn Miranda. "Edna O'Brien Profile Is Sexist and Cold Hearted." *The Irish Times*, 6 October 2019. https://www.irishtimes.com/culture/books/the-new-yorker-s -edna-o-brien-profile-is-sexist-and-cold-hearted-1.4051169.

Slivka, Jennifer A. "Irishness and Exile in Edna O'Brien's *Wild Decembers* and *In the Forest*." *New Hibernia Review* 17, no. 1 (2013): 115–131.

Smyth, Ailbhe. Introduction to *Wildish Things: Anthology of New Irish Women's Writing*, edited by Ailbhe Smyth, 7–16. Dublin: Attic, 1989.

Spenser, Edmund. *View of the Present State of Ireland*. London: Eric Partridge, 1934.

Stockton, Kathryn Bond. "'God' between Their Lips: Desire between Women in Irigaray and Eliot." *NOVEL: A Forum on Fiction* 25, no. 3 (Spring 1992): 348–359.

Thomas, Neil. "The Celtic Wild Man Tradition and Geofffrey of Monmouth's *Vita Merlini*: Madness or *Contemptus Mundi*?" *Arthuriana* 10, no. 1 (2000): 27–42.

Thompson, Helen. "Hysterical Hooliganism: O'Brien, Freud, and Joyce." In *Wild Colonial Girl: Essays on Edna O'Brien*, edited by Lisa Colletta and Maureen O'Connor, 31–57. Madison: University of Wisconsin Press, 2006.

———. "Uncanny and Undomesticated: Lesbian Desire in Edna O'Brien's 'Sister Imelda' and *The High Road*." *Women's Studies: An Interdisciplinary Journal* 32, no. 1 (2003): 21–44.

Ussher, Jane. *Managing the Monstrous Feminine: Regulating the Reproductive Body*. New York: Routledge 2006.

Wills, Clair. "Coda: Edna O'Brien and Eimear McBride." In *Ireland in Transition, 1980–2020*, edited by Eric Falci and Paige Reynolds, 295–303. Cambridge: Cambridge University Press, 2020.

———. "Women, Domesticity and the Family: Recent Feminist Work in Irish Cultural Studies." *Cultural Studies* 15, no. 1 (2001): 33–57.

Woodard, Ben. *Slime Dynamics: Generation, Mutation, and the Creep of Life*. Winchester, UK: Zero Books, 2012.

Woods, Michelle. "Red, Un-Red and Edna: Ernest Gébler, and Edna O'Brien." In *Edna O'Brien: New Critical Perspectives*, edited by Kathryn Laing, Sinéad Mooney, and Maureen O'Connor, 54–67. Dublin: Carysfort, 2006.

Woolf, Virginia. *A Room of One's Own*. New York: Harcourt Brace Jovanovich, 1989.

Yeager, Patricia. "The Death of Nature and the Apotheosis of Trash; or, Rubbish Ecology." *Publication of the Modern Language Association* 123, no. 2 (March 2018): 321–339.

Zipes, Jack. "A Second Gaze at Little Red Riding Hood's Trials and Tribulations." *Lion and the Unicorn* 7–8 (1983): 78–109.

INDEX

Abbey Theatre, 7, 56

abortion, 28, 61, 93, 98, 99, 108, 110–111; as assault, 53, 139n81; legislation in Ireland, 14, 16, 20, 109, 122n15; self-abortion, 20. *See also* pregnancy and childbirth

abuse: clerical, 14, 19, 63, 69, 75, 104, 108; domestic, 5, 10, 18, 20, 25, 27–29, 39, 45, 53–54, 59, 61, 63, 65, 71, 74, 86, 87, 88, 101, 102, 108, 131n55, 139n81; emotional, 51, 52, 53; institutional, 19, 52–53, 60, 69, 72, 73, 74, 75, 79, 80, 96; physical, 8, 24, 35, 37, 79; sexual, 9, 25–27, 37, 77. *See also* trauma. *See also* violence. *See also* rape

Ackroyd, Peter, 124n85

Adams, Gerry, 14

adultery, 10, 19, 21, 27, 8, 29, 30, 87, 100, 102

Agamben, Giorgio, 95

alcohol, 8, 19, 25, 41, 53, 59, 75, 90, 96, 105, 108, 139n81

Amis, Kingsley, 7, 117n33

Anderson, Susan Heller, 99, 124n85

androgyny, 31–33, 89–92, 93, 106

Annan, Gabriele, 57

Aosdána, 3, 116n24

Ashley, Melissa, 135n43

Banville, John, 134n27

Barad, Karen, 58, 80, 89

BBC (British Broadcasting Corporation), 4, 15, 18, 30

Beatty, Aidan, 127n23

Beckett, Samuel, 13

Bell, Pearl, 12, 26

Bell, The, 5

Benjamin, Walter, 99

Bennett, Jane, 40, 41, 49, 51, 60, 78

Bergonzi, Bernard, 11, 118n58

Big House fiction, 37–38, 126–127n22; birds, 8, 52, 53, 58, 76, 78, 101–104; death and, 35, 54, 92, 96, 100, 109, 112; mythology and, 773, 6, 91, 135n41; sex and, 61, 88–89, 90, 91; symbolic of freedom, 28, 65, 73, 101

Boko Haram, 15, 21, 60, 108

Bourke, Angela, 70, 133n15

Bourke, Fergus, 4

Bowen, Elizabeth, 38, 39

Boylan, Clare, 12, 35

Bragard, Véronique, 99

Braidotti, Rosi, 110, 112

Broderick, John, 57, 118n58

Brown, Bill, 36, 46, 47

Brownmiller, Susan, 76

Broyard, Anatole, 4, 12, 124n85

Burke, Edmund, 61, 96

Burke, Mary, 123n52, 124n71

Butler, Judith, 87

Byron, Kristi, 55, 97, 120n91

Cahill, Thomas, 57, 71

Cardin, Bertrand, 120n91

Carlson, Julia, 119n60

cattle, 27, 29, 44, 47, 53, 60, 62, 81, 88, 100, 106

censorship, 2, 6, 7, 8, 9, 10, 11, 12, 15, 18, 117n41, 118n47, 119n66. *See also* Irish Censorship Board

Chancer, Lynn, 15, 40

Chase, Elizabeth, 55

Chekhov, Anton, 2

Chrisler, Joan, 141n54

Cixous, Hélène, 103

Clark, Alex, 15

Cleary, Joe, 117n39

clerical sex abuse, 19, 63, 75, 104, 108

clothing, 8, 11, 15, 21, 22, 30, 35, 43–44, 46–47, 48, 66, 86, 107, 113

Connery, John, 12

Connolly, Linda, 121n7

convent, 2, 8, 11, 12, 21, 26, 62, 63

Cooke, Rachel, 11

Corless, Catherine, 19

corpse, 16, 48, 49, 53, 54, 59, 61, 62, 76, 77, 97, 98–100, 107–109. *See also* death

Coughlan, Patricia, 18, 86, 98, 123n52, 130n31

County Clare, 1, 7, 8, 14, 53, 67, 69, 72, 80, 134n26

Cronin, Michael G., 118n47, 118n55, 118n56

ABOUT THE AUTHOR

MAUREEN O'CONNOR lectures in the School of English in University College Cork. She is the author of *The Female and the Species: The Animal in Irish Women's Writing* (2010) and coeditor, with Derek Gladwin, of a special issue of the *Canadian Journal of Irish Studies*, "Irish Studies and the Environmental Humanities" (2018); with Kathryn Laing and Sinéad Mooney, of *Edna O'Brien: New Critical Perspectives* (2006); with Lisa Colletta, of *Wild Colonial Girl: Essays on Edna O'Brien* (2006); and, with Tadhg Foley, of *Ireland and India: Colonies, Culture, and Empire* (2006).